B.A.N.G!

Blacks Achieving Next-Level Growth
(The Official Guide To Black Entrepreneurship)

Written By Sholdon T. Daniels, Esq.

B.A.N.G!
Black Entrepreneurs Achieving Next-Level Growth
(The Official Guide To Black Entrepreneurship)

Copyright © 2023 by Sholdon T. Daniels, Esq.

All rights reserved.

No portion of this book may be reproduced in any form without written permission from the publisher or author, except as permitted by U.S. copyright law.

This publication is designed to provide accurate and authoritative information in regard to the subject matter covered. It is sold with the understanding that neither the author nor the publisher is hereby engaged in rendering legal, investment, accounting or other professional services. While the publisher and author have used their best efforts in preparing this book, they make no representations or warranties with respect to the accuracy or completeness of the contents of this book and specifically disclaim any implied warranties of merchantability or fitness for a particular purpose. No warranty may be created or extended by sales representatives or written sales materials. The advice and strategies contained herein may not be suitable for your situation. You should consult with a professional when appropriate. Neither the publisher nor the author shall be liable for any loss of profit or any other commercial damages, including but not limited to special, incidental, consequential, personal, or other damages.

Artwork by Sholdon Daniels
Edited by Alyse Daniels
Photography by Rocky Carter

ISBN XXXXXXXXX

First Edition 2023

ACKNOWLEDGMENTS

This book is dedicated to a few special individuals who have played an instrumental role in my journey as a Black entrepreneur and as a Black man.

First and foremost, to my dear friend Devon Campbell, who took me under his wing early on in my career and taught me the ins and outs of entrepreneurship and high fashion. He not only showed me the ropes, but also helped me to smooth out my rough edges and become the successful business person I am today. I will always be grateful for his guidance and mentorship. Bun and cheese, rice and peas, check please!

To Billy Carson, who not only inspired me to finish this book, but also has been a constant source of encouragement and support throughout my spiritual journey. His unwavering belief in me and my abilities has been a driving force behind my success. When the student is ready, the teacher will appear.

To my Uncle Rodney, the definition of black entrepreneurship, who gave me the space and support I needed to figure out my life and pursue my academic dreams. His belief in me and his constant push to achieve more, has been instrumental in helping me to reach my full potential. It's always love, Unk.

To my beautiful wife, who has been my rock through it all. Her unwavering love, support and encouragement have been invaluable in helping me to navigate the ups and downs of entrepreneurship and life in general. If God be for us, who can be against us?

To my children, SJ and Nova, who bring laughter and warmth into my life every day. Their love and joy has been an unending source of inspiration and motivation for me. To be your father is the highest honor of my life.

And last but definitely not least, to all the civil rights activists and icons that helped open the doors and manifest the opportunities that I enjoy as a black man in America today. To names like William J. Durham, Thurgood Marshall, Stokely Carmichael, Rosa Parks, Frederick Douglass, Malcolm X, Dr. Martin Luther King Jr., Harriet Tubman, Angela Davis, Maya Angelou, Fannie Lou Hamer, Ida B. Wells, Medgar Evars, W.E.B. Du Bois, Marcus Garvey, Colin Kaepernick and all the other brave individuals who fought for equality and justice for people of color. Their sacrifices and hard work have paved the way for me and countless others to achieve success and prosperity in a society that denied us those opportunities. This book is a tribute to their legacy and a reminder that their fight is not yet over.

This book is dedicated to all of you, for without your love, support, and guidance, this book would not have been possible.

Thank you.

Table of Contents

The Importance of Black Entrepreneurship   10
    ECONOMIC EMPOWERMENT   11
    REPRESENTATION   13
    COMMUNITY BUILDING   14
    CULTURAL PRESERVATION   15
    SOCIAL IMPACT   18
    INNOVATION   18

Defining Your Business Idea   20
    IDENTIFY YOUR PASSIONS AND STRENGTHS   20
    RESEARCHING YOUR MARKET   21
    EVALUATING YOUR COMPETITION   23
    DEFINING YOUR UNIQUE VALUE PROPOSITION   24
    EXPLORING NICHE MARKETS   24
    SEEKING FEEDBACK AND VALIDATION   25

Creating Your Business Plan   26
    DEFINING YOUR GOALS AND OBJECTIVES   26
    OUTLINING YOUR MARKETING AND SALES STRATEGIES   27
    DEVELOPING A FINANCIAL PLAN   27
    IDENTIFYING YOUR TARGET AUDIENCE   28
    RESEARCHING YOUR INDUSTRY AND COMPETITION   29
    SEEKING PROFESSIONAL ADVICE   29

Funding Your Startup   31
    IDENTIFYING FUNDING SOURCES   31
    DEVELOPING A FUNDING PLAN   32
    CRAFTING A PITCH   33
    SEEKING PROFESSIONAL ADVICE   34
    LEVERAGING YOUR PERSONAL AND PROFESSIONAL NETWORKS   34
    BUILDING A STRONG TEAM   35

Building A Strong Team   37
    IDENTIFYING YOUR TEAM NEEDS   37
    HIRING FREELANCERS AND CONTRACTORS   38
    UTILIZING INTERNS AND VOLUNTEERS   39
    BUILDING A VIRTUAL TEAM   39
    COLLABORATING WITH OTHER BUSINESSES   40
    SEEKING MENTORS AND ADVISORS   41

Marketing and Branding Strategies   43
    IDENTIFYING YOUR TARGET AUDIENCE   43

DEVELOPING A UNIQUE VALUE PROPOSITION	44
CRAFTING A COMPELLING BRAND MESSAGE	45
LEVERAGING SOCIAL MEDIA	46
BUILDING A PROFESSIONAL WEBSITE	47
PARTICIPATING IN TRADE SHOWS AND EVENTS	48
Networking To Build Professional Relationships	**50**
IDENTIFY NETWORKING OPPORTUNITIES	50
PARTICIPATE IN SOCIAL CIRCLES	51
PARTICIPATE IN PROFESSIONAL ORGANIZATIONS	52
GET INVOLVED WITH CHARITABLE ORGANIZATIONS	54
ACTIVELY MANAGE YOUR QUALITY CONNECTIONS	55
Time Management and Goal Setting	**57**
IDENTIFY YOUR PRIORITIES	59
CREATING A PLAN FOR TIME MANAGEMENT	60
SETTING SMART GOALS	60
DELEGATING AND OUTSOURCING	61
MANAGING DISTRACTIONS AND STAYING FOCUSED	62
MAKE TIME FOR THESE THINGS NO MATTER WHAT	63
Leading Your Team Effectively	**64**
COMMUNICATING CLEARLY	64
SETTING EXPECTATIONS AND GOALS	65
PROVIDING LEADERSHIP AND DIRECTION	66
BUILDING TRUST AND RESPECT	68
ENCOURAGING COLLABORATION AND TEAMWORK	69
PROVIDING FEEDBACK AND RECOGNITION	70
Overcoming Challenges and Setbacks	**72**
STAYING RESILIENT	72
SEEKING SUPPORT	73
REFRAMING CHALLENGES AS OPPORTUNITIES	74
SEEKING OUT RESOURCES	75
DEVELOPING A GROWTH MINDSET	75
BUILDING A STRONG SPIRITUAL SUPPORT SYSTEM	76
Financial Management and Budgeting	**78**
DEVELOPING A FINANCIAL PLAN	78
CREATING A BUDGET	79
MONITORING CASH FLOW	79
SEEKING PROFESSIONAL ADVICE	80
LEVERAGING FINANCIAL TOOLS AND RESOURCES	81
MANAGING DEBT	81

Legal Considerations For Black Entrepreneurs   **83**
    CHOOSING THE RIGHT BUSINESS STRUCTURE   83
    PROTECTING YOUR INTELLECTUAL PROPERTY   84
    COMPLYING WITH REGULATIONS   85
    DRAFTING LEGAL DOCUMENTS   86
    SEEKING PROFESSIONAL ADVICE   87
    MANAGING LEGAL DISPUTES   88

Building A Diverse And Inclusive Workplace   **90**
    COMMITTING TO DIVERSITY AND INCLUSION   90
    DEVELOPING A DIVERSITY AND INCLUSION PLAN   91
    RECRUITING A DIVERSE TEAM   92
    PROVIDING INCLUSIVE LEADERSHIP   93
    PROMOTING DIVERSITY AND INCLUSION   94

Managing Work-Life Balance   **97**
    SETTING BOUNDARIES   97
    PRIORITIZING SELF-CARE   98
    SEEKING EMOTIONAL SUPPORT   99
    MANAGING STRESS   99
    SEEKING PROFESSIONAL HELP   100
    FREE YOUR MIND   101

Leveraging Your Personal Brand   **103**
    DEFINING YOUR PERSONAL BRAND   103
    BUILDING YOUR ONLINE PRESENCE   104
    NETWORKING AND BUILDING RELATIONSHIPS   104
    DEVELOPING YOUR PERSONAL BRAND MESSAGE   105
    COLLABORATING WITH OTHERS   106

Using Social Media To Promote Your Business   **108**
    IDENTIFY YOUR TARGET AUDIENCE   108
    CHOOSING THE RIGHT PLATFORM   109
    DEVELOPING A SOCIAL MEDIA STRATEGY   110
    CREATING ENGAGING CONTENT   112
    BUILDING A COMMUNITY   112
    ANALYZING AND IMPROVING PERFORMANCE   113

Finding Mentors And Advisors   **115**
    IDENTIFY YOUR NEEDS   115
    RESEARCH POTENTIAL MENTORS   116
    BUILDING A RELATIONSHIP   117
    MENTORSHIP PROGRAMS   118

ADVISORY SERVICES	119
Developing Your Leadership Skills	**120**
IDENTIFYING YOUR LEADERSHIP STRENGTHS	120
IMPLEMENTING CHANGE	121
SEEKING LEADERSHIP TRAINING	122
BUILDING YOUR CONFIDENCE	123
LEADING WITH AUTHENTICITY	124
LEADING BASED ON BEST PRACTICES	124
Socializing For Black entrepreneurs	**126**
UNDERSTANDING THE PURPOSE OF SOCIAL ETIQUETTE	126
DEVELOPING GOOD CONVERSATION SKILLS	127
BEING RESPECTFUL AND COURTEOUS	128
BEING CONFIDENT	129
BEING AUTHENTIC	129
FOLLOWING SOCIAL NORMS	130
Staying Up-To-Date On Industry Trends	**131**
IDENTIFYING RELEVANT INDUSTRY TRENDS	131
STAYING CONNECTED TO YOUR INDUSTRY	132
READING INDUSTRY PUBLICATIONS	132
FOLLOWING INDUSTRY INFLUENCERS	133
PARTICIPATING IN PROFESSIONAL DEVELOPMENT OPPORTUNITIES	134
SEEKING PROFESSIONAL ADVICE	135
Crafting A Compelling Elevator Pitch	**136**
UNDERSTANDING THE PURPOSE OF AN ELEVATOR PITCH	136
IDENTIFYING YOUR UNIQUE VALUE PROPOSITION	137
KEEPING IT SHORT AND SWEET	138
BEING CLEAR AND CONCISE	138
PRACTICING YOUR PITCH	139
BEING AUTHENTIC	140
Negotiating And Closing Deals	**141**
PREPARING FOR NEGOTIATIONS	141
COMMUNICATING CLEARLY	142
BUILDING TRUST AND RAPPORT	142
BEING FLEXIBLE	143
ADVANCED NEGOTIATING TACTICS	144
CLOSING THE DEAL	144
Protecting Your Intellectual Property	**146**
UNDERSTANDING INTELLECTUAL PROPERTY	146

CONDUCTING A TRADEMARK SEARCH	147
FILING FOR TRADEMARKS	148
PROTECTING COPYRIGHTS	149
FILING FOR PATENTS	149
SEEKING PROFESSIONAL ADVICE	150

Expanding Your Business Internationally — **151**

RESEARCHING INTERNATIONAL MARKETS	151
UNDERSTANDING CULTURAL DIFFERENCES	152
DEVELOPING A GLOBAL MARKETING STRATEGY	153
ESTABLISHING A LOCAL PRESENCE ABROAD	153
COMPLYING WITH REGULATIONS	154
SEEKING PROFESSIONAL ADVICE	155

Building Strong Customer Relationships — **157**

PROVIDING EXCELLENT CUSTOMER SERVICE	157
BUILDING TRUST	158
LISTENING TO CUSTOMER FEEDBACK	159
SHOWING APPRECIATION	159
BUILDING LOYALTY	160
SEEKING PROFESSIONAL ADVICE	161

Leveraging Partnerships And Collaborations — **162**

IDENTIFYING POTENTIAL PARTNERS	162
NEGOTIATING PARTNERSHIPS	163
BUILDING STRONG WORKING RELATIONSHIPS	164
COMMUNICATING CLEARLY	165
ENLISTING THE PROS	166
EXPANDING YOUR REACH	167

Developing A Growth Mindset — **169**

UNDERSTANDING THE CONCEPT OF A GROWTH MINDSET	169
EMBRACING CHALLENGES	170
SEEKING FEEDBACK	171
FOCUSING ON PROCESS RATHER THAN OUTCOME	172
SEEKING PROFESSIONAL DEVELOPMENT OPPORTUNITIES	172
SURROUNDING YOURSELF WITH LIKEMINDED PEOPLE	173

Giving Back To Your Community — **175**

IDENTIFYING WAYS TO GIVE BACK	175
SUPPORTING BLACK CAUSES IS IMPORTANT	176
INCORPORATING SOCIAL RESPONSIBILITY	176
SUPPORTING RURAL BLACK COMMUNITIES	177
SCHOLARSHIPS AND GRANTS	179

POLITICAL ACTIVISM PART 1	179
POLITICAL ACTIVISM PART 2	180
USING TECHNOLOGY TO SERVE BLACK INTERESTS	181

Mentoring The Next Generation Of Entrepreneurs — **182**

IDENTIFYING OPPORTUNITIES TO MENTOR	182
SHARING YOUR KNOWLEDGE AND EXPERIENCE	183
BEING A SUPPORTIVE AND ENCOURAGING ROLE MODEL	183
SETTING EXPECTATIONS	184
BE GENEROUS BUT DISCERNING	185
GIVE CREDIT WHERE CREDIT IS DUE	185

Celebrating Your Success While Staying Grounded — **187**

RECOGNIZING YOUR ACCOMPLISHMENTS	187
SHARING YOUR SUCCESS	188
STAYING GROUNDED	188
RECOGNIZING YOUR LIMITATIONS	189
SEEKING FEEDBACK	190
DON'T GIVE UP!	190

Chapter One:
The Importance of Black Entrepreneurship

Black entrepreneurship has a long and rich history in the United States, and has played a vital role in the economic, social, and political advancement of the Black community in America. Despite facing numerous obstacles and discrimination, Black entrepreneurs from all walks of life have consistently found ways to start and grow successful businesses. In recent years, the importance of Black entrepreneurship and the contributions of Black entrepreneurs to the global economy has gained greater recognition, as it has the potential to not only benefit the individual entrepreneur, but also the larger community by creating jobs and fostering economic development. African Americans, in particular, have a unique way of churning out the creativity and innovation that often sparks global trends. This chapter will delve into the significance of Black entrepreneurship to modern society, both historically and in modern times.

One of the most important aspects of Black entrepreneurship is the ability to create jobs and stimulate economic development within the black community, which has a positive effect on the greater community at large. When Black entrepreneurs succeed, they not only benefit personally, but they also provide employment and other economic opportunities for other members of their community. This can have a ripple effect, as those employees then have the financial means to support other businesses and contribute to the local economy. We see this all the time in other ethnic communities.

At this time, in Dallas, Texas, the local Korean business community has mounted a significant push to encourage tourism and patronage in their proposed "Koreatown," an area in northwest Dallas ripe with businesses owned by Korean entrepreneurs[1]. When you go to any of these Korean-owned businesses you will find that many if not most of the employees are korean. This is not by chance.

According to a study by the National Bureau of Economic Research, ethnic enclaves, such as Asian and Hispanic communities, have played a significant role in the economic ascent of these groups in America over the past few decades. These enclaves, characterized by the concentration of a specific ethnic group in a geographic area, have provided new immigrants with access to social networks, information, and resources that have helped them to integrate into the labor market and start their own businesses. The study found that these ethnic enclaves have had a positive effect on the economic success of immigrant groups by providing them with a "head start" in the job market and by creating an environment that encourages the formation of new businesses. This has led to higher rates of entrepreneurship and self-employment

---

[1] Choi, Hojun. 2022. "Korean American business leaders push for recognition of Koreatown in northwest Dallas." Dallas Morning News. https://www.dallasnews.com/news/2022/12/29/korean-american-business-leaders-push-for-recognition-of-koreatown-in-northwest-dallas/.

among these groups, as well as increased wages and economic mobility[2]. The potential success for Black entrepreneurs is limitless, and the blueprint for Black entrepreneurs to become successful is all around us.

Historically and for whatever reason, Black entrepreneurs have often been vilified for banding together for the betterment of the black community[3]. For example, in the 1920s, the National Negro Business League, led by black businessman and civil rights leader, Booker T. Washington, was criticized for promoting the economic advancement of black people through the development of black-owned businesses. The organization was active for more than 50 years and had thousands of members across the United States. Similarly, in the 1960s and 1970s, the Black Economic Development Conference, an organization of black business leaders, was accused of promoting "black capitalism" at the expense of the broader civil rights movement. More recently, the "Buy Black" movement, which encourages black consumers to support black-owned businesses, has been criticized for promoting racial segregation and failing to address the systemic issues that contribute to economic inequality.

In addition to providing employment opportunities, Black entrepreneurship also has the potential to increase wealth and financial stability within the black community. Historically, black Americans have had less access to wealth-building opportunities, such as homeownership and higher education, leading to a significant wealth gap between black and white Americans. Black entrepreneurship can help to narrow this gap by providing an avenue for individuals to build their own wealth and financial security.

Black entrepreneurship is also important in terms of representation and visibility. Seeing successful black business owners can serve as a source of inspiration and motivation for aspiring entrepreneurs within the black community. It can also help to challenge and dispel negative stereotypes about the abilities and potential of black individuals.

Despite the numerous benefits of Black entrepreneurship, Black entrepreneurs still face significant barriers and challenges. These can include discrimination in access to capital, lack of access to networks and resources, and disproportionate representation in certain industries. It is crucial that these barriers be addressed in order to fully realize the potential of Black entrepreneurship to create economic opportunity, and to advance the black community and ultimately the world at large.

I want to give you six key takeaways from this book about the importance of Black entrepreneurship. These six ideas will help you better understand the great impact that Black entrepreneurs have on the world at large. These concepts include: economic empowerment, representation, community building, cultural preservation, social impact, and innovation. I will discuss them individually in this chapter.

ECONOMIC EMPOWERMENT

Black entrepreneurship can provide an opportunity for economic empowerment and wealth creation in communities that have historically been marginalized and disadvantaged. It

---

[2] Edin, Per-Aders, Peter Fredriksson, and Olaf Aslund. 2003. "Ethnic Enclaves and the Economic Success of Immigrants—Evidence from a Natural Experiment." The Quarterly Journal of Economics 118, no. 1 (February): 329-357. https://doi.org/10.1162/00335530360535225.
[3] Painter, Nell I. 2011. The History of White People. N.p.: W. W. Norton.

creates the flow of dollars that can then be used to create new homeowners, pay for weddings, hire new employees, and donate to political causes. This is due to a number of factors, including the ability to create jobs and stimulate economic development, the potential for increased wealth and financial stability, and the representation and sheer visibility of successful black business owners is always going to be a good look.

One of the most significant ways in which Black entrepreneurship can contribute to economic empowerment is through the creation of jobs and economic development. When Black entrepreneurs succeed, they not only benefit personally, but they also provide employment opportunities for other members of their community. This can have a ripple effect, as those employees then have the financial means to support other black-owned businesses and contribute to the local economy. In addition, black-owned businesses can help to revitalize underserved communities like rural communities, and stimulate economic growth in blighted urban areas.

Black entrepreneurship obviously has the potential to increase wealth and financial stability within the black community. Historically, black Americans have had less access to wealth-building opportunities, such as homeownership and higher education, leading to a significant wealth gap between black and other Americans. Black entrepreneurship can help to narrow this gap by providing an avenue for individuals to build their own wealth and financial security. Owning a business can provide a stable source of income, as well as opportunities for asset accumulation and wealth creation.

In addition to the economic benefits, Black entrepreneurship is also important in terms of representation and visibility. Seeing successful black business owners can serve as a source of inspiration and motivation for aspiring entrepreneurs within the black community. It can also help to challenge and dispel negative stereotypes about the abilities and potential of black individuals. This increased representation can also lead to greater diversity and inclusion in the business world, which can ultimately benefit all members of society.

This is why I made the commitment to maintain a presence as a black attorney in my hometown of Sherman, Texas. Sherman is a rural town situated about an hour north of Dallas. It used to have a bustling and prominent black business community in what I refer to as "The Mulberry Business District," but due to racism and its lasting effects, Sherman now has only a handful of successful black businesses. For instance, growing up, I never had a black attorney to look up to in my county. The only black lawyer to ever office in my hometown was the famed William J. Durham, friend and colleague to the late great Supreme Court Justice Thurgood Marshall. He and almost all of the other Black entrepreneurs in Sherman were forced out of business and out of town shortly after an infamous race riot that occurred in Sherman in 1930[4]. Today, I am the only African-American attorney serving the black community in Grayson County on an ongoing basis,[5] but I hope that one day this is no longer the case.

It is important to note that Black entrepreneurship is not without its challenges. Black entrepreneurs often face significant barriers and discrimination, such as lack of access to capital, limited access to networks and resources, and disproportionate representation in certain

---

[4] Phillips, Edward H. "The Sherman Courthouse Riot of 1930." East Texas Historical Journal 25, no. 2 (1987): 6.

[5] "Sherman native becomes city's only African American Attorney." 2015. KTEN News. https://www.kten.com/story/27863756/sherman-native-becomes-citys-only-african-american-attorney.

industries. These barriers can make it more difficult for Black entrepreneurs to start and grow their businesses, and can hinder their ability to achieve economic success. Fifty percent of all new businesses fail within their first five years of operation, and for black-owned businesses that percentage is even higher.[6]

I experienced these challenges when I first opened my law firm. I couldn't get a loan to float my business for the first year or to hire an assistant like many of my white colleagues did. However, I had anticipated this happening and I saved and invested much of my money into real estate and used a large chunk of my savings to launch an investment fund that I actively manage. I knew I couldn't depend on the current system completely, so I made plans to compensate for the shortcomings of society in order to make my business a success.

Despite these challenges, the importance of Black entrepreneurship cannot be overstated. Black entrepreneurs have the potential to empower the Black community as a whole by braving the business world as leaders. But in order to fully realize the potential of Black entrepreneurship, it is imperative that these barriers Black entrepreneurs face be addressed and obliterated. This can be achieved through a variety of means, including targeted funding and resources for black-owned businesses, increasing representation and diversity in the business world, providing education and support for aspiring Black entrepreneurs, and political reform. By fostering a supportive and inclusive environment for Black entrepreneurship, we can help to level the playing field and create greater economic opportunity for all.

REPRESENTATION

Black entrepreneurs can serve as role models and provide representation in industries where they are traditionally underrepresented. This is important because representation and visibility can have a significant impact on the aspirations and opportunities of individuals within a given community. Seeing successful role models who look like them can inspire and motivate aspiring entrepreneurs, and can help to challenge and dispel negative stereotypes about the abilities and potential of black individuals.

When I was coming of age during the late 1980's and 1990's, like many of my friends and classmates of African-American ethnicity, I lived in a single parent home and my father was incarcerated in the fallout of the American War on Drugs. So, rather than emulating the ways of my entrepreneurial albeit misguided father, I looked to my idols for guidance. I looked up to Black entrepreneurs like Puff Daddy or Diddy, Jay-Z, Master P, Dieon Sanders, and Oprah Winfrey. I still remember the radio advertisements I would hear on K104fm as a child when Dieon would promote his Dallas nightclub, Primetime21. I thought to myself as I rode in the back of my mother's red Geo Metro, "one day I'm going to have my own business too."

Black entrepreneurs can serve as role models merely through their success in building and growing their businesses. This can provide a sense of pride and accomplishment within the black community, and can serve as a source of inspiration for others. When I passed the bar on the first attempt and opened a law firm in Sherman, everyone treated me like a hero freshly returned from the battlefield. Just by the sheer act of opening my doors for business, my beloved Black community made me feel like I had already been inducted into the Black Man

---

[6] Bruno, Albert V., Joel K. Leidecker, and Joseph W. Harder. "Why firms fail." Business Horizons 30, no. 2 (1987): 50-58.

Hall of Fame. Other Black entrepreneurs who are able to overcome the numerous challenges and barriers they face can serve as an example of resilience and determination, and can demonstrate that it is possible to succeed despite the odds.

Besides serving as role models through their success, Black entrepreneurs can also provide representation and visibility within their industries. This is particularly important in industries where black individuals are traditionally underrepresented, such as in tech, law and government, finance, and the media. Seeing successful black business owners in these industries can help to increase diversity and inclusion, and can provide a sense of belonging and recognition for black individuals within these fields.

Representation and visibility can also have a positive impact on the greater community at-large. For too long, the world has seen Black people portrayed by American media as dangerous, classless, ignorant, and often more into alternative lifestyles than the more socially acceptable ones. Seeing successful black business owners and their beautiful Black families can foster a sense of pride and accomplishment within the black community, and can help to challenge and dispel negative stereotypes about the abilities and potential of black individuals. This is the thinking that underlies the cultural relevance of Black celebrities like Angela Simmons, EJ Johnson, and Justin Combs. Blue Ivy is only 11 years old as of the writing of this book, but I can say with almost unshakable certainty that she will grow up to become a successful entrepreneur–purely based on who her parents are. But the more beautiful thing is that there is a new generation with millions of little black girls who have a potential role model for business success in Blue. They can grow with her, follow her journey, and be inspired.

Black entrepreneurship can also lead to greater diversity and inclusion in the business world, which can ultimately benefit all members of society. However, it is important to note that representation and visibility alone are not enough to overcome the numerous challenges and barriers faced by Black entrepreneurs. It is crucial that these barriers be addressed and overcome in order to create a level playing field and provide equal opportunities for Black entrepreneurs and ultimately Black people. This can be achieved through a variety of means, including targeted funding and resources for black-owned businesses, increasing representation and diversity in the business world, political reform, and providing education and support for aspiring Black entrepreneurs.

So, now you know that Black entrepreneurs can serve as role models and provide representation in industries where they are traditionally underrepresented. Their success and visibility can have a positive impact on the aspirations and opportunities of individuals within the black community, and can lead to greater diversity and inclusion in the business world. Barriers still remain in place for aspiring Black entrepreneurs trying to gain access to capital, networking and resources, and high-level contacts in a given industry that look like them and share their cultural background. It is crucial that these barriers be addressed and overcome in order to create a level playing field and provide equal opportunities for Black entrepreneurs.

COMMUNITY BUILDING

Black-owned businesses can serve as economic anchors in their communities, providing jobs, goods, a myriad of services, and by contributing to the local economy. This is important because businesses–particularly small businesses–play a vital role in the economic health and vitality of a given community. When black-owned businesses succeed, they not only benefit the individual entrepreneur, but they also provide a range of benefits to the community-at-large.

One of the most significant ways in which black-owned businesses can serve as anchors in their communities is through the creation of jobs. When Black entrepreneurs succeed, they tend to grow their businesses and expand their teams. This provides employment opportunities for other members of their community. The new job opportunities can have a ripple effect, as those new employees then have the financial means to support other businesses and contribute even more to the local economy. Additionally, black-owned businesses can help to revitalize underserved neighborhoods and stimulate economic growth in both rural and urban areas.

Black-owned businesses contribute to their communities by providing goods and services that meet the needs and wants of local residents and by generally improving the quality of life for the greater community at large. Offerings can range from basic necessities, such as food and clothing, to more specialized products and services, such as beauty salons, home repair, bookkeeping services, and law firms. By meeting the needs of the local community, black-owned businesses can help to create a sense of vibrancy and vitality within the community at-large.

In addition to providing jobs and goods and services, black-owned businesses can also contribute to the local economy through their spending and tax contributions. When Black entrepreneurs succeed, they are able to reinvest their profits back into their businesses and the community, supporting other local businesses and contributing to the local tax base. This can help to create a stronger and more sustainable local economy by directly affecting the bottom line of county and city governments.

How can we as Black entrepreneurs face the significant barriers and challenges before us? How do we eviscerate barriers like discrimination in access to capital, lack of access to networks and resources, and disproportionate representation in certain vital industries? We join forces and combine our social capital and our collective economic power to bring the change we seek. We need a new generation of Black business alliances and a push for more black ownership in industries like professional sports, music and entertainment, medicine, finance, law, engineering. It is crucial that these barriers be addressed in order to fully realize the potential of black-owned businesses to serve as anchors in their communities and contribute to the world in a more meaningful and productive way.

So, now you know that black-owned businesses can serve as anchors in their communities by providing jobs, goods, services, and by contributing to the local economy. Their success has the potential to provide a range of benefits to the community at-large, including employment opportunities, meeting the needs and wants of local residents and businesses, and contributing to the local tax base. It is important that barriers to black-owned businesses be addressed in order to fully realize their potential and benefits.

CULTURAL PRESERVATION

Black entrepreneurship can help to preserve and celebrate cultural traditions and values, and provide a platform for sharing these values with a wider audience. This is important because cultural traditions and values are an integral part of the black community, and serve as a source of pride, identity, and community.

We don't own any of the platforms on which our people, cultural traditions, and values are portrayed. We don't own mainstream terrestrial hip-hop and RnB radio stations–old white guys do. We don't own major newspapers and television news stations to tell the stories that matter to us–old white guys control the flow of information relevant to the black community on that scale. We don't own or control major film studios, NBA and NFL teams, or giant record labels–old white guys do. Sure, we have Tyler Perry, Oprah, and RocNation, but having a handful of successful Black entrepreneurs in major areas of influence is not enough to uplift the black community as a whole. We need all hands on deck. By starting and growing businesses that are rooted in these traditions and values, Black entrepreneurs can help to preserve and celebrate these cultural practices, and share them with a wider audience.

Black creativity and athleticism has captured the attention of the masses for ages. Our colloquialisms and vernacular are appropriated and exploited by multinational corporations and political parties all the time. Our Black sons, brothers, and cousins compose the rosters and put up the performances that sell the tickets in the big sports arenas, but we don't own the teams or the stadiums. Black creatives make the music and play the characters that enrich lives all over the world on a daily basis–but we don't own the record labels, the production companies, the casting agencies, the distribution companies, the licensing agencies, the performing rights organizations, or the radio stations–old white guys do.

One way in which Black entrepreneurship can help to preserve cultural traditions and values is through the creation of businesses that are centered around these practices. For example, a black entrepreneur might start a business that specializes in traditional African-inspired clothing, or a restaurant that serves dishes that are rooted in African cuisine. By starting businesses that are connected to their cultural traditions and values, Black entrepreneurs can help to keep these practices alive and relevant, and share them with a wider audience.

Another way–one that requires an effort from our black celebrities and influencers–is to use the platforms that we have to advocate for improvement in conditions for Black entrepreneurs in America. We need a new movement amongst our best, brightest, and most successful members of the black community. Colin Kaepernick attempted to inspire a movement amongst black NFL players to rise up against current systems of institutional racism by staging peaceful protests during the national anthem of his football games. But rather than take a knee and take a stand with their brother in his act of brave defiance that would have ultimately benefited us all as black people, the other prominent Black players took their paychecks and then took their lilly-asses home. The saga concluded with Colin being black-balled from the NFL. This was just of many lost opportunities, and a powerful example of the untapped potential in the black community to spark change for the better.

In addition to preserving cultural traditions and values, Black entrepreneurship can also provide a platform for sharing these practices with a wider audience. This can be achieved through a variety of means, such as social media, online marketing, and traditional advertising. By sharing their products and services with a wider audience, Black entrepreneurs can help to introduce others to their cultural traditions and values, and help to increase understanding and appreciation for these practices.

The portrayal of black culture and the curation of black art is practically controlled by–you guessed it–old white guys. The strongest parts of any culture are usually based upon family and spiritual traditions. The strength of the black community depends entirely upon the strength of the network of individual black family units within the black community. One of the main reasons we don't have a strong and united black community in America is because we don't have strong black individual family units. Our families are often fractured and estranged. But this was not always the case within the black community. Through slavery, the reconstruction, the great migration, and other socio-political phenomena like the American War on The Black Family Unit, the American black family has largely been left in tatters compared to our brethren in Africa. The war on the black family is largely an economic one perpetrated by the American government, but the American media's way of portraying and preserving our culture also plays a huge role in that war as well.

Take the portrayal of the modern black family unit in American media, for example. When you look at television shows, advertisements, and movies take care to notice the American mainstream's portrayal of us. You will see black people in families composed of everything besides a black man married to a black woman with happy, healthy, heterosexual black children. You will see various commercials and films with a black woman with a non-black man, or a black man married to a non-black woman. When I do see two black people in love on television, it's usually portrayed as homosexual love. Don't believe me? Go onto Youtube and pull up any pharmaceutical commercial and see how many purely black families you see that are being portrayed as completely healthy and happy. It's as if Hollywood has an agenda because producers and directors go to great lengths to show black families as anything other than straight black.

There is tremendous strength to be found in a giant network of black families, but America has been waging war on the black family since the transatlantic slave trade. Black musicians with themes of hope and inspiration, or with pro-black messaging in their music are passed over by white record executives for those that sing tales of black death and destruction. But Black entrepreneurship can change this. Black-owned major record labels and radio stations would help to empower the black community to take back control of its narrative and its destiny from those who seek to usurp it. We need more black ownership in music, film and tv.

Black entrepreneurship also helps to celebrate cultural traditions and values within the black community. By starting and growing successful businesses that are rooted in these traditions, Black entrepreneurs can create a sense of pride and accomplishment within the community, and provide a platform for sharing these practices with others. This can help to strengthen the bonds within the community and foster a sense of unity and belonging.

This can be achieved through the creation of businesses that are centered around cultural traditions and values, sharing these practices with a wider audience, and celebrating these traditions within the black community. Black-owned businesses that provide event services, restaurants, travel agencies, museums, and art galleries, parade and festival companies, production studios, and black-owned private schools are all businesses with the potential to make immense profits while celebrating black cultural traditions.

The production house that tells black stories, restaurants that serve fine cuisine originating within the black community, travel agencies that specialize in black cultural tours that enlighten and create bonds among all people, local black history museums and art galleries that showcase black talent in different mediums, and companies that host parades and festivals celebrating black achievement and heroism could all be deployed to uplift the black community while enriching the world at large. Black-owned lifestyle magazines and television networks can show us black opulence and tell black stories free from the coercive influence of political parties controlled by old white guys. Black-owned radio stations could play music by talented black artists that speak truth to power and tell stories that inspire hope and activism. Black entrepreneurship is a formidable tool against the well-embedded institutional racism that still affects our the black community today.

SOCIAL IMPACT

Black entrepreneurs have the opportunity to create positive social impact through their businesses, whether through their products and services, or through initiatives that give back to their communities. This is important because businesses can have a significant impact on the well-being and prosperity of their communities, and Black entrepreneurs have the ability to use their businesses as a platform for making a positive difference.

One way in which Black entrepreneurs can create positive social impact through their businesses is through the products and services they offer. For example, a black entrepreneur might start a business that provides healthy and affordable food options in a food desert, or a business that offers products made by black artisans that helps to increase market visibility for black businesses, or a company that creates eco-friendly products to help protect the environment. By offering products and services that address pressing social issues and meet the needs of their communities, Black entrepreneurs can help to make a positive difference in the lives of all those around them.

In addition to creating positive social impact through their products and services, Black entrepreneurs also have the opportunity to give back to their communities through initiatives that are specifically focused on making a difference. This can include things like volunteering time and resources to support local causes, or starting a business that is specifically designed to benefit the community, such as a social enterprise. By actively working to make a positive impact in their communities, Black entrepreneurs can help to create a sense of social responsibility and purpose within their businesses.

It is important to note that creating positive social impact is not limited to businesses that are focused on social causes. All businesses, regardless of their focus, have the opportunity to make a positive difference in their communities. This can be achieved through things like supporting local suppliers and vendors, providing employment and training opportunities, and contributing to the local black organizations. By taking a proactive approach to giving back to their communities, Black entrepreneurs can help to create a more vibrant and prosperous society for all.

INNOVATION

Black entrepreneurs can bring fresh perspectives and new ideas to their industries, leading to innovation and progress. This is important because diversity of thought and experience is crucial for driving innovation and progress in any field. By bringing their unique perspectives and experiences to their industries, Black entrepreneurs can help to challenge the status quo and bring new ideas and approaches to the table.

One way in which Black entrepreneurs can bring fresh perspectives and new ideas to their industries is through their personal experiences and backgrounds. For example, a black entrepreneur who has grown up in a low-income neighborhood might bring a unique perspective to the field of affordable housing, or a black entrepreneur who has experienced discrimination might bring a different perspective to the field of criminal justice or diversity and inclusion. By bringing these unique experiences and perspectives to their industries, Black entrepreneurs can help to spark new ideas and approaches that might not have otherwise been considered.

In addition to their personal experiences, Black entrepreneurs also bring new ideas and approaches to their industries through their cultural traditions and values. For example, a black entrepreneur might draw on African-inspired design elements to create innovative fashion products, or incorporate traditional African healing practices into their wellness business. By bringing these cultural influences into their industries, Black entrepreneurs can help to bring fresh perspectives and new ideas to the table.

Black entrepreneurs also contribute to innovation and progress in their industries by serving as role models and providing representation in fields where they are traditionally underrepresented. By succeeding in these fields and serving as an example for others to follow, Black entrepreneurs can help to increase diversity and inclusion, and can serve as the voice for sharing new ideas and approaches. However, it is crucial that the barriers discussed earlier be addressed in order to fully realize the potential of Black entrepreneurship in this regard.

Chapter Two:
Defining Your Business Idea

As a black entrepreneur in America, the process of defining your business idea is no doubt a daunting and potentially fraught undertaking. Not only are you faced with the same challenges that all entrepreneurs must confront when trying to conceptualize and bring a new venture to fruition, but you also most likely have to navigate the unique set of barriers and biases that are the unfortunate reality for black business owners today. Despite these challenges, many Black entrepreneurs are still able to not only survive, but thrive, by finding creative ways to turn their ideas into successful enterprises. In this chapter, we will explore the process of defining your business idea and offer insights and guidance for how you can successfully bring your own vision to life.

Obviously, the process of defining your business idea is a crucial first step towards building a successful enterprise. You can't build a business if you have no idea what you're bringing to the marketplace. It requires not only a deep understanding of your own passions, skills, and values, but also a comprehensive analysis of the market and industry in which you hope to operate. This chapter is designed to provide you with the tools and resources you need to confidently and effectively define your business idea and set the stage for future growth and success. We will begin by exploring the importance of self-assessment and market research in the idea definition process, and then move on to discuss how to refine and articulate your concept in a clear and compelling manner. Throughout the chapter, we will draw on the experiences and insights of successful Black entrepreneurs to offer practical guidance and inspiration as you work to bring your own vision to fruition.

IDENTIFY YOUR PASSIONS AND STRENGTHS

It's important for Black entrepreneurs to identify their passions and strengths in order to create a business that is meaningful and fulfilling to them. Making money in business is cool and all, but if you're not happy or not passionate about your livelihood, then it will only end up becoming another monotonous station that you dread tending everyday. So, do something you would do for free if you had all the money in the world.

So, again, the first step in defining your business idea is to take a thorough inventory of your passions and strengths. This involves examining what truly excites and motivates you, as well as what you are naturally good at. Some questions to consider as you reflect on your passions and strengths might include:

- What activities or hobbies do you enjoy in your free time?
- What subjects or topics do you love learning about or discussing?
- What skills or abilities do you have that others frequently compliment or seek out?

- What values or principles are most important to you, and how do they inform your decision-making?

It is important to be honest and candid with yourself as you consider these questions, as your passions and strengths will form the foundation of your business idea. For example, if you are passionate about cooking and have a natural talent for creating delicious, innovative recipes, starting a food-related business might be a great fit. On the other hand, if you are not particularly interested in cooking and do not consider yourself a particularly skilled chef, it is unlikely that a food-related business would be a good fit for you in the long term.

Once you have identified your passions and strengths, it is time to start thinking about how you can translate them into a viable business idea. This requires a combination of creativity and strategic thinking. Consider the following steps as you work to define your business idea:

1. Research the market: Before you can develop a solid business idea, you need to have a good understanding of the market in which you will be operating. This includes identifying potential customers, competitors, and trends in your industry. You can gather this information through online research, market reports, and by speaking with industry experts.
2. Identify a problem or need: A successful business idea addresses a problem or need that customers are willing to pay to solve. As you research the market, pay close attention to areas where there is a gap in the offerings of existing businesses. This could be an unmet need, a pain point, or an opportunity for innovation.
3. Develop a solution: Once you have identified a problem or need, it is time to brainstorm ways to solve it. Consider how your passions and strengths can be leveraged to create a unique and compelling solution. This might involve developing a new product or service, or offering an existing product or service in a novel way.
4. Test and refine your idea: Before you fully commit to your business idea, it is important to test it out on a small scale to see if it is viable. This might involve conducting market research to gauge customer interest, or creating a prototype or sample of your product or service to show to potential customers. Based on the feedback you receive, you may need to make adjustments to your idea in order to make it more attractive or effective.

Defining your business idea as a black entrepreneur can be a challenging but rewarding process. By taking the time to identify your passions and strengths, and using them to develop a unique and compelling solution to a problem or need in the market, you can set the stage for future success and create a business that aligns with your values and goals.

RESEARCHING YOUR MARKET

Conducting market research helps entrepreneurs understand the needs and preferences of their target audience, and identify opportunities within their industry. As a black entrepreneur, it is essential to conduct thorough market research. This process involves gathering and analyzing data about your potential customers, competitors, and the market as a whole in order to inform your business decisions and strategy. Here, I will uncover how you can effectively research your market as a black entrepreneur in order to set the stage for success.

One of the key benefits of market research is that it allows you to gain a deep understanding of your target audience and their needs. This is especially important if you are targeting a specific demographic, such as black consumers, as their preferences and purchasing habits may differ from those of the general population. Some ways to research your target audience might include:

- **Surveying potential customers**: One of the most effective ways to gather data about your target audience is to ask them directly. Consider creating a survey that asks questions about their needs, preferences, and purchasing habits. You can distribute the survey through social media, online forums, or in-person at events or locations where your target audience is likely to be.
- **Conducting focus groups**: Another way to gather data about your target audience is to bring a small group of people together for a focused discussion about your product or service. Focus groups can be a valuable source of insights, as they allow you to observe how people interact with your concept and get a sense of their thoughts and feelings about it.
- **Analyzing industry data**: In addition to gathering data directly from potential customers, it is also helpful to review industry reports, market research studies, and other sources of data to get a broader understanding of your target audience. This can provide valuable insights into trends, patterns, and opportunities within your industry.

Once you have a solid understanding of your target audience, the next step is to identify opportunities within your industry. This involves looking for areas where there is a gap in the offerings of existing businesses, or where you can differentiate your product or service in a meaningful way. Some ways to identify opportunities within your industry might include:

- **Analyzing competitors**: It is important to keep an eye on what your competitors are doing in order to understand the landscape of your industry and identify areas where you can differentiate yourself. Consider creating a competitive analysis that compares your product or service to those of your competitors in terms of features, pricing, and marketing efforts.
- **Identifying unmet needs**: Look for areas where there is a need or demand that is not being adequately addressed by existing businesses. This could be a pain point, an unfulfilled desire, or an opportunity for innovation.
- **Seeking out trends**: Pay attention to emerging trends in your industry, as they can often signal new opportunities for growth. This might involve looking at consumer behavior, technological advancements, or shifts in regulations or policies.

Effective market research is a crucial component of success for any black entrepreneur. By taking the time to understand the needs and preferences of your target audience and identify opportunities within your industry, you can develop a business strategy that is grounded in data and positioned for success. Don't make the mistake of trying to force a product or service down people's throats. Instead, do your research and offer people products and services that they desire or need.

EVALUATING YOUR COMPETITION

Understanding the competition can be a key factor in helping Black entrepreneurs identify areas where they can differentiate their business and stand out in the market. By analyzing the competition, Black entrepreneurs can gain a better understanding of the market, identify any gaps or opportunities, and develop strategies to set themselves apart from the competition.

One of the first steps in understanding the competition is to conduct a thorough market analysis. This involves researching the market and gathering information about the current state of the industry, including the size and growth of the market, the major players and their market share, and any trends or changes that may be affecting the market.

Once you have a good understanding of the market, you can then start to analyze your competition. This involves examining the products or services offered by your competitors, their pricing and marketing strategies, and their strengths and weaknesses. By understanding what your competitors are doing, you can identify any areas where you may be able to differentiate your business and stand out in the market.

One way that Black entrepreneurs can differentiate their business is by focusing on a specific niche or target market. By identifying a specific group of customers or a particular need or problem that is not being adequately addressed by the competition, you can tailor your products or services to meet these specific needs and stand out in the market.

Another way to differentiate your business is by offering a unique value proposition. This can be achieved by offering a superior product or service, or by providing added value through exceptional customer service or a memorable brand experience. By offering something that the competition does not, you can differentiate your business and stand out in the market.

In addition to these strategies, Black entrepreneurs can also differentiate their business by building strong relationships with their customers. This can involve going above and beyond to ensure customer satisfaction, being responsive to customer needs and concerns, and building a loyal customer base through excellent service and support.

Another way to differentiate your business is by leveraging your unique experiences and perspectives as a black entrepreneur. By bringing a fresh perspective and unique insights to your products or services, you can differentiate your business and stand out in the market. For example, I have the ability to write a book from the perspective of a black entrepreneur because I am a black entrepreneur. Entrepreneurship–from an author's perspective–is a pretty broad topic. However, an entrepreneurship book geared specifically towards black and marginalized entrepreneurs is a more narrow niche. Black entrepreneurs looking for a book that can help them become bosses and give them guidance on how to manage their lifestyle at the same time–that's an even smaller niche.

Hopefully, you now see that understanding the competition is an important aspect of running a successful business, and it can be particularly beneficial for Black entrepreneurs looking to differentiate their business and stand out in the market. By conducting a thorough market analysis and understanding the competition, Black entrepreneurs can identify areas where they can differentiate their business and develop strategies to set themselves apart from the competition.

DEFINING YOUR UNIQUE VALUE PROPOSITION

A unique value proposition is a clear and concise statement that explains the unique benefits of your business and what sets it apart from the competition. It is a key component of your marketing strategy, and it can help Black entrepreneurs clearly communicate the value of their business to potential customers.

Developing a unique value proposition can be a challenging task, but it is an essential step in building a successful business. To create an effective unique value proposition, it is important to first identify your target market and understand their needs and pain points. This will help you tailor your value proposition to meet the specific needs of your target audience.

Once you have a clear understanding of your target market, you can start to brainstorm potential value propositions. Some questions to consider include: What makes your product or service unique? How does it solve a specific problem or meet a specific need for your customers? What value does it offer that the competition does not?

It is important to keep your unique value proposition concise and to the point. A good unique value proposition should be able to clearly communicate the value of your business in a single sentence or phrase.

In addition to clearly communicating the benefits of your business, a unique value proposition can also help you differentiate your business from the competition. By offering something that the competition does not, you can stand out in the market and attract potential customers.

Once you have developed your unique value proposition, it is important to consistently incorporate it into all aspects of your marketing efforts. This includes your website, social media profiles, marketing materials, and any other communications with potential customers.

So, now you know that defining your unique value proposition is an essential step in building a successful business. By clearly communicating the benefits of your business and what sets it apart from the competition, you can effectively attract potential customers and differentiate your business in the market. By consistently incorporating your unique value proposition into all aspects of your marketing efforts, you can effectively communicate the value of your business and stand out from the competition.

EXPLORING NICHE MARKETS

As a black entrepreneur, you may want to consider exploring niche markets within your industry as a way to differentiate your business and stand out in the market. A niche market is a specific segment of a larger market that has unique needs or characteristics. By specializing in a particular niche, you can focus your efforts on meeting the specific needs of this group of customers and differentiate your business from the competition.

There are several benefits to specializing in a niche market. First, niche markets are often less competitive than larger markets, which can make it easier for you to stand out and differentiate your business. Additionally, because niche markets are typically smaller, you can focus on building strong relationships with your customers and providing exceptional service to meet their specific needs.

To explore niche markets, it is important to first identify your target market and understand their needs and pressure points. This will help you determine which niche markets may be a good fit for your business. You can then research these markets to gather information about the size and growth of the market, the major players and their market share, and any trends or changes that may be affecting the market.

Once you have identified a potential niche market, it is important to develop a marketing strategy that targets this specific group of customers. This may involve developing specialized products or services that meet the specific needs of this market, or targeting your marketing efforts to reach potential customers within this market.

In addition to specializing in a particular niche market, it is also important to keep an eye on trends and changes in the larger market. By staying up to date on industry trends and changes, you can identify opportunities to expand your business and reach new customers.

I've just summed up how exploring niche markets can be a valuable strategy for Black entrepreneurs looking to differentiate their business and stand out in the market. By specializing in a particular niche and targeting your marketing efforts to meet the specific needs of this group of customers, you can build a successful business and differentiate yourself from the competition. By staying up to date on industry trends and changes, you can also identify opportunities to expand your business and reach new customers.

SEEKING FEEDBACK AND VALIDATION

As a black entrepreneur, seeking feedback and validation from potential customers and industry experts can be an important step in refining and validating your business idea. By gathering input and perspectives from others, you can gain valuable insights into your business concept and identify any potential weaknesses or areas for improvement.

One way to seek feedback and validation is by conducting market research. This can involve surveying potential customers to gather insights into their needs and preferences, or conducting focus groups to get more in-depth feedback on your business idea. Market research can help you understand the potential demand for your products or services and identify any potential challenges or obstacles you may face in bringing your idea to market.

In addition to conducting market research, you can also seek feedback and validation from industry experts and advisors. This can include reaching out to business mentors, joining industry associations or networking groups, or seeking the guidance of industry professionals. These individuals can provide valuable insights and guidance, and they can help you identify potential opportunities or challenges that you may not have considered.

It is also important to be open to feedback and be willing to make changes or adjustments to your business idea based on the feedback you receive. While it is natural to be attached to your business idea, being open to feedback and willing to make changes can help you refine your idea and increase the chances of success. The main point is to ask for the feedback because, as the old adage goes, "a closed mouth don't get fed."

If a successful launch is what you're looking for, seeking feedback and validation is an important step in the process of launching a business. By gathering input and insights from potential customers and industry experts, you can validate and refine your business idea and increase your chances of success. By being open to feedback and willing to make changes based on the feedback you receive, you can improve your business concept and increase your chances of success in the market.

Chapter Three:
Creating Your Business Plan

As a black entrepreneur, creating a solid business plan is essential to the success of your business. A well-crafted business plan not only serves as a roadmap for your business, but it also helps you to clearly articulate your vision, goals, and strategies to potential investors, partners, and customers. A business plan can also help you to secure funding, attract top talent, and stay organized and on track as you work to grow and scale your business. In this chapter, we will explore the key elements of a business plan and discuss how Black entrepreneurs can leverage this valuable tool to achieve success. I will cover topics such as defining your goals, planning your marketing strategy, developing ways to pay for stuff, researching your industry and more.

DEFINING YOUR GOALS AND OBJECTIVES

Defining your goals and objectives is an essential step in creating a business plan, and it can be particularly important for Black entrepreneurs as they work to establish and grow their businesses. A clear set of goals and objectives can help you stay focused and motivated, and it can also provide a roadmap for your business, helping you to stay on track and measure your progress.

To define your goals and objectives, it is important to start by considering your long-term vision for your business. What do you hope to achieve in the long run? This might include goals such as increasing sales, expanding your customer base, or achieving profitability.

Once you have identified your long-term vision, you can start to break down your goals into more specific and achievable objectives. This might include short-term goals such as launching a new product line, increasing your social media presence, or improving customer satisfaction. It is important to make your objectives measurable, so that you can track your progress and know when you have achieved them.

In addition to setting specific goals and objectives, it is also important to consider the resources and support you will need to achieve them. This might include financial resources, staff, marketing efforts, or partnerships. By considering the resources and support you will need to achieve your goals, you can ensure that you have a solid foundation for your business.

As you work to define your goals and objectives, it is also important to be flexible and open to change. The business landscape is constantly evolving, and your goals and objectives may need to adapt as your business grows and changes. By being open to change and adjusting your goals and objectives as needed, you can ensure that your business remains lean, agile and well-positioned for success.

Clearly, defining your goals and objectives is an essential step in creating a business plan and establishing a successful venture. By setting specific and measurable objectives and considering the resources and support you will need to achieve them, you can stay focused and motivated as you work to grow your business. By being open to change and adapting your goals and objectives as needed, you can ensure that your business remains agile and well-positioned for success.

OUTLINING YOUR MARKETING AND SALES STRATEGIES

As a black entrepreneur, a strong marketing and sales plan can be a crucial factor in attracting and retaining customers. A well-crafted marketing and sales plan should outline your target market, your marketing and sales channels, and your marketing and sales tactics, as well as your budget and resources. By outlining these key elements, you can create a roadmap for building and maintaining a successful customer base.

One of the first steps in outlining your marketing and sales strategies is to identify your target market. This involves understanding the demographics, needs, and preferences of your potential customers. By understanding your target market, you can tailor your marketing and sales efforts to effectively reach and engage with your audience.

Once you have identified your target market, you can then consider your marketing and sales channels. This might include traditional channels such as print and broadcast advertising, as well as digital channels such as social media and email marketing. By considering a range of channels, you can reach your target market through the channels that they are most likely to use.

You then need to consider your marketing and sales channels, you should also outline your marketing and sales tactics. This might include specific campaigns or promotions, as well as tactics such as content marketing or lead generation. By outlining specific tactics, you can create a roadmap for executing your marketing and sales efforts.

Finally, it is important to consider your budget and resources when outlining your marketing and sales strategies. This includes both financial resources, as well as staff and other resources that you will need to execute your marketing and sales efforts. By considering your budget and resources, you can ensure that you have the support you need to effectively implement your marketing and sales strategies.

So, a strong marketing and sales plan is essential for attracting and retaining customers as a black entrepreneur. By identifying your target market, considering a range of marketing and sales channels, outlining specific marketing and sales tactics, and considering your budget and resources, you can create a roadmap for building and maintaining a successful customer base. By regularly reviewing and refining your marketing and sales strategies, you can stay attuned to the needs and preferences of your customers and stay ahead of the competition.

DEVELOPING A FINANCIAL PLAN

Developing a financial plan is an essential step in forecasting your revenue and expenses, and making informed business decisions. A financial plan should outline your current financial position, your financial goals, and your strategies for achieving those goals. By creating a financial plan, you can gain a better understanding of your financial resources and needs, and you can make informed decisions about how to allocate those resources to achieve your business objectives.

One of the key components of a financial plan is understanding your current financial position. This includes examining your current assets, liabilities, and cash flow, as well as any outstanding debts or obligations. By understanding your current financial position, you can identify any potential challenges or opportunities that may impact your business.

Once you have a clear understanding of your current financial position, you can then set financial goals for your business. These goals might include increasing revenue, improving profitability, or achieving a certain level of cash flow. It is important to make your financial goals specific, measurable, achievable, relevant, and time-bound (SMART) to ensure that they are realistic and achievable.

In addition to setting financial goals, your financial plan should also outline the strategies you will use to achieve those goals. This might include strategies such as increasing sales, reducing expenses, or seeking additional funding. By outlining specific strategies, you can create a roadmap for achieving your financial goals.

Again, developing a financial plan is an essential step in forecasting your revenue and expenses and making informed business decisions as a black entrepreneur. By understanding your current financial position, setting financial goals, outlining strategies for achieving those goals, and considering your budget and resources, you can create a roadmap for achieving financial success and meeting your business objectives. By regularly reviewing and updating your financial plan, you can stay abreast of changes in your financial position and adjust your strategies as needed.

IDENTIFYING YOUR TARGET AUDIENCE

Clearly defining your target audience is an essential step in tailoring your marketing and sales efforts to reach your desired customers. By identifying your target audience, you can focus your efforts on reaching and engaging with the specific group of customers that are most likely to be interested in your products or services.

To identify your target audience, it is important to start by considering the characteristics of your ideal customer. This might include factors such as demographics, interests, needs, and purchasing habits. By understanding the characteristics of your ideal customer, you can more effectively reach and engage with this group.

Once you have a clear understanding of your ideal customer, you can then start to segment your target audience into smaller groups. This might include dividing your audience by age, gender, income, location, or other factors that are relevant to your business. By segmenting your audience, you can tailor your marketing and sales efforts to more effectively reach specific groups of customers.

In addition to considering the characteristics of your target audience, it is also important to consider the channels that they are most likely to use. This might include traditional channels such as print and broadcast advertising, as well as digital channels such as social media and email marketing. By considering the channels that your target audience is most likely to use, you can more effectively reach and engage with them.

Once you have identified your target audience and the channels they are most likely to use, you can then start to develop marketing and sales strategies that are tailored to this specific group of customers. This might include developing targeted campaigns or promotions, or creating content that is specifically designed to appeal to your target audience. By developing strategies that are tailored to your target audience, you can more effectively reach and engage with this group.

So remember, clearly defining your target audience is an essential step in tailoring your marketing and sales efforts to reach your desired customers. By understanding the characteristics of your ideal customer and the channels they are most likely to use, you can develop targeted strategies that are more likely to be successful in reaching and engaging with this group. By regularly reviewing and updating your target audience, you can stay attuned to changes in your customer base and adjust your strategies as needed.

RESEARCHING YOUR INDUSTRY AND COMPETITION

Conducting industry and competitive research is an essential step for any entrepreneur, but it is especially important for Black entrepreneurs. By understanding the landscape they are operating in, Black entrepreneurs can make informed decisions that increase their chances of success.

To start, it is important to research your industry. This means learning about the trends, challenges, and opportunities that exist within your industry. There are many resources available to help you do this, including trade publications, industry reports, and online databases like IBISWorld or Hoover's.

One key aspect of industry research is understanding the market size and growth potential of your industry. This information can help you gauge the potential demand for your products or services and make decisions about how to position your business in the market.

It is also important to research your competitors. This means learning about the other businesses that offer products or services similar to yours. By understanding your competitors, you can identify their strengths and weaknesses and determine how to differentiate your own business.

To research your competitors, you can start by looking at their websites, reading their press releases and articles, and conducting online searches. You can also use tools like Google Alerts to stay updated on your competitors' activities. Additionally, you may want to consider talking to customers or suppliers to get a sense of what they think of your competitors.

Another important aspect of competitive research is understanding your competitors' pricing strategies. By knowing how your competitors price their products or services, you can determine whether you need to adjust your own pricing to remain competitive.

In addition to conducting research on your industry and competitors, it is also important to research potential customers. This means learning about their needs, preferences, and behaviors. You can do this through market research surveys, focus groups, or online research. By understanding your target customers, you can tailor your products or services to better meet their needs and increase your chances of success.

Overall, conducting industry and competitive research is an important step for any entrepreneur, but it is especially important for Black entrepreneurs. By understanding the landscape they are operating in, Black entrepreneurs can make informed decisions that increase their chances of success. By researching their industry, competitors, and customers, Black entrepreneurs can gain valuable insights that help them position their business for success in a competitive market.

SEEKING PROFESSIONAL ADVICE

Seeking advice from industry experts, mentors, and advisors can be an invaluable step in the process of developing a solid business plan. By drawing on the knowledge and experience of others, you can gain valuable insights and a perspective that can help you identify potential challenges and opportunities, and make informed decisions about your business.

One key advantage of seeking professional advice is that it can help you develop a business plan that takes into account all the necessary considerations. This includes everything from financial projections and marketing strategies, to operational plans and risk management strategies. It's always good to have someone that can see into your blind spots and help you stay prepared for things you yourself cannot see coming.

To get started, you may want to consider reaching out to industry experts or consultants who have experience in your specific industry. They can provide valuable insights on market trends, customer needs, and regulatory considerations, as well as help you develop a realistic financial plan.

In addition to industry experts, mentors and advisors can also be a valuable source of advice and guidance. Whether you are just starting out or have been in business for a while, having someone to bounce ideas off of and get feedback from can be incredibly helpful. Mentors and advisors can also provide valuable perspective on business challenges and opportunities, and help you identify potential solutions.

Another important consideration when seeking professional advice is to make sure you are working with individuals or organizations that understand the unique challenges and opportunities faced by Black entrepreneurs. This can be especially important for those who are just starting out and may not have as much experience or knowledge about the business landscape.

Overall, seeking professional advice from industry experts, mentors, and advisors is an important step for any entrepreneur, but it is especially important for Black entrepreneurs. By drawing on the knowledge and experience of others, you can develop a solid business plan that takes into account all the necessary considerations, and increase your chances of success. So, it is always better to seek professional advice before starting a business or making any major business decisions.

Chapter Four:
Funding Your Startup

As a black entrepreneur, securing funding for your startup can often feel like an uphill battle. Despite the numerous resources and opportunities available for entrepreneurship, black business owners still face significant barriers when it comes to accessing capital. These challenges can be particularly daunting for those who are just starting out and may not have the connections or resources of more established entrepreneurs. However, it is important to remember that funding is crucial for the success and growth of any business, and there are steps you can take to increase your chances of securing the financial support you need. This chapter will explore some of the options available to Black entrepreneurs looking to find funding for their startup and provide tips and strategies for maximizing your chances of success.

IDENTIFYING FUNDING SOURCES

As a black entrepreneur, it is important to research and identify potential sources of funding for your startup. This may include grants, loans, and investment opportunities that are specifically targeted towards minority-owned businesses or those that have a history of supporting diverse entrepreneurs. Here are some steps you can take to identify funding sources:

1. Research online: There are numerous online resources that can help you find funding opportunities for your startup. Websites like Grants.gov, the Minority Business Development Agency, and the National Association of Investment Companies (NAIC) are all good places to start. You can also search for grants and loans specifically designed for minority-owned businesses on the U.S. Small Business Administration (SBA) website.
2. Look into government grants: The government offers a range of grants specifically designed to support minority-owned businesses. The SBA has a number of programs that provide financial assistance to minority-owned businesses, including the 7(j) Management and Technical Assistance Program and the 8(a) Business Development Program.
3. Consider crowdfunding: Crowdfunding platforms like Kickstarter and Indiegogo allow you to raise money from a large number of people in exchange for a product or service. This can be a great way to get your business off the ground and test the market for your product or service.
4. Explore angel investing: Angel investors are individuals who invest their own money in startups in exchange for an ownership stake in the company. Many angel investors are looking for innovative and diverse startups to support, and there are organizations like the Pipeline Angels and the New Voices Fund that specifically support Black entrepreneurs.

5. Look into venture capital: Venture capital firms invest in high-growth startups in exchange for an ownership stake in the company. Although venture capital can be difficult to secure, it can provide a significant amount of funding for your startup. There are venture capital firms that focus on investing in diverse startups, such as Kapor Capital, Black Angel Tech Fund, Backstage Capital, Humble Ventures, Cross Culture Venture Capital, 500 Startups, The Harriet Fund, and Reach Capital to name a few.
6. Explore small business loans: Small business loans can provide the capital you need to get your startup off the ground. The SBA offers a number of loan programs for small businesses, including the 7(a) Loan Program and the 504 Loan Program. You can also consider applying for a business loan from a bank or alternative lender.
7. Network with other entrepreneurs: Connecting with other entrepreneurs and business owners can be a great way to learn about funding opportunities. You can join entrepreneurship groups or attend industry events to meet potential investors or lenders.

By researching and identifying potential sources of funding, you can increase your chances of securing the financial support you need to grow your startup. It is important to be proactive and take advantage of any opportunities that may be available to you. With persistence and determination, you can find the funding you need to achieve your business goals.

DEVELOPING A FUNDING PLAN

Once you have identified potential sources of funding for your startup, it is important to develop a funding plan. A funding plan is a detailed outline of the specific sources of funding you plan to pursue, the amount of funding you need, and how it will be used. Here are some key steps you can take to develop a funding plan:

- Determine your funding needs: The first step in developing a funding plan is to determine the amount of funding you need to get your startup off the ground and achieve your business goals. This will involve creating a budget that outlines your expected expenses, including costs for rent, salaries, marketing, and other business-related expenses.
- Identify your funding sources: Once you know how much funding you need, you can start identifying the specific sources of funding you plan to pursue. This may include grants, loans, investment opportunities, or a combination of these options. Make sure to research the requirements and application process for each potential funding source to ensure that you are a good fit and have a strong chance of success.
- Develop a timeline: It is important to have a clear timeline for securing funding for your startup. This will help you stay organized and ensure that you are making progress towards your funding goals. Your timeline should include deadlines for

applying for grants and loans, as well as any other key milestones related to securing funding.
- Create a pitch: A strong pitch is crucial for convincing investors or lenders to support your startup. Your pitch should include an overview of your business, your target market, and the value proposition of your product or service. You should also include financial projections and a clear plan for how you will use the funding you receive.

Develop a plan for using the funding: Once you have secured funding, it is important to have a clear plan for how you will use it. This should include specific goals and milestones that you plan to achieve with the funding, as well as a budget for how you will allocate the funds.

Developing a funding plan is an important step for any entrepreneur, but it can be especially crucial for Black entrepreneurs who may face additional challenges when it comes to accessing capital. By putting together a clear and well-thought-out plan, you can increase your chances of success and set your startup up for long-term growth.

CRAFTING A PITCH

As a black entrepreneur, you will likely need to pitch your business to potential funders in order to secure the financing you need to get your startup off the ground. A strong pitch is crucial for convincing investors or lenders to support your business, and it can be the difference between securing funding or coming up empty-handed. Here are some tips for crafting a compelling pitch:

1. Identify your value proposition: Your value proposition is the unique benefit that your product or service offers to customers. It is important to clearly communicate this value in your pitch, as it will help potential funders understand the potential return on investment (ROI) they can expect from supporting your business. I will cover value propositions in more detail later.
2. Highlight your competitive advantage: In order to stand out from the competition, it is important to highlight any unique advantages that your business has. This could include a proprietary technology, a unique business model, or a strong team.
3. Explain your target market: It is important to clearly define your target market in your pitch, as this will help potential funders understand the size and potential of your market. Be specific and use data to back up your claims.
4. Present your financial projections: Financial projections are estimates of your business's future financial performance. They can include estimates of your revenue, expenses, and profits. It is important to present realistic and well-reasoned financial projections in your pitch, as they will help potential funders understand the potential ROI of supporting your business.
5. Practice, practice, practice: A strong pitch is the result of careful preparation and practice. It is important to rehearse your pitch in front of a test audience and get

feedback on what works and what doesn't. This will help you refine your pitch and improve your chances of success.

Crafting a compelling pitch is an essential skill for any entrepreneur, but it can be especially important for Black entrepreneurs who may face additional barriers when it comes to accessing capital. By highlighting the value of your product or service and the potential return on investment, you can increase your chances of securing the financing you need to succeed.

SEEKING PROFESSIONAL ADVICE

As a black entrepreneur, you may find it beneficial to seek the advice of financial advisors, business consultants, or legal professionals as you navigate the funding process. These professionals can provide valuable guidance and support as you work to secure the financing you need to grow your business. Here are some reasons why you may want to consider seeking professional advice:

- Financial advisors can help you create a budget and financial plan: Financial advisors can help you create a budget and financial plan that takes into account your current financial situation and your business goals. They can provide advice on how to allocate your resources and manage your finances to maximize your chances of success.
- Business consultants can provide guidance on business strategy and growth: Business consultants can help you develop a solid business strategy and identify opportunities for growth. They can also provide guidance on how to scale your business and navigate challenges as you grow.
- Legal professionals can help you navigate the legal aspects of starting a business: For instance, I help my clients navigate the legal aspects of starting a business, including incorporating their business, drafting contracts, and protecting their intellectual property.
- Professional advisors can help you create a strong pitch: Financial advisors, business consultants, and legal professionals can all provide valuable input as you craft a strong pitch to present to potential funders. They can help you clarify your business concept, identify your target market, and develop financial projections that are realistic and well-reasoned.

Seeking professional advice can be especially important for Black entrepreneurs, who may face additional barriers when it comes to accessing capital. By working with financial advisors, business consultants, and legal professionals, you can increase your chances of success and set your startup up for long-term growth. These services are worth the money.

LEVERAGING YOUR PERSONAL AND PROFESSIONAL NETWORKS

As a black entrepreneur, it can often be difficult to access funding and resources, as well as to build support for your business. One way to overcome these challenges is to leverage your personal and professional networks.

Here are some tips for leveraging your personal and professional networks as a black entrepreneur:

1. Identify key connections: Take some time to think about the people in your life who might be able to help you in your business endeavors. These might include friends, family members, colleagues, and other professionals who have relevant expertise or connections.
2. Reach out and ask for help: Once you have identified key connections, don't be afraid to reach out and ask for help. People are often willing to lend a helping hand, especially if they believe in your vision and are invested in your success.
3. Attend networking events: Networking events are a great way to meet new people and make valuable connections. Look for events that are relevant to your industry or target market, and be sure to follow up with any connections you make after the event.
4. Join professional organizations: Joining professional organizations can provide you with access to a larger network of professionals and potential funding sources. Many organizations also offer training and development opportunities, which can help you to grow your skills and knowledge.
5. Build relationships: Building relationships is key to leveraging your personal and professional networks. Take the time to get to know people, and be sure to follow up and stay in touch. This will help to build trust and establish a strong foundation for future collaborations.

Overall, leveraging your personal and professional networks is an important strategy for Black entrepreneurs. By building and nurturing relationships with key connections, you can increase your chances of finding funding and building support for your business.

BUILDING A STRONG TEAM

As a black entrepreneur, it can often be difficult to access funding and resources, as well as navigate through the various challenges that come with starting and running a business. One way to increase your chances of success is to build a strong team of advisors and supporters who can help you along the way.

There are several key components to building a strong team:

1. Identify individuals with relevant expertise and experience: Look for individuals who have experience in your industry, as well as those who have expertise in areas such as finance, marketing, and legal affairs. These individuals can provide valuable guidance and support as you navigate the challenges of starting and growing your business.

2. Build a diverse team: A diverse team brings a range of perspectives and experiences to the table, which can help you to better understand and serve your target market. In addition, a diverse team can help to create a more inclusive and welcoming environment for your employees and customers.
3. Foster open communication and collaboration: Strong teams are built on open communication and collaboration. Encourage team members to share their ideas and feedback, and make sure that everyone feels heard and valued. This will help to build trust and strengthen the team dynamic.
4. Set clear goals and expectations: Establishing clear goals and expectations for your team can help to ensure that everyone is working towards the same objectives. This will help to keep the team focused and motivated, and can help to prevent misunderstandings and conflicts.
5. Provide support and resources: As a leader, it is important to provide your team with the support and resources they need to succeed. This might include training and development opportunities, access to technology and tools, and other forms of support as needed.

Overall, building a strong team of advisors and supporters is an important step in the journey of any black entrepreneur. By putting in the effort to assemble a diverse and capable team, you can increase your chances of success and navigate the challenges of starting and growing a business more effectively. Building a strong team is so important to the black entrepreneur that I'm going to delve a little bit deeper into the idea in the next chapter. Plus, having people work for you is technically what makes you a boss.

Chapter Five:
Building A Strong Team

As an entrepreneur, building a strong and effective team is crucial to the success of your business. From identifying your team's needs to hiring freelancers and contractors, there are many factors to consider when building your team. Utilizing interns and volunteers can be a cost-effective way to bring new ideas and energy to your team, while building a virtual team can help you to tap into a global pool of talent. Seeking out mentors and advisors can provide valuable guidance and support as you navigate the challenges of starting and growing your business. In this chapter, we will delve into these topics and provide practical strategies for building a team that will help your business thrive.

But before we get started, here's a little joke to lighten the mood: Why was the math book sad? Because it had too many problems. (I know, I know, it's a bit cringey. But don't worry, the rest of this chapter will be much more insightful!)

IDENTIFYING YOUR TEAM NEEDS

As a black entrepreneur, it is important to carefully assess your business needs in order to determine the types of team members you need to bring on board. This will help to ensure that you have the necessary skills and expertise to support the growth and success of your startup.

Here are some steps to take when identifying your team needs:

1. Evaluate your current team: Take some time to review the strengths and weaknesses of your current team. Identify any gaps in skills or expertise that need to be filled in order to support the growth of your business.
2. Determine your business needs: Consider the various tasks and responsibilities that need to be carried out in order to run and grow your business. Think about the types of skills and expertise that will be required to fulfill these tasks.
3. Prioritize your needs: Once you have identified your business needs, prioritize them based on which are most essential to the success of your startup. This will help you to focus on the most important hires first.
4. Consider the long-term: As you build your team, it is important to think about the long-term needs of your business. Consider what types of skills and expertise will be needed as your business grows and evolves over time.

By taking the time to assess your team needs and determine the types of team members you need to bring on board, you can ensure that you have the necessary skills and expertise to support the growth and success of your startup.

HIRING FREELANCERS AND CONTRACTORS

You may find that your business has specific needs that are not met by your current team. In these cases, hiring freelancers or contractors can be a cost-effective way to bring in specialized skills and expertise on a short-term basis.

Here are some considerations to keep in mind when hiring freelancers and contractors:

- Determine the scope of work: Clearly define the scope of work for the freelancer or contractor, including specific tasks, deadlines, and any other requirements. This will help to ensure that everyone is on the same page and that the work is completed to your satisfaction.
- Negotiate terms: Be sure to negotiate terms such as payment, timing, and any other important details with the freelancer or contractor. This will help to avoid misunderstandings and ensure that everyone is clear on their responsibilities.
- Use a contract: It is important to use a contract when hiring freelancers or contractors. A contract will clearly outline the terms of the relationship and protect both parties in the event of any disputes.
- Communicate regularly: Regular communication is key to maintaining a successful working relationship with freelancers and contractors. Make sure to keep them in the loop and provide any necessary feedback or guidance as needed.

Overall, hiring freelancers and contractors can be a cost-effective way to fill short-term or specialized needs and build a team. By clearly defining the scope of work, negotiating terms, using a contract, and communicating regularly, you can build successful relationships with these professionals. Here are some practical steps you can take to hire freelancers or contractors to fill short-term or specialized needs:

1. Search for candidates: There are many resources available for finding freelancers and contractors, including online job boards, social media platforms, and professional networks. Use these resources to search for candidates who have the skills and expertise you are looking for.
2. Review resumes and portfolios: Once you have identified a pool of candidates, review their resumes and portfolios to get a sense of their experience and capabilities. Consider reaching out to references or previous clients to learn more about the candidates.
3. Interview candidates: Conduct interviews with the top candidates to further assess their skills and fit for your business. Be sure to ask specific questions about their experience and how they would approach the work you need done.
4. Negotiate terms: Once you have selected a candidate, be sure to negotiate terms such as payment, timing, and any other important details. A written contract

outlining these terms can help to protect both parties in the event of any disputes. I provide these types of agreements all the time in my law practice.

By following these steps, you can effectively hire freelancers or contractors to fill short-term or specialized needs and build a cost-effective team for your business.

UTILIZING INTERNS AND VOLUNTEERS

As a black entrepreneur, you may find that your business has specific needs that are not met by your current team. In these cases, utilizing interns and volunteers can be a cost-effective way to bring in new ideas and energy while also providing valuable support to your business.

Here are some considerations to keep in mind when utilizing interns and volunteers:

1. Determine your needs: Take some time to assess your business needs and determine what types of tasks and responsibilities could be handled by interns or volunteers. This will help you to identify the types of interns or volunteers you should be looking for.
2. Search for candidates: There are many resources available for finding interns and volunteers, including online job boards, social media platforms, and professional networks. Use these resources to search for candidates who are interested in gaining experience in your industry.
3. Review resumes and portfolios: Once you have identified a pool of candidates, review their resumes and portfolios to get a sense of their experience and capabilities. Consider reaching out to references or previous internships to learn more about the candidates.
4. Interview candidates: Conduct interviews with the top candidates to further assess their fit for your business. Be sure to ask specific questions about their goals and interests, as well as their availability and commitment level.
5. Set expectations: It is important to clearly communicate your expectations for interns and volunteers. Make sure they understand the tasks and responsibilities they will be taking on, as well as any policies and procedures they will need to follow.

By utilizing interns and volunteers, you can bring in new ideas and energy while also providing valuable support to your business. This can be a cost-effective way to build a team, especially if you are operating on a tight budget like me when I first started out as an entrepreneur.

BUILDING A VIRTUAL TEAM

As a black entrepreneur, you may also find that your business needs access to a wide range of skills and expertise in order to succeed, and those skills might not be readily available to you if you're only searching within your local workforce. This need is especially pronounced if you operate your business in a remote or rural part of the world. One way to meet these needs is by building a virtual team, which allows you to leverage technology to access talent from anywhere in the world.

There are several key benefits to building a virtual team:

- Access to a global pool of talent: A virtual team allows you to tap into a global pool of talent, rather than being limited to hiring locally. This can be especially beneficial if you are operating in an industry where certain skills are scarce in your area.
- Greater flexibility: A virtual team allows you to be more flexible in terms of how you structure your team. You can bring on team members as needed, rather than committing to long-term hires.
- Cost savings: Building a virtual team can be more cost-effective than hiring employees, as you don't need to provide office space or other physical resources.
- Improved productivity: Studies have shown that virtual teams can be just as productive, if not more productive, than in-person teams. This is because virtual team members often have greater autonomy and can choose to work at times when they are most productive.

There are also a few challenges to consider when building a virtual team:

- Communication: Effective communication is key to the success of any team, and this can be more challenging in a virtual setting. It is important to establish clear channels of communication and to make an effort to stay connected with team members.
- Trust and accountability: Building trust and ensuring accountability can be more challenging in a virtual setting. It is important to establish clear expectations and to provide team members with the support and resources they need to be successful.

Overall, building a virtual team can be a powerful way for Black entrepreneurs to access a global pool of talent and leverage technology to build a successful and productive team. By overcoming the challenges of communication and trust, you can build a virtual team that is well-equipped to support the growth and success of your business.

COLLABORATING WITH OTHER BUSINESSES

As a black entrepreneur, you may find that your business has specific needs that are not met by your current team, virtual assistants, or other resources. In these cases, collaborating with other businesses can be a way to access the expertise and resources you need without having to hire additional staff.

There are several benefits to collaborating with other businesses:

- Access to specialized expertise: Collaborating with other businesses can give you access to specialized expertise that you may not have in-house. This can be especially beneficial if you are operating in a niche industry or if you need access to specialized equipment or technology.
- Shared resources: Collaborating with other businesses can allow you to share resources such as office space, equipment, and staff. This can be a cost-effective way to access the resources you need without having to invest in them yourself.
- New perspectives: Collaborating with other businesses can bring new perspectives and ideas to your business, which can help you to think outside the box and come up with innovative solutions.
- Increased credibility: Collaborating with well-respected businesses in your industry can increase your credibility and help you to build a stronger reputation.

There are also a few challenges to consider when collaborating with other businesses:

- Maintaining control: Collaborating with other businesses can require you to give up some control over certain aspects of your business. It is important to carefully consider any agreements and ensure that you are comfortable with the level of control you are relinquishing.
- Managing expectations: Clearly communicating and managing expectations is crucial when collaborating with other businesses. Make sure that everyone is on the same page in terms of goals, roles, and responsibilities.
- Protecting your interests: It is important to protect your interests when collaborating with other businesses. Be sure to carefully review any agreements and consider seeking legal counsel if necessary.

Though it seems counterintuitive, collaborating with other businesses can actually be a powerful way for Black entrepreneurs to access the expertise and resources they need without having to hire additional staff. By overcoming the challenges of maintaining control, managing expectations, and protecting your interests, you can build successful and mutually beneficial collaborations that will support your growth and success.

SEEKING MENTORS AND ADVISORS

You may find that you need access to expertise and guidance as you navigate the challenges of building and growing your business as a black entrepreneur. Seeking mentors and advisors can be a powerful way to tap into this expertise without the need to bring on additional employees. In this chapter, we will explore the various benefits of seeking mentors and advisors, as well as some of the challenges to consider. We will also provide practical strategies for finding and working with mentors and advisors to support the growth and success of your business.

There are several benefits to seeking mentors and advisors:

- Expert guidance: Mentors and advisors can provide valuable guidance and support as you build and grow your business. They can offer insight and advice based on their own experiences and expertise, which can help you to make more informed decisions.
- Networking opportunities: Seeking mentors and advisors can provide access to a larger network of professionals and resources. This can be especially beneficial if you are just starting out and are looking to build connections in your industry.
- Improved decision-making: Having access to the insights and guidance of mentors and advisors can help you to make better decisions for your business. They can provide perspective and help you to consider different options and approaches.
- Personal and professional growth: Working with mentors and advisors can provide opportunities for personal and professional growth. They can help you to identify areas for improvement and provide guidance and support as you work to develop your skills and knowledge.

There are also a few challenges to consider when seeking mentors and advisors:

- Finding the right fit: It is important to find mentors and advisors who are a good fit for your business and goals. Take the time to research potential mentors and advisors and consider reaching out to multiple individuals to see who might be the best fit.
- Managing expectations: Clearly communicate your expectations and goals when seeking mentors and advisors. This will help to ensure that everyone is on the same page and that you are able to make sure you don't expect too much from your mentor.

I have many contacts within the business world, and my office is available to assist you if you need guidance on who to turn to for help with your business. Visit me at sholdondaniels.com for more information.

Chapter Six:
Marketing and Branding Strategies

Marketing and branding are crucial components of any business, but they can be especially challenging for Black entrepreneurs. One of the key reasons for this is that identifying and targeting the right audience can be difficult, as the market is often saturated with competition and there may be cultural barriers that need to be overcome. In this chapter, I will discuss the importance of identifying your target audience as a black entrepreneur and provide strategies and techniques for effectively reaching and engaging that audience. I will also explore the unique challenges and opportunities that Black entrepreneurs face in the world of marketing and branding, and offer solutions for overcoming those challenges. With the right marketing and branding strategies, Black entrepreneurs can achieve success and grow their businesses in a competitive marketplace. I might have touched on some of these concepts in different sections of this book, but the nature of marketing requires an integration of interests and ideas, so you will see it often throughout this book.

IDENTIFYING YOUR TARGET AUDIENCE

Marketing and branding are crucial to the success of any business, and Black entrepreneurs are no exception. However, identifying and targeting the right audience can be particularly challenging for black business owners, as the market is often saturated with competition and there may be cultural barriers that need to be overcome. In order to effectively reach and engage their target audience, Black entrepreneurs need to understand the unique challenges and opportunities that they face in the world of marketing and branding, and develop strategies that are tailored to their specific needs.

One effective way to identify your target audience as a black entrepreneur is to conduct market research. Market research involves gathering information about your target customers, such as their demographics, interests, and purchasing habits. This information can be collected through surveys, focus groups, and interviews, and can help you to better understand the needs and preferences of your target audience. Additionally, it can give you an idea of your customer needs and where to find them.

Another way to identify your target audience is to identify and analyze your competitors. Take note of their target audience, branding and marketing strategies, pricing, and sales tactics. This can provide valuable insight into what works and what doesn't in your particular industry, and can help you to develop strategies that will set your business apart from the competition.

To help illustrate these concepts, let's consider the case of a black entrepreneur who wants to start a hair care line targeted towards black women. A great starting point would be to understand the market of the product and what is being offered currently. By conducting market research, she may discover that there is a high demand for hair care products that cater to the specific needs of black women's hair, such as products that address dryness, breakage, and heat damage. Additionally, she would find the specific stores, salons, and online platforms where these products are being sold and target those channels for her sales and marketing efforts.

The entrepreneur would also analyze the competitors and what their target audience is. How are they branding themselves and how are they pricing their products? This can help her determine how she wants to brand and market her hair care line, for instance, the line could be marketed as a "natural, high-quality product" with a message of self-care and confidence for black women, And pricing strategy could be that it is not too expensive, but also not being too cheap as to be considered low quality.

Another key factor to consider when identifying your target audience as a black entrepreneur is cultural context. As a black business owner, it's important to understand and be able to appeal to the cultural values and preferences of your target audience. For example, the hair care line could appeal to a customer's preference for natural hair care or have testimonials of successful customers with similar hair type or texture, that establishes a sense of cultural relevance.

Clearly, identifying your target audience as a black entrepreneur is essential to the success of your marketing and branding efforts. By conducting market research, analyzing competitors, and understanding cultural context, you can develop strategies that are tailored to the unique needs and preferences of your target audience, and set your business apart from the competition. Keep in mind that, as an entrepreneur you should always be ready to adjust and adapt to new information and changes in your target audience preferences.

DEVELOPING A UNIQUE VALUE PROPOSITION

As I mentioned earlier, a unique value proposition (UVP) is a clear statement that explains the unique benefits that your business offers to its customers. It is a key component of effective marketing and branding, and is essential for Black entrepreneurs who want to stand out in a competitive market. Developing a UVP can be challenging, but by understanding the unique needs and preferences of your target audience, and leveraging your competitive advantage, you can create a powerful message that resonates with your customers.

Let's consider the case of a black entrepreneur who wants to start a clothing line for plus-size women. Developing a UVP for this business might involve identifying the specific pain points and challenges that plus-size women face when it comes to finding fashionable clothing options. This could include issues such as limited availability in larger sizes, lack of options in trendy styles, or limited representation in fashion media.

To create a unique value proposition, the entrepreneur could focus on offering fashionable, high-quality clothing options in a range of sizes that are specifically designed to fit and flatter plus-size women's bodies. By emphasizing the importance of inclusivity and self-expression, she could appeal to her target audience's desire for stylish clothing that makes them feel confident and proud of their bodies.

Additionally, the entrepreneur could also leverage her own personal experience as a plus-size woman to create a UVP that resonates with her target audience. For instance, she could create a message that emphasizes her personal understanding of the difficulties that plus-size women face in finding fashionable clothing, and her commitment to creating a brand that addresses those issues.

Another way to develop a unique value proposition is to differentiate the brand by offering a unique service or providing a unique experience to the customers. This could involve offering personal styling advice, hosting events and pop-up shops that provide customers with an immersive shopping experience, or offering custom tailoring services. This can help to create an emotional connection with customers that goes beyond the product itself, and it also helps in promoting loyalty.

Another key consideration when developing a UVP as a black entrepreneur is to identify and leverage your competitive advantage. This could involve highlighting the unique cultural perspective that your business offers, or emphasizing your commitment to supporting and uplifting the black community. For example, the plus-size clothing line could emphasize the cultural relevance of the clothing styles and patterns, or support charitable causes that empower black women.

Hopefully you see now that a unique value proposition is a powerful tool for Black entrepreneurs who want to stand out in a competitive market. By understanding the unique needs and preferences of your target audience, and leveraging your competitive advantage, you can create a message that resonates with your customers and differentiates your business. Additionally, by offering unique services and experiences, you can create a strong emotional connection with your customers that goes beyond the product itself, and that helps foster loyalty.

CRAFTING A COMPELLING BRAND MESSAGE

Creating a compelling brand message is an essential part of successful marketing and branding, especially for Black entrepreneurs. A well-crafted brand message can help to attract customers, build trust, and establish a unique identity for your business. In this chapter, we will explore the process of crafting a compelling brand message within the context of marketing and branding for a black-owned barber shop.

First and foremost, it's important to understand your target audience and what they are looking for in a barber shop. For a black-owned barber shop, this may include a focus on traditional barbering techniques and a welcoming atmosphere for the black community. Additionally, consider the values and mission of your business and how these can be incorporated into your brand message. For example, if your shop places a high emphasis on community and culture, this should be reflected in your message.

Once you have a clear understanding of your target audience and business values, you can start to craft your brand message. A strong brand message should be concise, clear, and consistent across all of your marketing materials. One effective way to do this is to use a tagline or slogan that encapsulates the essence of your brand. For a black-owned barber shop, this might be something like "Where tradition meets modern style" or "Making the community look and feel their best."

In addition to your tagline, it's important to use consistent branding elements across all of your marketing materials, such as your logo, colors, and imagery. Using these elements consistently will help to create a strong visual identity for your business and make it easy for customers to recognize and remember your brand.

When it comes to the actual message, think about what makes your business stand out from the competition. For a black-owned barber shop, this might include the focus on modern barbering techniques, knowledgeable barbers with a deep understanding of black hair, or a welcoming and inclusive atmosphere. Highlighting these unique selling points in your message will help to differentiate your business from the competition and attract customers who are looking for something specific.

Another important aspect of crafting a compelling brand message is to make it relatable to your target audience. For black-owned businesses, this means understanding the unique experiences and perspectives of the black community, and how your brand can speak to them. For example, you could highlight the importance of the barbershop as a community gathering place and a safe space for black men to come together. Additionally, incorporating customer testimonials or highlighting customer-centric policies can also be helpful to establish trust and relatability.

Finally, it's important to stay true to your brand message and remain consistent in its delivery across all of your marketing materials and interactions. This can be achieved by maintaining a consistent tone and voice across all of your materials, and being clear and transparent about the values and mission of your business. Additionally, it may be helpful to have detailed brand guidelines that sets standards for messaging and visual elements. I use branding guidelines in all my companies and it helps when commissioning marketing materials from freelancers.

Now you should pretty much see why crafting a compelling brand message is an essential part of marketing and branding for Black entrepreneurs. By understanding your target audience and business values, and using consistent branding elements and relatable message, you can create a strong visual identity and attract customers to your business. A barber shop can take advantage of its community-gathering aspect and its focus on traditional techniques to stand out from the competition and build a loyal customer base. Remember to stay true to your message and remain consistent in its delivery, and your brand will be poised for success.

LEVERAGING SOCIAL MEDIA

In today's digital age, social media has become an essential tool for businesses of all sizes and industries, and in this section I will use a black-owned online fitness apparel business as an example. By leveraging social media, Black entrepreneurs can effectively reach their target audience, build brand awareness and loyalty, and ultimately, drive sales and growth.

One key way that a black-owned online fitness apparel business can leverage social media to improve their marketing and branding efforts is by creating a strong visual identity. The power of visual storytelling through videos, images, and graphics is huge on social media. By using high-quality, visually appealing workout-themed images and fitness-related videos to showcase their products, a black-owned fitness apparel business can create a strong visual identity that grabs the attention of their target audience. Additionally, by highlighting the brand's core values and messages through visually appealing graphics, a black-owned online fitness apparel business can also create a deeper connection with their target audience.

Another way that a black-owned online fitness apparel business can leverage social media to improve their marketing and branding efforts is by creating engaging and interactive content. This can be done by hosting giveaways, contests, and other promotions on social media platforms, encouraging customers to post reviews and testimonials, or by using live streaming to showcase product demos or behind-the-scenes footage. By creating interactive content, a black-owned online fitness apparel business can foster engagement and build stronger connections with their target audience.

It's also important to note that black-owned online fitness apparel businesses can leverage social media to be a part of larger conversations and movements. By highlighting the brand's support for black culture, wellness, and fitness movements, a black-owned online fitness apparel business can show that they're not only a business, but also an important part of the community. Additionally, by amplifying the voices and stories of black athletes, entrepreneurs, and community leaders through social media, a black-owned online fitness apparel business can build a sense of community and belonging around their brand.

Another powerful way to leverage social media for black-owned online fitness apparel businesses is by using influencer marketing. Identifying social media influencers in the fitness, wellness, and fashion spaces that align with the brand's values can help to reach and resonate with a new target audience. Influencers can help to promote the brand, showcase their products, and help to build brand awareness and trust. Additionally, working with influencers who have diverse backgrounds, body types, and abilities can also help to build inclusivity and diversity within the brand.

It's also essential to mention the importance of analyzing social media metrics and data. By tracking metrics such as engagement rates, click-through rates, and website traffic, a black-owned online fitness apparel business can gain insight into which social media strategies are working and which ones aren't. This can help them to make data-driven decisions about how to improve their marketing and branding efforts going forward.

Clearly, social media is a powerful tool for black-owned businesses looking to improve their marketing and branding efforts. By creating a strong visual identity, engaging interactive content, and participating in relevant movements and conversations, leveraging influencer marketing and analyzing metrics, Black entrepreneurs can build brand awareness, loyalty and ultimately drive sales and growth.

BUILDING A PROFESSIONAL WEBSITE

A professional website is an essential component of any business, but in this section, I'll use a black-owned snack vending machine business as an example. A well-designed website can help to build brand awareness and credibility, establish trust with customers, and ultimately, drive sales and growth.

One key aspect of building a professional website for a black-owned snack vending machine business is to create a clear and user-friendly design. This can be done by using simple, clean layouts and easy-to-read typography, as well as by using high-quality images and graphics to showcase products and services. A user-friendly design will help to create a positive user experience, which can be important for building trust and credibility with customers.

Another important aspect of building a professional website for a black-owned snack vending machine business is to ensure that it is mobile-responsive. Today, more and more people are using smartphones and tablets to browse the internet, and a mobile-responsive website will ensure that customers can access the website easily regardless of the device they're using. This will also help to improve the user experience and can help to increase conversions.

It's also important to consider the search engine optimization (SEO) when building a professional website. SEO can help a website to rank higher in search engines like Google, which can be important for driving traffic to the website. This can be achieved by including relevant keywords on the website, optimizing meta tags, and building high-quality backlinks. Additionally, having a clear navigation, and organized structure and effective site speed can also help with SEO efforts.

Another key aspect of building a professional website for a black-owned snack vending machine business is to include clear and detailed information about the products and services offered, as well as easy-to-find contact information. This includes information about the different types of vending machines available, the brands and products that are available, and any additional services that are offered, such as vending machine maintenance or restocking. Additionally, easy-to-find contact information, such as a phone number, email address, and contact form, can help to build trust with customers by making it easy for them to get in touch with the business.

It's also important to consider the security and reliability of the website when building a professional website for a black-owned snack vending machine business. This means including secure payment options and implementing SSL encryption to protect customer data, as well as regularly backing up the website to prevent data loss. Having a clear and specific privacy policy also adds to the trustworthiness of the website.

Finally, building a professional website for a black-owned snack vending machine business should also consider the use of social media and e-commerce capabilities. Integrating social media platforms and having easy-to-use e-commerce functionality can help to increase brand awareness and drive sales. By using the website as a platform to advertise the vending machines, products and services, and additional services, along with the possibility to make purchases or inquiries, black-owned snack vending machine businesses can expand their reach and accessibility.

Again, building a professional website is essential for a black-owned snack vending machine business looking to establish trust and credibility, and drive sales and growth. By focusing on a user-friendly design, mobile-responsive design, SEO, detailed product and service information, security and reliability, and utilizing social media and e-commerce capabilities, any black-owned business can create a website that not only looks professional but also effectively communicates and serves the business to its target audience on a silver platter.

PARTICIPATING IN TRADE SHOWS AND EVENTS

Participating in trade shows and events is an effective way for businesses to market and brand their products and services, but in this example I will use a black-owned hair salon. These events can help to increase brand awareness, generate new leads, and ultimately, drive sales and growth.

One of the key benefits of participating in trade shows and events is the opportunity to connect with potential customers face-to-face. This can be an effective way to build trust and credibility with potential customers, and to showcase the salon's products and services. During the trade show, hair salon businesses can showcase their expertise by providing demonstrations and mini-consultations to visitors. This can help to generate leads and interest in the salon's products and services.

Another important benefit of participating in trade shows and events is the opportunity to network with other professionals in the industry. Trade shows and events often bring together professionals from different companies and industries, and this can be a great opportunity to learn about the latest trends and best practices in the industry. Additionally, this can be a great way for black-owned hair salon businesses to connect with other black-owned businesses, and build a sense of community.

Additionally, participating in trade shows and events can help a black-owned hair salon business to increase their brand awareness by exposing the salon's brand to a large number of potential customers. By having a professional booth setup, with branded materials and well-trained staff, the salon can make a lasting impression on visitors and can help to create a memorable experience that can ultimately lead to more customers.

Furthermore, trade shows and events can be an effective way to gather market research and feedback. By conducting surveys and questionnaires at the event, or by having one-on-one conversations with visitors, businesses can gain valuable insights into the needs and preferences of their target audience, which can be used to improve their products and services.

It's also important to mention that trade shows and events can be an effective way to generate media coverage. By reaching out to the media and inviting them to cover the salon's participation at the event, a black-owned hair salon business can get their brand featured in the local or national press, which can help to increase brand awareness and credibility.

When it comes to black-owned hair salon business, it's also important to participate in events that are specific to the black community. These can be events that focus on hair and beauty for black women, or events that showcase black-owned businesses. This can be a great way to connect with potential customers, as well as to get involved in the black community.

Participating in trade shows and events is an effective way for black-owned businesses to market and brand their products and services to customers and potential partners. These events can help to increase brand awareness, generate new leads, and ultimately, drive sales and growth. By participating in the right trade shows and events, having a professional booth setup, networking, gathering market research and feedback, and generating media coverage, any black-owned business can gain a competitive edge and make lasting connections with potential customers.

Chapter Seven:
Networking To Build Professional Relationships

Welcome to the chapter on networking and building professional relationships within the context of Black entrepreneurship. The journey of a black entrepreneur is not always an easy one, and as such, building a strong network of support is vital to the success of any black-owned business. The ability to connect with like-minded individuals, learn from industry leaders, and gain access to valuable resources is essential for any entrepreneur, and is especially important for Black entrepreneurs who may face additional challenges in building their businesses.

Networking can take many forms, from attending industry events and trade shows to connecting with other entrepreneurs online or through mentorship programs. The key is to be strategic and intentional in your approach, identifying the people and organizations that can help to advance your business goals. Building professional relationships is also about giving back and being a resource for others. By providing value and supporting others in your network, you can foster mutually beneficial relationships that will help you to achieve your own goals.

In this chapter, I will explore the various ways in which Black entrepreneurs can build a strong network of support, including networking strategies and tactics, building relationships with industry leaders and influencers, and ways to support and uplift other Black entrepreneurs.

I will also discuss the importance of mentorship in Black entrepreneurship, as well as the ways in which Black entrepreneurs can find, connect and engage with a mentor. It's also important to touch on the benefits of joining organizations and groups that support the growth and development of Black entrepreneurs, and how to leverage them to build your network.

I hope that the information and insights provided in this chapter will help you to develop a comprehensive networking strategy that will enable you to build a strong network of support and advance your business goals. Thank you for following along, and I wish you all the best as you continue to build your black-owned business.

IDENTIFY NETWORKING OPPORTUNITIES

Networking is a crucial aspect of building and growing any black-owned business, but in this example I will use a bookkeeping business to illustrate. Networking allows entrepreneurs to connect with potential clients, learn from industry leaders and gain access to valuable resources. Identifying networking opportunities is an essential step in building a strong network of support and growing a business.

One effective way to identify networking opportunities is to attend industry events and trade shows. These events provide a platform for business owners to showcase their products and services, connect with other professionals in their industry and gain insights into the latest trends and best practices. For example, attending a conference for small business owners or a trade show specific to accounting and finance industries can help a black-owned bookkeeping business reach a large number of potential clients and gain valuable insights into the industry.

Another way to identify networking opportunities is by joining a professional association or trade organization. Many professional associations offer networking events, educational opportunities, and resources for members. Joining organizations that support the growth and development of Black entrepreneurs can be particularly beneficial for black-owned businesses as it can provide opportunities to connect with other black business owners and gain access to valuable resources and mentorship opportunities.

Networking can also be done virtually by using social media and online platforms. Joining online groups, forums, and professional communities for bookkeeping and accounting can be a great way to connect with other professionals in the industry, reach a large number of potential clients and learn from other professionals in the industry. Platforms such as LinkedIn and Facebook have professional groups specifically for bookkeeping and accounting that can be a great way to reach a large number of potential clients and learn about the latest trends and best practices in the industry.

Participating in mentorship programs can also be an effective way to identify networking opportunities. A mentorship program provides an opportunity to connect with an experienced professional who can offer guidance and support as you grow your business, and it also provides a valuable learning opportunity for the mentee. A mentorship program can be an excellent way to gain access to new resources and learn about the latest trends and best practices in the industry.

Networking can also take place by giving back and supporting other black-owned businesses. This can be done by volunteering in local black-owned business communities, attending and supporting events that showcase black-owned businesses and providing support and resources to other Black entrepreneurs. Giving back and supporting other black-owned businesses can be a valuable way to build relationships, connect with other Black entrepreneurs and build a sense of community among Black entrepreneurs.

Identifying networking opportunities is an essential aspect of building and growing a black-owned bookkeeping business. Attending industry events and trade shows, joining professional associations and trade organizations, using social media and online platforms, participating in mentorship programs, and giving back and supporting other black-owned businesses are all effective ways to identify and connect with the right people and organizations that can help advance your business goals. By being strategic and intentional in your approach and providing value and support to others in your network, you can foster mutually beneficial relationships that will help you achieve your business goals.

PARTICIPATE IN SOCIAL CIRCLES

Participating in social circles can be an effective way for Black entrepreneurs to network and build professional relationships, especially for those in the legal industry like me. As a black-owned law firm, actively engaging in certain social circles can provide opportunities to connect with potential clients, learn from other professionals in the industry, and gain access to valuable resources that I might not have known about otherwise. This is that old saying, "It's not always what you know, but who you know."

One way to participate in social circles is by joining professional organizations and associations. These organizations often host events and gatherings that provide opportunities to connect with other professionals in the legal industry. Joining organizations that specifically cater to black legal professionals can be especially beneficial, as it can provide a sense of community and support for Black entrepreneurs in the field. Additionally, these organizations often provide resources and opportunities for continuing education and professional development. Join one and be active. Be active when it comes to serving the mission of the organization and be active when it comes to making new friends.

Another way to participate in social circles is by attending networking events and conferences. These events can also provide an opportunity to meet and connect with potential clients, as well as other legal professionals. Attending events specific to the legal industry or to black-owned businesses can help you to reach a specific target audience, and gain insights into the latest trends and best practices in the field.

Participating in social circles can also be done virtually by using social media and online platforms. Joining online groups, forums, and professional communities for the legal industry can be a great way to connect with other professionals in the field. Social media platforms such as Reddit and Twitter can be a great tool to find, connect and engage with other legal professionals, black-owned law firms, and related organizations. You can follow me on Twitter at @SholodonDaniels and on Instagram @EntertainmentLawya.

Another way to participate in social circles is by joining local business groups and chambers of commerce. These groups can provide opportunities to connect with other business owners and professionals in the area, and can also provide resources and support for businesses. Additionally, participating in these groups can also help to establish your law firm as a valuable member of the local community, which can help you to build a strong reputation and attract potential clients.

Participating in social circles can also involve giving back to the community and supporting other black-owned businesses. This can be done by volunteering at local organizations, attending and supporting events that showcase black-owned businesses, and by providing support and resources to other Black entrepreneurs. Giving back and supporting others in the community can help establish your business as a reputable and responsible member of the community, while also helping to build relationships and connect with other Black entrepreneurs.

To recap, participating in social circles is an effective way for Black entrepreneurs to network and build professional relationships. Joining professional organizations and associations, attending networking events and conferences, participating in online communities and forums, joining local business groups, and giving back to the community are all effective ways to participate in social circles and connect with potential clients, other legal professionals, and build relationships that can benefit your business. By being strategic and intentional in your approach and providing value to others in your network, you can foster mutually beneficial relationships that will help your law firm to grow and thrive.

PARTICIPATE IN PROFESSIONAL ORGANIZATIONS

Participating in professional organizations is an effective way for Black entrepreneurs to network and build professional relationships, gain access to valuable resources, and stay informed about the latest trends and best practices in their industry. As a black entrepreneur, it's important to be strategic and intentional in your approach to joining professional organizations, and to select those that align with your business goals and align with the interests of the black community.

One of the first steps in participating in professional organizations is to research and identify organizations that align with your industry and business goals. This can involve attending networking events, speaking with industry leaders, and researching online.

Here are some prominent organizations that Black entrepreneurs may consider joining:

- National Black MBA Association (NBMBAA) - this organization provides networking opportunities, career development resources, and professional development programs for black business professionals.
- The National Association of Black Accountants (NABA) - this organization provides networking opportunities, resources, and educational programs for black professionals in the accounting and finance industry.
- National Black Chamber of Commerce (NBCC) - this organization provides resources and advocacy for black-owned businesses, as well as networking and business development opportunities.
- Black Women's Roundtable - this organization provides opportunities for black women entrepreneurs to connect, advocate and educate each other, providing support and resources.
- The Executive Leadership Council (ELC) - this organization provides leadership development and networking opportunities for black executives across all industries.

Another way to participate in professional organizations is to attend events and conferences hosted by the organization. Again, these events can provide opportunities to connect with other members of the organization, learn about the latest trends and best practices in the industry, and gain insights into the resources and support available to members. It's how you can keep your business on the cutting edge of your industry.

Additionally, participating in professional organizations can also involve volunteering and getting involved in committees or boards. This can be a great way to gain leadership experience, build relationships with other members, and make a meaningful impact within the organization. After all, you're reading this book because you want to become a boss. Being a boss in business is almost always going to entail sitting on a few boards and making some high level decisions. Get your foot in the door by serving on the board of your local industry organization.

Finally, participating in professional organizations can also involve giving back and supporting other black-owned businesses. This can be done by volunteering in local black-owned business communities, attending and supporting events that showcase black-owned businesses and providing support and resources to other Black entrepreneurs.

Giving back and supporting other black-owned businesses is a meaningful way to build relationships and connect with other Black entrepreneurs, and it also helps to build a sense of community among Black entrepreneurs in general.

To sum it up, participating in professional organizations is an effective way for Black entrepreneurs to network and build professional relationships, gain access to valuable resources and stay informed about the latest trends and best practices in their industry. Joining organizations such as NBMBAA, NABA, NBCC, Black Women's Roundtable, and The Executive Leadership Council can be a great way to connect with other black professionals and business owners, while also gaining access to resources and support that can help to grow your business. By being strategic and intentional in your approach, and by providing value and support to others in your network, you can foster mutually beneficial relationships that will help you achieve your business goals.

GET INVOLVED WITH CHARITABLE ORGANIZATIONS

Participating in charitable organizations can be an important way for Black entrepreneurs to build professional relationships and advance their careers. In addition to the personal fulfillment that comes from giving back to one's community, participating in these organizations can provide valuable networking opportunities, and a chance to connect with other like-minded individuals who are also committed to making a difference.

One of the key benefits of participating in charitable organizations as a black entrepreneur is the ability to build relationships with other professionals in your field. By working together on a common cause, you can create opportunities to collaborate and build trust with other business leaders, which can lead to new business opportunities and partnerships down the road. Additionally, by participating in a charitable organization, you can demonstrate your commitment to community and social responsibility, which can be a valuable asset when seeking funding or other support for your business.

Another benefit of charitable organizations is that they can provide a platform to develop and showcase your leadership skills. Many charitable organizations rely on volunteers to help run their operations, and by taking on leadership roles within these organizations, you can gain valuable experience in project management, team building, and fundraising. These skills can be transferable to your business, and will be assets to you as a business leader.

When looking for a charitable organization to get involved with, it's important to find one that aligns with your personal values and interests. Some other organizations that support black causes include:

- The National Black Chamber of Commerce
- The NAACP
- The National Black Arts Festival
- The United Negro College Fund
- Black Girls Code
- The National Black Theatre
- The Black Women's Health Imperative
- The Black Economic Council

- The National Black Child Development Institute

These organizations work on a variety of issues such as economic empowerment, education, health, and representation and advocacy in arts, business and other fields. By finding a group that you are passionate about and that resonates with your personal and professional goals, you can make a more meaningful impact, while also receiving the greatest benefits from your participation.

Participating in charitable organizations can be a powerful way for Black entrepreneurs to build relationships and advance their careers. By volunteering your time and talents to support the black community, you can create opportunities to connect with other like-minded individuals who are also committed to making a difference, while also developing valuable skills that can help you achieve your business goals. However, It's also important to be mindful of the impact and representation of these organizations, and to consider and support the local and grassroots organizations as well as the national and well-established ones. By finding an organization that aligns with your personal values and interests, you can make the most of your time and resources while also making a meaningful difference in the lives of others.

ACTIVELY MANAGE YOUR QUALITY CONNECTIONS

Maintaining strong professional relationships is an important aspect of building and growing a business, and this is especially true for Black entrepreneurs, who may face additional challenges and barriers in the business world. Building and nurturing professional connections can help Black entrepreneurs gain access to new opportunities, resources, and networks that can aid in the growth and success of their businesses.

Here are some tips for actively maintaining your business connections as a Black entrepreneur:

- Network strategically: Networking events and organizations can be great places to meet other business professionals and make new connections. However, it's important to be strategic in your networking efforts. Seek out events and organizations that are focused on Black entrepreneurship or that are likely to have a significant number of Black attendees. This will increase the likelihood of making connections with people who understand the unique challenges and opportunities that Black entrepreneurs face.
- Use social media effectively: Social media can be a powerful tool for connecting with other business professionals and building your brand. Utilize platforms such as LinkedIn and Twitter to engage with other entrepreneurs, business leaders, and potential customers. By consistently sharing valuable content and engaging with others, you can establish yourself as an authority in your industry and build a strong online presence.
- Be proactive: Don't wait for opportunities to come to you - actively seek out new connections and opportunities. Reach out to other business professionals and entrepreneurs, and offer to meet for coffee or lunch to discuss your businesses and how you might be able to collaborate.

- Follow up and stay in touch: After making a new connection, make sure to follow up and stay in touch. Send a quick email or message to thank the person for their time, and ask if there is anything you can help them with. Following up will help keep the relationship alive and open the door for potential collaborations in the future.
- Join Professional organizations: Joining professional organizations in your industry can be a great way to connect with other business professionals and stay informed about the latest industry trends and best practices. Look for organizations that cater to black professionals specifically or have a large presence of black members.
- Focus on Building long-term relationships: Building strong, long-term relationships takes time and effort. It's important to understand that it's not about the immediate benefit or outcome but about the potential for future collaborations, support, and mutual growth.

Building and maintaining professional relationships as a Black entrepreneur can be challenging, but it is an important aspect of growing and succeeding in business. By being strategic, proactive, and building strong, long-term relationships, Black entrepreneurs can gain access to new opportunities, resources, and networks that can help them achieve success.

Chapter Eight:
Time Management and Goal Setting

    Time management and goal setting are crucial elements of running a successful business, and Black entrepreneurs face unique challenges in balancing the demands of their businesses with the realities of systemic inequality. In this chapter, I will explore the importance of time management and goal setting for Black entrepreneurs, and examine strategies for effectively managing time and setting goals in the face of additional barriers and obstacles. I will begin by discussing the ways in which systemic racism and discrimination impact the daily lives and work of Black entrepreneurs, and how this can make time management and goal setting more difficult. I will then delve into practical tips and techniques for setting and achieving goals, managing time, and building effective systems for staying organized and productive. Through a combination of research and real-world examples, I will examine the various ways in which Black entrepreneurs can overcome the challenges they face and use time management and goal setting to create a more equitable and successful business environment.

    Systemic racism and discrimination have a significant impact on the daily lives and work of Black entrepreneurs. Black entrepreneurs are more likely to face challenges in accessing capital, networking opportunities, and other resources that are essential for starting and growing a business. This can make it more difficult for Black entrepreneurs to effectively manage their time and set meaningful goals for their businesses because they simply cannot afford to delegate tasks or hire help.

    One of the most significant ways in which systemic racism and discrimination impact Black entrepreneurs is through the lack of access to capital. According to a study by the National Bureau of Economic Research[7], Black-owned businesses are less likely to receive funding from traditional sources, such as banks and venture capitalists, than white-owned businesses. This lack of access to capital can make it more difficult for Black entrepreneurs to invest in the resources and equipment they need to run their businesses, and can also make it more difficult to plan for the future and set meaningful goals.

    Discrimination in networking opportunities is another significant way in which systemic racism and discrimination impact Black entrepreneurs. As a result of lack of representation, Black entrepreneurs often don't have the same access to industry events, business associations, and mentorship opportunities as their white counterparts. This can make it more difficult for Black entrepreneurs to make valuable connections and gain access to the resources they need to grow their businesses.

---

[7] Robb, Alicia M., and Robert W. Fairlie. 2007. "Access to financial capital among US businesses: The case of African American firms." The Annals of the American Academy of Political and Social Science 613 (1): 47-72.

Additionally, systemic racism and discrimination can also impact Black entrepreneurs in terms of harassment and prejudice[8]. Studies have found that Black entrepreneurs are more likely to face discrimination in the form of harassment or hostility from customers, suppliers, and other business partners. This can lead to additional stress and distractions that can make it more difficult for Black entrepreneurs to focus on their work and achieve their goals.

Furthermore, Black entrepreneurs are more likely to experience burnout and mental health issues, as a result of dealing with the additional stressors from systemic racism and discrimination which can lead to a poor work-life balance and make it difficult to set and achieve goals[9].

It is irrefutable that systemic racism and discrimination have a significant impact on the daily lives and work of Black entrepreneurs, making it more difficult for them to access capital, networking opportunities, and other resources that are essential for starting and growing a business. These challenges can make it more difficult for Black entrepreneurs to effectively manage their time and set meaningful goals for their businesses. As a result, Black entrepreneurs must be even more strategic, resilient and persistent in their efforts to overcome these barriers and achieve success in their business ventures.

Here are some additional statistics that can provide more context on how systemic racism and discrimination impact the daily lives and work of Black entrepreneurs:

- According to a 2020 report by the National Black Chamber of Commerce, Black-owned businesses only receive approximately 1.4% of all venture capital funding[10].
- A study by the Center for Global Policy Solutions found that Black-owned businesses are more likely to be denied loans than white-owned businesses, even when controlling for creditworthiness and business plans[11].
- A study by the SBA found that Black-owned businesses are disproportionately affected by COVID-19 pandemic and are more likely to be closed down permanently than white-owned businesses[12].

These statistics provide context for the gap in access to capital for Black entrepreneurs which make it difficult for them to grow their business and set and achieve their goals. Additionally, these numbers demonstrate the significant impact of COVID-19 on Black-owned

---

[8] Feagin, Joe R., and Nikitah Imani. "Racial barriers to African American entrepreneurship: An exploratory study." Social Problems 41, no. 4 (1994): 562-584.

[9] Feagin, Joe. Systemic racism: A theory of oppression. Routledge, 2013.

[10] Braswell, Porter. 2022. "Black investors make up only 3% of the VC industry—here's how to change that." Fast Company. https://www.fastcompany.com/90777034/black-founders-only-receive-1-4-vc-funds-heres-how-to-change-that.

[11] Fairlie, Robert W., and Alicia M. Robb. 2008. Race and Entrepreneurial Success: Black-, Asian-, and White-owned Businesses in the United States. N.p.: MIT Press.

[12] Fairlie, Robert W. 2022. "The Impacts of COVID-19 on Racial Disparities in Small Business Earnings." SBA. https://cdn.advocacy.sba.gov/wp-content/uploads/2022/08/16104005/Report_COVID-and-Racial-Disparities_508c.pdf.

businesses specifically, and how the pandemic exacerbates the existing disparities and difficulties that Black entrepreneurs face daily.

It's important to note that these statistics are not exhaustive and might not reflect the specific experiences of every Black entrepreneur but they provide a general overview of the scale of the issue and the impact of systemic racism and discrimination on Black entrepreneurs.

IDENTIFY YOUR PRIORITIES

As a Black entrepreneur, it can be difficult to manage your time and set meaningful goals due to the additional barriers and obstacles you may face in the business world. Identifying your priorities as a Black entrepreneur can help you focus your efforts on the most important tasks and move your business forward.

Here are some practical tips for identifying your priorities as a Black entrepreneur:
- Create a list of your long-term goals: Start by identifying the big-picture goals you want to achieve for your business. This can include things like increasing revenue, expanding your customer base, or growing your team.
- Break down your goals into smaller, more manageable tasks: Once you have identified your long-term goals, break them down into smaller, more manageable tasks that you can work on day-to-day. For example, if your goal is to increase revenue, you can set specific targets for sales and create a plan to reach those targets through marketing efforts, networking, or developing new products or services.
- Prioritize based on urgency and importance: Once you have a list of tasks, prioritize them based on their level of urgency and importance. Identify which tasks need to be completed first in order to move your business forward.
- Eliminate low-priority tasks: Take a hard look at your list of tasks and eliminate any that are not essential to your business's success. This can include things like meetings or tasks that can be delegated.
- Set weekly and daily goals: Set specific goals for each week and each day to help you stay focused and on track. Make sure they align with your long-term goals and take into account your prioritized task list.
- Use tools to track your progress: Utilize tools such as calendars, to-do lists, and project management software to help you stay organized and on track. These tools can help you see your progress and stay motivated.
- Reflect and reassess regularly: Make sure to set aside some time regularly to reflect on your progress, evaluate your priorities and adjust as necessary.

Being efficient at identifying your priorities as a Black entrepreneur is essential for effectively managing your time and setting meaningful goals. By breaking down your goals into smaller, more manageable tasks, prioritizing based on urgency and importance, eliminating low-priority tasks, and using tools to track your progress, Black entrepreneurs can stay focused and on track to achieve success. Remember to reflect and reassess regularly to make sure you're still on the right track.

CREATING A PLAN FOR TIME MANAGEMENT

Creating a time management plan is essential for staying organized and focused as an entrepreneur, especially in light of the additional barriers and obstacles that Black entrepreneurs may face. A well-crafted time management plan can help Black entrepreneurs use their time more efficiently and achieve their goals more effectively.

First and foremost, it's important to understand that time management is a personal endeavor. As Stephen Covey, author of "The 7 Habits of Highly Effective People" states, "The key is not to prioritize what's on your schedule, but to schedule your priorities." This means that it's important to identify your most important goals and tasks and make sure that you are dedicating enough time to work on them.

One strategy for creating an effective time management plan is to use the Eisenhower Matrix, developed by President Eisenhower, which helps you to prioritize tasks based on their level of importance and urgency. According to Eisenhower, "What is important is seldom urgent, and what is urgent is seldom important." By identifying and focusing on important tasks that are not urgent, you can work on building a sustainable business that can weather any challenges that come your way. (A fun tidbit: President Eisenhower and I were both born in the same Texas town near the red river–Denison.)

Another strategy is to set specific, measurable and achievable goals, as advised by Peter Drucker, a management consultant and author of "Effective Executive", he said "What gets measured gets managed." By setting measurable goals, you can better track your progress and stay motivated.

It's also important to have a realistic view of time availability, and to manage your energy, not just your time. Tony Schwartz, author of "The Power of Full Engagement" states "Manage energy, not time. It is a valuable lesson that if we don't manage energy effectively, time will become irrelevant." This means recognizing that some periods in the day you may be more productive than others and planning your schedule accordingly.

Another effective strategy for managing time efficiently is to use tools such as calendars, to-do lists, and project management software. These tools can help you stay organized and on track, and can also be a valuable resource for prioritizing and tracking progress on your goals.

Finally, it's important to be flexible and adaptable. Tim Ferriss, author of "The 4-Hour Work Week" states "The best plan is only as good as its execution. The most efficient and effective method of conveying information to and within a development team is face-to-face conversation" Being open to changing your plan as necessary and checking in regularly to ensure that you're still on the right track can help you stay flexible and achieve your goals.

It is widely accepted that time management is a critical element of achieving success as a Black entrepreneur. By understanding that time management is a personal endeavor, prioritizing tasks, setting specific, measurable and achievable goals, managing your energy efficiently, utilizing tools to stay organized and focusing on flexibility, Black entrepreneurs can use their time more efficiently and achieve success.

SETTING SMART GOALS

Setting SMART goals is an effective strategy for Black entrepreneurs to create clear, actionable objectives that will help them achieve success. The SMART criteria, which stands for specific, measurable, achievable, relevant and time-bound, is a widely recognized framework that can help Black entrepreneurs set effective goals.

First, it's essential that your goals be specific. According to Earl G. Graves Sr., founder of Black Enterprise magazine, "You have to set your objectives, and then you have to work to achieve them. It's the only way to measure success." Setting specific goals allows Black entrepreneurs to be clear about what they want to achieve, and it also allows them to identify the steps they need to take to achieve their goals.

Additionally, goals should be measurable. This means that entrepreneurs must be able to track their progress and determine whether they are on track to achieve their goals. As Robert L. Johnson, founder of BET and The RLJ Companies, said "Being able to measure the success of a business is the key to long-term success." Measurable goals allow Black entrepreneurs to see their progress and make necessary adjustments.

The goals should also be achievable, in other words, they should be realistic and within reach. It's important to set goals that are challenging but not impossible. As Daymond John, founder of FUBU and Shark Tank investor, said "When you're starting a business, you have to set attainable goals for yourself. You can't just say, 'I'm going to be a millionaire in a year.' You have to set small, achievable goals."

Relevance is also an essential criteria in goal-setting, it means that the goals should align with the overall vision and mission of the business. As Janice Bryant Howroyd, founder of ACT-1 Group, said "Your goals must be clear, specific, and aligned with your mission, values, and long-term vision" Setting relevant goals helps Black entrepreneurs stay focused and motivated.

Finally, goals should be time-bound, meaning they should have a deadline. As Strive Masiyiwa, founder of Econet Wireless said "In order to have any chance of achieving anything, you have to have goals and a plan for reaching them." Setting a deadline helps entrepreneurs stay on track and achieve their goals within a specific timeframe.

Setting SMART goals is an effective strategy for Black entrepreneurs to create clear, actionable objectives that will help them achieve success. By using the SMART criteria, Black entrepreneurs can ensure that their goals are specific, measurable, achievable, relevant and time-bound. This can help them stay focused and motivated and increase the likelihood of achieving success. And setting and reaching them can bring an added sense of accomplishment and a boost of self-esteem. We could all use a little more of that.

DELEGATING AND OUTSOURCING

Delegating and outsourcing tasks are critical strategies for Black entrepreneurs looking to optimize their time and focus on the most important activities. Delegating and outsourcing can free up time and energy for Black entrepreneurs, allowing them to focus on what they do best and grow their business.

One of the biggest benefits of delegating and outsourcing is the ability to free up time for more important activities. As a Black entrepreneur, it's essential to focus on the tasks that are core to your business and that you are best equipped to handle. As Warren Buffett, CEO of

Berkshire Hathaway said "The best thing a leader can do is to pick good people and let them do their jobs." By delegating or outsourcing tasks that are not core to your business, you can focus on the most important tasks that will help you grow your business.

Another key benefit of delegating and outsourcing is the ability to bring in expertise and new perspectives. Outsourcing certain tasks, such as accounting, legal, or IT can allow Black entrepreneurs to bring in experts who can help them make better decisions and optimize their business. As Mark Zuckerberg, CEO of Facebook said "move fast and break things." Outsourcing allows entrepreneurs to bring in experts who can get things done faster and with high quality.

Additionally, outsourcing can help to lower costs and increase efficiency. By outsourcing certain tasks, Black entrepreneurs can benefit from lower labor costs and access to specialized tools and resources. As Bill Gates, founder of Microsoft, said "It's fine to celebrate success but it is more important to heed the lessons of failure" Outsourcing allows Black entrepreneurs to focus on their strengths and outsource tasks that are not core to their business.

In conclusion, delegating and outsourcing are powerful strategies that Black entrepreneurs can use to free up time and focus on the most important activities. By identifying tasks that are not core to their business, Black entrepreneurs can free up time and bring in new perspectives and expertise, which can help to lower costs and increase efficiency. This can ultimately help Black entrepreneurs to optimize their time and focus on the most important activities that will help them grow their business.

MANAGING DISTRACTIONS AND STAYING FOCUSED

Managing distractions and staying focused is essential for entrepreneurs, as we face unique challenges that can impede our productivity and success. Identifying and eliminating distractions, and developing strategies for staying focused on our goals, can help us achieve success and reach our full potential.

One of the most important steps in managing distractions is to identify the sources of those distractions. This can include things like social media, email, phone calls, or even people. Once the sources of distractions are identified, you can take steps to eliminate them. For example, turning off notifications for social media or email when you're working on a specific task can help reduce distractions.

Another strategy for managing distractions is to set boundaries and create a conducive working environment. This can involve things like creating a designated workspace that is free from distractions, and creating a daily schedule that allows for concentrated work sessions. It can also involve setting a schedule for checking and responding to emails and phone calls, rather than letting them interrupt your focus throughout the day.

Developing strategies for staying focused on your goals is also crucial. This can involve setting specific and measurable goals, breaking them down into smaller tasks, and prioritizing them based on importance and urgency. The Pomodoro Technique is a widely used strategy in which one works on a single task for 25 minutes with a short break then a longer break after four cycles. Also, developing a daily routine that includes activities that help you focus, such as meditation or exercise can also be useful.

Creating a sense of accountability can also be an effective way to stay focused. This can involve working with a mentor or accountability partner, or even sharing your goals with a trusted friend or family member. This can help you stay motivated and focused, and hold you accountable for reaching your goals. Just be sure to take steps to optimize your productivity and you will achieve success.

MAKE TIME FOR THESE THINGS NO MATTER WHAT

As an entrepreneur, it is essential to make time for taking care of yourself, not only for the well-being of yourself, but also for the success of your business. Black entrepreneurs often experience higher levels of stress and burnout due to systemic racism and a long history of discrimination. Therefore, it's important for Black entrepreneurs in particular to make time for activities that promote mental, physical, and spiritual health. This is often referred to as "self-care."

Here are a few essential things that all Black entrepreneurs should make time for in their lives in order to maintain their mental, physical, and spiritual health:

- **Mental health**: Make time for activities that help you relax and reduce stress, such as meditation, yoga, or journaling. These activities can help you manage anxiety and depression, which can be exacerbated by the stress of being a Black entrepreneur. Oprah Winfrey, media executive and philanthropist once said "*Create the highest, grandest vision possible for your life, because you become what you believe.*"
- **Physical health**: Make time for regular exercise and proper nutrition. Regular exercise can help to reduce stress, improve cardiovascular health, and increase energy levels. Proper nutrition can also help to improve energy levels and overall health.
- **Spiritual health**: Make time for activities that connect you with your spiritual or religious beliefs. This can include things like prayer, reading spiritual texts, or participating in religious practices. Spirituality can be a powerful source of strength, support, and resilience for Black entrepreneurs, it also can help to build a sense of purpose, meaning, and understanding of events and challenges. Your faith is what gives you real substance, not just the worldly things. Faith is what will sustain you when everything else falls apart.
- **Social connections**: Make time for social connections with family and friends. Strong social connections can provide a sense of community, and can also serve as a source of emotional support.

Chapter Nine:
Leading Your Team Effectively

Leading a team is a critical aspect of entrepreneurship, and it is especially important for Black entrepreneurs who often lack the formal leadership training and experience due to lack of opportunities to lead. In this chapter, we will explore strategies for leading your team effectively, with a focus on best practices for Black entrepreneurs. As Nelson Mandela, the first President of South Africa once said, "It is better to lead from behind and to put others in front, especially when you celebrate victory and when nice things occur. You take the front line when there is danger. Then people will appreciate your leadership."

An old riddle goes: "I am not a leader, but I am responsible for their lives. Who am I?" The answer is "a captain of a ship". Leading a team effectively is not just about being the leader, it's about being the captain of the ship, guiding and taking care of the people that are in your charge. In this chapter, we will look at the ways in which you can develop the skills and qualities of a good leader to navigate and reach success.

COMMUNICATING CLEARLY

Effective communication is a critical aspect of leading a team and it is especially important for Black entrepreneurs. Clear communication can foster a sense of unity and purpose among team members, which is essential for achieving success. In this chapter, we will explore strategies for communicating clearly with your team, with a focus on best practices for Black entrepreneurs.

First and foremost, it's essential for them to communicate their vision and expectations clearly. A clear vision and a clear set of expectations can help to ensure that everyone is on the same page and working towards the same goals. As a leader, it's important to communicate your vision in a way that is both inspiring and easy to understand. This can be achieved by using simple, clear language, and by providing examples that help to illustrate your vision.

Furthermore, Black entrepreneurs should create a culture of open and transparent communication within their organization. By fostering an environment where team members feel comfortable sharing their thoughts and ideas, they can tap into the collective wisdom of the group and make better decisions. It's important for Black leaders to be approachable and open to feedback and for team members to understand that honest and direct feedback is expected and encouraged.

Effective communication also involves active listening. It's important for Black entrepreneurs to make sure they understand the perspective of their team members, and to take their thoughts and ideas into consideration when making decisions. By actively listening to team members, Black bosses can build trust and respect and can show that they value the contributions of each team member.

It's also important for Black entrepreneurs to communicate clearly and effectively with stakeholders outside the organization. This can include customers, vendors, and investors. By communicating clearly and effectively with these stakeholders, Black entrepreneurs can build strong relationships and ensure that their business is well-positioned for success.

Clear communication can foster a sense of unity and purpose among team members, which is essential for achieving success. If your team is not performing up to snuff, first look at yourself as a leader and see how you can better communicate your goals and expectations. Black entrepreneurs should ensure that they are communicating their vision and expectations clearly, fostering a culture of open and transparent communication, actively listening and communicating effectively with stakeholders. By following these strategies, Black entrepreneurs can effectively lead their team and position their business for success.

SETTING EXPECTATIONS AND GOALS

As the captain of a ship, it is essential for Black entrepreneurs to set clear expectations and goals for their team and provide the support and resources necessary for them to succeed. Setting clear expectations and goals can help to ensure that everyone is on the same page and working towards the same destination.

Again, it's important for Black entrepreneurs to set clear and specific goals for their team. These goals should be aligned with the overall vision and mission of the business, and should be measurable and achievable. This way, team members will know exactly what they are working towards, and how their efforts contribute to the success of the business.

In addition, bosses should set clear expectations for their team, including what is expected in terms of performance, accountability, and communication. By setting clear expectations, Black entrepreneurs can help to ensure that everyone is on the same page, and that team members understand their role in the organization.

To support their team, Black leaders should provide the necessary resources and support to help team members achieve their goals. This can include things like training, tools and equipment, and access to information and expertise. Don't just hire a team and throw them to the proverbial wolves. Rear them. By providing the necessary resources and support, Black entrepreneurs can empower their team to take ownership of their work and achieve their goals.

Yes, Black entrepreneurs should be prepared to provide guidance and support when needed, and be accessible to their team members for questions and feedback. This can involve providing regular check-ins, providing regular feedback and coaching, and providing opportunities for team members to continue their development. Keeping an open-door policy for your team is usually a good strategy.

It's also important for Black entrepreneurs to provide recognition and rewards for a job well done. You want to increase retention rates and morale? Give your team props often. This can include things like bonuses, promotions, and public recognition. By recognizing and rewarding the efforts and achievements of team members, Black entrepreneurs can help to create a sense of engagement and motivation among their team.

I hope you see now why setting clear expectations and goals, and providing the support and resources necessary for success, is crucial for Black entrepreneurs as the captain of the ship. Black bosses have to ensure that their team members are aligned with the business vision, are aware of their roles and are motivated to work towards achieving the set goals. By doing so, they can position their business for success and navigate through the voyage.

PROVIDING LEADERSHIP AND DIRECTION

Leading a team is a critical aspect of entrepreneurship, and it is especially important for Black entrepreneurs who seek to become bosses and dominant in their industry. In this chapter, we will explore strategies for leading your team effectively, with a focus on best practices for Black entrepreneurs.

One key aspect of effective leadership besides setting clear expectations and goals for the team includes providing a clear vision and mission for the business, as well as specific, measurable goals that align with that vision. You need to come to the table each day with a clear vision that you can rally your team behind. Your team cannot be on the same page and working towards the same goal if you are not clear on your vision.

Another important aspect of effective leadership is serving as a role model for the team. Black entrepreneurs should lead by example, demonstrating the values and behavior that they expect from the team. This includes things like a strong work ethic, integrity, and a commitment to excellence. By serving as a role model, Black entrepreneurs can inspire their team to strive for success and greatness.

You need to show your team that you're passionate about your business as well as the success of your team. One story of a black entrepreneur that comes to mind is that of Tristan Walker. Born and raised in the projects of New York, Tristan had a passion for entrepreneurship from a young age. He always had an interest in the beauty industry, and after college, he landed a job at Foursquare building partnerships with consumer packaged goods companies. He quickly realized that while the industry had many products catering to people with different hair types and textures, there were very few options for people with tight curls and kinks, which is a very common trait among black people.

Determined to fill this gap in the market, Tristan left Foursquare and started researching the hair care industry. He spent months talking to people and learning about the unique needs of black hair, and eventually came up with the idea for Bevel, a line of shaving products specifically designed for men with coarse, curly hair.

Tristan was incredibly passionate about his business, and his passion was contagious. He worked tirelessly to build Bevel from the ground up, traveling to trade shows and speaking at events to spread the word about his products. Despite facing numerous obstacles, including skepticism from investors, Tristan persevered, and Bevel quickly gained a devoted following. Eventually, Tristan was able to secure funding and build a successful business.

Today, Bevel is a well-known brand, and Tristan continues to inspire other Black entrepreneurs with his story of passion, determination and hard work.

You need to be resilient and bounce back from setbacks that are inevitably going to arise. One black entrepreneur who was incredibly resilient in regards to their business is Earl G. Graves Sr, the founder of Black Enterprise Magazine.

Graves was born in Brooklyn, New York and grew up in a working-class family. He attended Morgan State College, and then served in the United States Army before starting a career in advertising. However, he always felt that there was a lack of representation of black-owned businesses in mainstream media, and he decided to take action by starting Black Enterprise Magazine. The magazine was launched in 1970, during a time of great racial and economic turmoil. He faced many obstacles, including lack of funding and advertising, but he never gave up on his vision. He persisted and kept pushing forward, and as a result, Black Enterprise Magazine became one of the leading publications for black business owners and entrepreneurs.

Despite the many challenges he faced, Graves Sr. always remained resolute and committed to his goal of providing a platform to showcase and support black-owned businesses. He also was an advocate for financial literacy and economic empowerment for black communities until his death in 2020.

Use your innovative mindset to display for your team why you deserve to be their leader. This means thinking outside the box when it comes to solving problems or forming an idea. One black entrepreneur who was incredibly innovative in regards to their business is Dr. Lonnie G. Johnson, inventor of the Super Soaker water gun.

Dr. Johnson is a former NASA engineer and inventor who has over 80 patents to his name. He invented the Super Soaker water gun in the early 90s, which revolutionized the water gun industry and became one of the best-selling toys of all time. The Super Soaker uses pressurized air to shoot water, which was a new and innovative approach to water guns that made it more powerful and accurate than previous models.

Dr. Johnson's innovation not only led to the creation of a popular toy, but also paved the way for the development of other pressurized water-based products, such as fire extinguishers and power washers. He is also a proponent for STEM education and has founded several organizations to promote science and technology education for underprivileged students, including the Johnson STEM Activity Center[13], which provides hands-on learning experiences in science, technology, engineering, and math. Dr. Lonnie Johnson continues to be an inspiration for young inventors and entrepreneurs who wish to make a difference with their innovations.

A strong work ethic is a trait indicative of great leaders throughout history, too. There's a story about a black entrepreneur named Tariq Farid and his company which used to be called Edible Arrangements. He originally started a small flower shop in a strip mall in Connecticut. When he first started, Tariq would wake up at 4 am every day to go to the flower market, handpick the freshest flowers, and then open his shop at 8 am. He would work in the shop all day, and then go home at night to work on the books and plan for the next day.

As the years went by, Tariq's flower shop became increasingly successful and he began to expand his business. He opened several more stores and eventually even started a wholesale division, supplying flowers to other florists. Despite the growth of his business, Tariq's work ethic never wavered. He was still at the flower market every morning at 4 am, and he still worked in the shop every day.

Tariq's dedication and hard work paid off, and today his company, "Edible" is one of the largest floral retailers in the country, with over 100 stores across the United States[14]. His story is a testament to the power of hard work and dedication in achieving success as an entrepreneur.

---

[13] n.d. Lonnie Johnson | Johnson STEM Activity Center | United States. Accessed January 17, 2023. https://www.johnsonstem.org/.

[14] "Edible Arrangements® - CEO, Tariq Farid." n.d. Edible Arrangements. Accessed January 17, 2023. https://www.ediblearrangements.com/about/tariq-farid-ceo-edible-arrangements/.

I personally believe that Black entrepreneurs should place a priority on hiring veterans, as they often have experience working in a rank structure, and a deep understanding of how to work as a cohesive unit with limited resources. In my experience, veterans make great team members and can be a valuable asset to any startup or business as veterans have a history of discipline, perseverance, and leadership. Take one of my personal inspirations, Evan Hafer, who is a successful entrepreneur and a US Army veteran who has made a significant impact in the business world.

Evan Hafer is a U.S. Army veteran and the founder and CEO of Black Rifle Coffee Company (BRCC). He started the company in 2012 and it has quickly grown into one of the most popular and successful specialty coffee companies in the US. Evan is a strong advocate for hiring veterans and has made it a priority to employ veterans and active-duty military personnel at BRCC. He believes that veterans bring valuable skills and experience to the workforce, such as leadership, discipline, and the ability to adapt to changing situations. He also believes that hiring veterans is a way to give back to those who have served their country.

Black Rifle Coffee Company is a great example of how a business can be built by hiring veterans. By providing jobs for veterans, Evan is not only helping vets to re-enter the civilian workforce but also creating a strong, dedicated and efficient team that can bring a lot of value to the company. Additionally, his company has been able to use the veteran-hiring as a differentiator in the market, which helped to build a loyal customer base that values the company's mission.

Evan Hafer's story and the success of Black Rifle Coffee Company, is a great example of how hiring veterans can be a smart decision for entrepreneurs, and how it can be a powerful tool for building a successful and sustainable business.

Understand that effective leadership is essential for the success of a business, especially for Black entrepreneurs. Setting clear expectations and goals, serving as a role model, providing guidance and support, recognizing and rewarding team members, and considering hiring veterans are all strategies that can help Black entrepreneurs lead their team effectively and achieve success.

BUILDING TRUST AND RESPECT

Building trust and respect with your team is essential for the success of any business, and it is particularly important for Black entrepreneurs. In this section, we will explore strategies for building trust and respect with your team, with a focus on best practices for Black entrepreneurs.

First, Black entrepreneurs should lead by example and consistently demonstrate the values and behaviors that they expect from their team. This includes things like transparency, integrity, a strong work ethic, and a commitment to excellence. By leading by example, Black entrepreneurs can demonstrate that they are invested in the success of the business and are worthy of respect. A great leader won't ask his team to do anything he himself would not do.

Next, Black entrepreneurs should make an effort to understand and address any issues that the team members may have, whether personal or work related. Showing that you care about the well-being of your team members, can foster a sense of loyalty and respect towards you. People won't care about your business until they know you care about them. This goes for team members, customers, and potential partners alike.

Additionally, Black entrepreneurs should also provide opportunities for team members to grow and develop both professionally and personally. This can include things like training, mentorship, and networking opportunities. By providing these opportunities, Black entrepreneurs can demonstrate that they are invested in the success of their team members and that they value their contributions to the business.

Finally, Black entrepreneurs should recognize and reward the efforts and achievements of their team members. This can include things like bonuses, promotions, and public recognition. By recognizing and rewarding the efforts and achievements of team members, bosses can help to create a sense of engagement and motivation among their team.

Let's recap. Building trust and respect with your team is essential for the success of any business, and it is particularly important for Black entrepreneurs. Clear and open communication, leading by example, addressing team member issues, providing opportunities for growth and development and recognizing the efforts of the team are all strategies that can help Black entrepreneurs build trust and respect with their team and position the business for success.

ENCOURAGING COLLABORATION AND TEAMWORK

Encouraging collaboration and teamwork is crucial for the success of any business, and it is particularly important for Black entrepreneurs. A culture of collaboration and teamwork can help to foster a sense of unity and purpose within the team, and can lead to more creative and effective solutions to challenges faced by the business. In this section, we will explore strategies for encouraging collaboration and teamwork within your team.

First, entrepreneurs should create an environment that encourages open communication and idea-sharing among team members. This can include things like regular team meetings, open-door policies, and online platforms where team members can share ideas and collaborate on projects. By fostering an environment that encourages open communication and idea-sharing, Black entrepreneurs can help to create a sense of community and collaboration among their team.

Secondly, Black entrepreneurs should establish clear roles and responsibilities for each team member and make sure everyone is aware of them. This will help to ensure that everyone knows what is expected of them and how their work contributes to the overall success of the business. Also, this will reduce infighting, redundancy, resentment, and people stepping on each other's toes in the workplace. Remember, disagreements within the office are bound to happen, so do what you can as a boss to reduce the odds of them occurring if it is within your power. This takes me to my third point.

Thirdly, entrepreneurs should establish a system for managing conflicts and disagreements among team members, it can be in the form of a team leader or a designated person for such matters, to ensure that conflicts are resolved in a timely and effective manner and that the team can continue to work together effectively. The main thing you want is a team that can work together as a unit. So this will require a culture of support and sharing, not competitiveness and individualism. This takes me to my next point.

Fourthly, Black entrepreneurs should provide opportunities for team members to learn and grow together, whether it is through team building activities, workshops, or mentorship programs. By providing these opportunities, Black entrepreneurs can help to create a sense of unity and shared purpose among their team and foster a culture of collaboration and teamwork.

Finally, Black entrepreneurs should recognize and reward the efforts and achievements of their team as a whole and not just as individuals. Again, rewards can include things like bonuses, promotions, and public recognition. By recognizing and rewarding the team's achievements and contributions, entrepreneurs can help to create a sense of engagement and motivation among their team.

Summarily, encouraging collaboration and teamwork is crucial for the success of any business, and it is particularly important for Black entrepreneurs. Fostering an environment that encourages open communication and idea-sharing, establishing clear roles and responsibilities, managing conflicts, providing opportunities for growth and recognizing the efforts of the team are all strategies that can help Black entrepreneurs to maintain a culture of collaboration and inspiration within their team and position the business for success. I will discuss in more detail how Black entrepreneurs can provide feedback and recognition in the next section.

PROVIDING FEEDBACK AND RECOGNITION

Providing feedback and recognition is a crucial aspect of leading a team and is essential for the success of any business, particularly for Black entrepreneurs. In this section, we will explore strategies for providing feedback and recognition to your team, with a focus on best practices for Black entrepreneurs.

First, it is important for Black entrepreneurs to provide timely and constructive feedback to their team members. This feedback should be specific, actionable, and focused on helping team members to improve their skills and performance. Providing feedback regularly, whether it is positive or corrective, can help to create a sense of trust, engagement and motivation among the team, as it shows that the entrepreneur cares about their development and progress.

Secondly, it is important for Black entrepreneurs to provide recognition for a job well done. Give them an extra few hundred bucks one pay period as a thank you. Or publish an article in the local paper lauding them and thanking them for their hard work. Host a company party or trip to show appreciation to your team. Let them taste some of the best fruits of the business with you, and treat them all with equal respect. Recognizing and rewarding the efforts and achievements of team members can help to create a sense of engagement and motivation among the team, and foster a sense of loyalty towards the entrepreneur and the business.

Additionally, bosses should also establish a system for tracking progress and accomplishments, whether it's through performance evaluations, progress reports, or regular check-ins. By having a system in place, it helps the entrepreneur to identify areas of success, as well as areas that need improvement and tailor the feedback accordingly. All negative feedback should be backed up with empirical evidence, written records, and witness statements if necessary. Let your team know that if you come to them with a grievance, it will not be frivolous. With respect to employee discipline, this will foster an understanding that your system is "tough but fair," with fairness being the main point.

Thirdly, Black entrepreneurs should encourage their team members to share their feedback on their work, providing an avenue for them to share what they have done, what they did well, and where they struggled. By actively listening to their team members, it can help identify areas that need improvement and give the entrepreneur a chance to provide feedback on those areas.

So, providing feedback and recognition is a crucial aspect of leading a team and is essential for the success of any business, particularly for Black entrepreneurs. Providing timely and constructive feedback, recognizing and rewarding efforts, and encouraging team members to share their feedback can all help Black entrepreneurs to foster a sense of engagement, motivation and loyalty among their team and position the company for success.

Chapter Ten:
Overcoming Challenges and Setbacks

Entrepreneurship is not for the faint of heart. It takes grit, determination, and a willingness to take risks to start and grow a successful business. However, even the most successful entrepreneurs will encounter challenges and setbacks along the way. The difference between those who succeed and those who don't is often their ability to stay resilient in the face of adversity and actively seek out the support and resources they need to overcome those obstacles.

In this chapter, we will delve into the topic of overcoming challenges and setbacks as a Black entrepreneur. We will discuss the importance of staying resilient, seeking support, reframing challenges as opportunities, and seeking out resources. Additionally, we will examine the power of developing a growth mindset and building a strong spiritual support system. Through the stories and insights of successful Black entrepreneurs, we will explore practical strategies for navigating the unique challenges faced by Black business owners and emerging victorious on the other side.

We will start by discussing the importance of staying resilient and maintaining a positive attitude, even in the face of setbacks. This includes the ability to bounce back from failure and to maintain a sense of hope and determination. We will also explore the importance of seeking support, both within and outside of your business. This can include seeking mentorship, networking with other entrepreneurs, and building a strong support system of family and friends.

We will also explore the concept of reframing challenges as opportunities for growth and learning. This mindset shift can help entrepreneurs see difficult situations in a new light, and find ways to turn them into opportunities for success. Along with this we will look at the importance of seeking out resources that can help you overcome challenges, such as financial assistance, business training programs, and networking events.

Finally, we will delve into the power of developing a growth mindset and building a strong spiritual support system. A growth mindset, which focuses on learning and improvement, can help entrepreneurs stay motivated and continue to push forward even in the face of adversity. Building a strong spiritual support system can provide a sense of inner peace and a foundation for resilience in difficult times.

Throughout this chapter, we will offer practical tips and actionable advice for overcoming the challenges and setbacks that Black entrepreneurs may face. By understanding the unique obstacles that Black business owners may face, and the strategies that have helped others succeed, you will be better equipped to navigate your own entrepreneurial journey with confidence and resilience.

STAYING RESILIENT

As a Black entrepreneur, it is important to maintain a resilient mindset and not let setbacks and challenges deter you from your goals. Resilience is the ability to bounce back from adversity and maintain a positive attitude even in the face of obstacles. This mindset is crucial for success as a Black business owner, as you may encounter unique challenges that can test your determination and resolve.

As the motivational speaker Les Brown said, "You must remain focused on your journey to greatness. It is not a matter of if you will get there, but a matter of when you will arrive." Remember, success is not a destination, it's a journey. And it will be full of ups and downs.

One key aspect of staying resilient is being able to handle and learn from failure. Failure is a natural part of the entrepreneurial process, and it is important to not let it discourage you. Instead, view it as a learning opportunity and use it to grow and improve your business. As Thomas Edison said, "I have not failed. I've just found 10,000 ways that won't work."

Another important aspect of resilience is maintaining a sense of hope and determination. Even in the face of obstacles, it is important to believe in your ability to succeed and to not give up on your goals. This can be difficult at times, but having a strong vision and mission for your business can help to keep you motivated and focused. As the author Maya Angelou said, "I have learned that people will forget what you said, people will forget what you did, but people will never forget how you made them feel."

It's also crucial to be able to have a support system, both within and outside of your business. Surrounding yourself with people who believe in your vision and who will support you through the ups and downs of entrepreneurship can be invaluable. It's important to have a mentor, a friend, or a family member who can provide guidance and encouragement when you need it most. Additionally, finding a community of other entrepreneurs who you can relate to and learn from can be a powerful way to gain perspective on the challenges you're facing, and to stay motivated.

Finally, it's important to take care of your well-being, both physically and mentally. Starting a business can be a stressful and demanding process, and it's important to make time for self-care and to prioritize your mental health. If you ever find yourself in a real mental health crisis, don't hesitate to reach out to emergency hotlines such as National Suicide Prevention Lifeline (1-800-273-TALK) which provide confidential and free support 24/7. I also like the app called ZocDoc, which allows you to visit with all kinds of doctors virtually from anywhere with internet access. I'll go further into seeking support in the next section.

By staying resilient and maintaining a positive attitude, Black entrepreneurs can overcome the challenges they face and achieve their goals. Remember to stay motivated and determined, lean on a supportive network, and take care of your well-being. With a resilient mindset, you can push through obstacles and come out on top as a successful Black entrepreneur.

SEEKING SUPPORT

As a Black entrepreneur, seeking support from a network of advisors, mentors, and colleagues is an important aspect of overcoming challenges and setbacks. Building a strong support system can provide guidance, encouragement, and a sounding board for ideas and feedback. Additionally, a network of contacts can be a valuable resource for connecting with potential customers, partners, and investors.

One key aspect of seeking support is identifying and building relationships with mentors. Mentors are experienced individuals who can provide guidance and advice based on their own successes and failures. They can also serve as role models and can help entrepreneurs stay motivated and focused on their goals. Finding a mentor that understands your experience as a black entrepreneur can be even more beneficial.

Another important aspect of seeking support is networking with other entrepreneurs and industry professionals. Networking provides an opportunity to connect with others who are facing similar challenges and to gain valuable insights and perspective. Additionally, networking can lead to potential business partnerships and collaborations.

Another aspect of seeking support is seeking feedback, both inside and outside of your organization. Seek feedback from customers, employees and suppliers. This feedback can be crucial in identifying areas for improvement and can provide valuable insights into the needs and wants of your target market.

It's also important to remember that seeking support doesn't have to be limited to individuals or groups within your industry or field. Consider seeking support from family and friends, or from community resources such as business incubators or accelerators, which can provide access to training and resources for small business owners.

By actively seeking support from a network of advisors, mentors, and colleagues, Black entrepreneurs can overcome challenges and setbacks more effectively. Remember, no one can do it all alone and it's important to ask for help when needed. By building a strong support system, you can gain valuable insights and resources that can help you navigate the unique challenges faced by Black business owners and emerge victorious on the other side.

REFRAMING CHALLENGES AS OPPORTUNITIES

As a black entrepreneur, you will inevitably face challenges along the way. Whether it's securing funding, navigating discrimination, or simply trying to stand out in a crowded market, there will be times when you feel like giving up. However, it's important to remember that these challenges can also be opportunities for learning and growth.

As the famous entrepreneur and motivator, Eric Thomas, once said, "When you want to succeed as badly as you want to breathe, then you'll be successful." This quote reminds us that true success comes from a deep-seated desire to overcome obstacles and keep moving forward, no matter what.

One ancient allegory that illustrates this point well is the story of the Phoenix, a mythical bird that is said to be able to rise from its own ashes. The Phoenix symbolizes the idea of rebirth and renewal, and can serve as a reminder that even when things seem bleak, there is always the possibility of rising from the ashes and starting anew.

We, as American descendants of slavery (ADOS), have been overcoming challenges since we took our first breaths. As a people, we are the phoenix. And just like the Phoenix, Black entrepreneurs have the ability to turn challenges into opportunities for growth. By reframing these challenges as opportunities for learning and growth, you can gain valuable insights, build resilience, and ultimately emerge stronger than before.

Moreover, one of the most valuable traits of any entrepreneur is the ability to adapt, rather than seeing any disruption as a threat. Don't be so quick to cut off team members for making mistakes. Show compassion. Business is not everything. It's important to not only adapt but also be empathetic and understand the human-side of any situation.

In conclusion, as a black entrepreneur, it's important to remember that challenges are a natural part of the journey to success. By reframing these challenges as opportunities for learning and growth, you can turn them into stepping stones on the path to achieving your goals. And, like the Phoenix, you can rise from the ashes and soar to new heights.

SEEKING OUT RESOURCES

As a black entrepreneur, you may feel like you're navigating a constantly shifting landscape of challenges and setbacks. But it's important to remember that you're not alone on your journey. There are many resources available to help you overcome the obstacles you'll encounter along the way.

One of the most important resources you can tap into is training and education. Whether it's taking a class or attending a workshop, learning new skills and strategies can help you stay ahead of the curve and better compete in your market. For example, if you're looking to start a business in a highly-technical field, it can be beneficial to take a class or pursue a certification to gain a deeper understanding of the industry.

Another valuable resource you can tap into is support programs. There are various programs that provide mentorship, networking opportunities, and other resources to help entrepreneurs from marginalized communities succeed. For example, the National Black Business Council and the National Association of Black Owned Broadcasters are organizations that provide support specifically for Black entrepreneurs.

Networking is also essential, so look for groups and events that connect Black entrepreneurs and Small Business Owners to each other. Many times, these types of groups have guest speakers, which can be a great opportunity to learn from successful entrepreneurs.

Additionally, there are a lot of financial resources available for businesses, like loans, grants, and tax incentives, that can help you get your business off the ground. Look for programs that are tailored to your specific needs and qualifications.

So, as a black entrepreneur, it's important to seek out resources that can help you overcome challenges and setbacks. From training and education to support programs and networking opportunities, there are many resources available to help you succeed. With the right tools, you'll be able to build a strong and sustainable business that will weather any storm.

DEVELOPING A GROWTH MINDSET

A growth mindset is a valuable asset for any entrepreneur, but it is particularly important for Black entrepreneurs, who often face unique challenges and barriers to success. Developing a growth mindset involves recognizing that setbacks and challenges are a natural part of the entrepreneurial journey, and that these difficulties can be used as opportunities to learn and grow.

One effective way to cultivate a growth mindset is through the metaphor of gardening. Just as a gardener must tend to their plants regularly, constantly nourishing and nurturing them, so too must an entrepreneur tend to their growth mindset. This means regularly engaging in activities and practices that promote learning and development, such as reading, seeking out new experiences, and seeking feedback from others.

Like a gardener, an entrepreneur must also be willing to make adjustments and take risks. A gardener may need to try different types of fertilizer or replant a crop if it isn't thriving in a particular location. Similarly, an entrepreneur may need to pivot their business strategy or try a new marketing approach if they are not seeing the results they desire.

Another important aspect of gardening is patience and persistence. A gardener cannot expect their plants to grow overnight, and must instead be patient and persistent in their efforts to cultivate a lush and bountiful garden. Similarly, an entrepreneur must be patient and persistent in their efforts to build and grow their business. Setbacks and challenges are inevitable, but with a growth mindset, they can be seen as opportunities to learn and grow, rather than as reasons to give up.

In sum, developing a growth mindset is a vital step for Black entrepreneurs looking to succeed in today's competitive business landscape. By cultivating a growth mindset, Black entrepreneurs can see setbacks and challenges as opportunities to learn and grow. To achieve this, the entrepreneurs should take inspiration from the daily effort of gardening by staying nourished and nurturing their mindset, seeking out new experiences, seeking feedback, and being patient with their progress.

BUILDING A STRONG SPIRITUAL SUPPORT SYSTEM

One of the key components of developing a growth mindset as a Black entrepreneur is building a strong support system. A support system can provide guidance and encouragement during the inevitable challenges and setbacks of the entrepreneurial journey. There are several key individuals and groups that can make up a strong support system for Black entrepreneurs.

- Advisors: Advisors can be valuable sources of information and guidance for Black entrepreneurs. These individuals can provide expertise in areas such as finance, marketing, or operations, and can help entrepreneurs make important decisions and navigate the complexities of running a business.
- Mentors: Mentors can be especially valuable for Black entrepreneurs, as they can provide guidance and support based on their own experiences in the industry. Black entrepreneurs can benefit from the guidance and support of mentors who have faced and overcome similar challenges.
- Colleagues: Colleagues can be a valuable source of support, encouragement, and inspiration. Networking with other Black entrepreneurs can provide opportunities to share resources, knowledge, and ideas, and can help entrepreneurs feel less alone on their entrepreneurial journey.

It is important to note that building a support system isn't always an easy task, especially for Black entrepreneurs that may have to navigate additional cultural, racial or economic biases.

For instance, you just may find yourself being the only Black person in the room while you're at a work function one day, and for some this is enough to cause anxiety. Having someone you can call that understands what that is like can be a tremendous boon to the mental health, confidence, and perspective of a Black entrepreneur. If you've been there, you know exactly what I mean. It may take some time and effort, but the benefits of having a support system in place can be immeasurable. Black entrepreneurs can seek out mentoring programs, networking groups, and other resources specifically for Black business owners to help connect with potential advisors, mentors, and colleagues.

Let's sum it up here. Building a strong support system is an essential aspect of developing a growth mindset for Black entrepreneurs. Having a network of advisors, mentors, and colleagues can provide guidance, encouragement, and a sense of community as we navigate the challenges of building and growing a successful business. A support system can help to provide the reassurance, guidance and accountability that we need to face and overcome obstacles, as well as fostering a sense of belonging and community as we navigate the often challenging landscape of commerce.

Chapter Eleven:
Financial Management and Budgeting

Welcome to the chapter on Financial Management and Budgeting for Black entrepreneurs. As a business owner, it is crucial to have a solid understanding of financial management in order to ensure the success and sustainability of your venture. I got lucky and married a CFO to a major corporation, but if you didn't, this next chapter should help get you going in the right direction. In this chapter, we will cover important topics such as developing a comprehensive financial plan, creating a budget that works for your business, closely monitoring cash flow, seeking professional advice, leveraging financial tools and resources, and effectively managing debt. We will explore each of these topics in detail and provide practical tips and strategies for implementing them in your own business. Whether you are just starting out or are an experienced entrepreneur, this chapter will provide valuable insights and knowledge to help you navigate the financial aspects of entrepreneurship.

DEVELOPING A FINANCIAL PLAN

A financial plan is a comprehensive document that outlines your business's financial goals, strategies, and projections. It serves as a roadmap for achieving financial success and helps you make informed decisions about managing your business's finances. I've helped many people start up new businesses over the years. Many of them fail, and a few of them succeed. I have noticed in my own experience that businesses with a written financial plan are more likely to secure funding and experience growth than businesses without a plan.

Creating a financial plan can seem daunting, but it doesn't have to be. The key is to start by identifying your business's financial goals, such as increasing revenue or reducing costs. From there, you can develop strategies for achieving those goals, such as expanding your product line or negotiating better deals with suppliers. Once you have your goals and strategies in place, you can then create financial projections, such as projected income statements and cash flow statements. These projections will help you identify potential challenges and opportunities and make adjustments to your plan as needed.

It's important to note that a financial plan is not a static document; it should be regularly reviewed and updated as your business evolves. Many experts recommend reviewing your financial plan at least once a quarter (Inc, 2019). When conducting a review, take the time to assess your actual performance against your financial projections and make any necessary adjustments to your plan.

In this section, we will take you step by step on how to develop a comprehensive financial plan that aligns with your business's goals and strategies. We will also provide information on financial tools and resources that can help simplify the process, including templates and software that can assist with creating financial projections. With the right financial plan in place, you will be well-equipped to navigate the financial aspects of entrepreneurship and achieve the success you desire for your business.

CREATING A BUDGET

Creating a budget is an essential step in financial management for any business, and it is especially important for Black entrepreneurs who may face additional financial challenges. A budget can help Black entrepreneurs track their spending, identify areas for cost savings, and allocate resources effectively. In this section, we will discuss the basics of creating a budget and provide tips for making the most of this valuable tool.

The first step in creating a budget is to gather all of your financial information, including income, expenses, and cash flow. This information should be organized and clearly recorded in a budget template or spreadsheet. There are many budget templates and tools available online, including those specifically designed for small businesses and entrepreneurs.

Once you have all of your financial information organized, you can begin to analyze your income and expenses. Start by identifying fixed expenses, such as rent and utility bills, as well as variable expenses, such as marketing and advertising costs. It's important to also include any debt payments and savings goals in your budget.

Next, compare your income and expenses to see if there are any areas where you can reduce costs. Look for areas where you can make cuts or find more cost-effective solutions. For example, you may be able to negotiate lower rates for services or find ways to reduce overhead costs. I used virtual services to bolster my law firm's capacity. You might be served well to do the same in your venture.

In addition to tracking and analyzing your spending, it's also important to establish goals and allocate resources accordingly. Identify what are the most important things you need to do or purchase to make your business grow, and prioritize them. This could include investing in marketing or hiring additional staff, for example. And remember that your goals and priorities may change over time as your business grows and evolves.

Creating a budget is a process that requires regular review and update. Make sure to regularly monitor your spending, income, and cash flow to ensure that you are on track to meet your financial goals. And don't be afraid to make adjustments as needed. As you gain a deeper understanding of your financial situation, you'll be better equipped to make informed decisions that will help your business thrive.

Nobody can argue with the fact that creating a budget is an essential tool for any business, especially for Black entrepreneurs, it can provide a clear picture of your financial situation, helping you to make informed decisions, prioritize your goals and cut on unnecessary expenses. Regularly monitoring and updating your budget will help you stay on track and achieve your financial goals.

MONITORING CASH FLOW

Cash flow is the lifeblood of any business, and it is especially critical for Black entrepreneurs to pay close attention to their cash flow. Black entrepreneurs often face additional challenges when it comes to securing funding, and it is essential that they take steps to manage their cash flow effectively to ensure that they have sufficient funds to meet their business needs.

One of the most important things that Black entrepreneurs can do to monitor their cash flow is to keep accurate financial records. This includes tracking all income and expenses, as well as maintaining detailed records of all transactions. This information can be used to create financial statements, such as balance sheets, income statements, and cash flow statements, which can provide valuable insights into the financial health of the business. Try using a software application to help you automate some tasks and generate some financial documents for you.

Another important step for monitoring cash flow is to create a budget and stick to it. A budget can help entrepreneurs forecast their cash flow, so they know how much money they are likely to have coming in and going out. This can help them plan for any shortfalls and take steps to mitigate them in advance. Meet regularly with your financial team to stay on top of your business. I like to meet with my team at least once or twice per week.

Additionally, it is important to regularly review financial performance and projections of the business to identify trends in the cash flow. For example, if business is cyclical and there are typically months with less cash inflows, planning to have enough cash reserves can ensure that the business does not run out of money during such months. This is the case with many of my clients who own landscaping businesses.

Their business is bustling during the spring and summer months from cutting yards and doing commercial landscaping gigs. But during Autumn and winter, business can get slow. This is why making keeping accurate financial records, and putting in the required financial planning time is crucial to helping you achieve your financial goals.

Finally, black bosses should be proactive in seeking out funding from a variety of sources, such as grants, loans, and investors. This can help to ensure that they have a consistent flow of funds to support their business operations and can take advantage of growth opportunities as they arise.

Overall, monitoring cash flow is crucial for the success of any business, and Black entrepreneurs should make it a priority to track their finances closely and take steps to manage their cash flow effectively. Regular monitoring and forecasting can help to ensure that they have the funds they need to meet their business needs and achieve their goals.

SEEKING PROFESSIONAL ADVICE

As a Black entrepreneur, managing your finances effectively is crucial to the success of your business. One way to ensure that you are on the right track financially is to seek the advice of a financial advisor or accountant. These professionals can provide guidance on budgeting, investing, and managing cash flow, all of which are important considerations for any business owner.

A financial advisor can help you create a long-term financial plan for your business, which can include setting financial goals and developing strategies to achieve them. They can also provide guidance on investments, such as stocks, bonds, and real estate, to help you grow your wealth over time.

An accountant, on the other hand, can provide more specific advice on budgeting and managing cash flow. They can help you create a budget for your business and track your spending to make sure you are staying within your means. An accountant can also help you navigate the tax laws and regulations that apply to your business, and make sure you are taking advantage of any deductions or credits that you may qualify for.

In addition to a financial advisor or accountant, Black entrepreneurs may also want to seek the advice of a business coach or mentor. These professionals can provide guidance on the operational and strategic aspects of running a business, such as marketing, sales, and management.

It's important to note, as a Black entrepreneur, you may also want to seek out professionals or resources that specifically caters to your community as they may have a better understanding of the unique financial challenges and opportunities you may face.

The main takeaway is that seeking professional advice can be an invaluable tool for Black entrepreneurs as they navigate the financial aspects of running a business. With the help of a financial advisor, accountant, or other professional, you can have the confidence and knowledge you need to make smart financial decisions for your business.

LEVERAGING FINANCIAL TOOLS AND RESOURCES

As a Black entrepreneur, there are a number of financial tools and resources available to help you manage your finances more efficiently. From budgeting software to financial planning apps, these resources can provide valuable insights and make it easier to track your expenses and income.

Budgeting software, such as Mint, can help you create and stick to a budget, and track your expenses. These tools allow you to categorize your spending and see where your money is going, which can help you identify areas where you can cut costs and reallocate funds.

Accounting software like QuickBooks, Xero, or Wave can help you keep track of income and expenses, create invoices, manage payroll, and generate financial reports. This can be particularly useful for tracking the financial health of your business, and making informed decisions.

Financial planning apps, like Credit Karma or Clarity Money, can help you track your credit and spending and spending, set financial goals, and develop a plan to achieve them. These apps provide a wide range of financial tools, including budgeting, saving, and investing.

Leveraging financial tools and resources can be an effective way for Black entrepreneurs to manage their finances and make informed business decisions. By taking advantage of these resources, you can improve your financial literacy and gain a better understanding of your business's financial health. It's important to have in mind that not all the financial apps and resources are created equal, it's important to explore the options and choose the one that works best for your specific needs and business model. And most importantly, it's always a good idea to seek professional advice when making important financial decisions.

MANAGING DEBT

As a Black entrepreneur, managing debt is an important aspect of maintaining financial stability. Whether you have taken out a loan to start your business or accumulated credit card debt, it is essential to develop strategies for managing and paying off your debt in a timely manner.

One popular online service for managing debt is National Debt Relief. This company offers a range of debt management services, including debt consolidation and settlement. This can be helpful if you have multiple credit cards or loans with high interest rates, as consolidating them into a single loan with a lower interest rate can make it easier to manage your payments.

Another popular online service is Credit Karma, which offers a wide range of financial tools and resources. One of their services is to provide you with personalized debt management plans, it'll give you a recommended strategy for paying off your debt, as well as a personalized budget plan.

In addition to online debt management services, there are a number of tips that Black entrepreneurs can follow to manage their debt:

1. Understand your debt: It's important to know exactly how much you owe, and to whom you owe it. This includes not just the total amount of debt, but also the interest rates, fees, and payment terms.
2. Prioritize your payments: If you have multiple debts, it can be helpful to prioritize which ones to pay off first. Consider paying off high-interest debts first, such as credit card debt, as these can quickly add up if left unpaid.
3. Create a budget: A budget can help you keep track of your expenses and ensure that you are putting enough money toward paying off your debt.
4. Get help if you need it: If your debt is becoming overwhelming, consider seeking the advice of a financial advisor or credit counselor. These professionals can help you develop a debt management plan and provide guidance on budgeting and saving. My office has contacts that can help you out with this.

Managing debt can be challenging, but with the right strategies in place, Black entrepreneurs can take control of their finances and achieve financial stability. By using online debt management services and following these tips, you can make progress in paying off your debt and securing a bright financial future for your business.

Chapter Twelve:
Legal Considerations For Black Entrepreneurs

Welcome to the chapter on legal considerations for Black entrepreneurs. This chapter will cover important topics such as choosing the right business structure, protecting your intellectual property, and managing legal disputes. As a black entrepreneur, it is essential to have a solid understanding of the legal considerations involved in starting and running a business. By understanding and proactively addressing these legal issues, you can set your business up for success and protect yourself from potential liabilities. In this chapter, we will explore the various legal options available to Black entrepreneurs and provide practical advice on how to navigate the legal landscape of owning a business.

CHOOSING THE RIGHT BUSINESS STRUCTURE

Choosing the right business structure is an important decision that all entrepreneurs, including Black entrepreneurs, must make when starting a business. The business structure you choose will affect the way you operate your business, your personal liability, and your tax obligations.

There are several different business structures to choose from, including sole proprietorship, partnership, limited liability company (LLC), corporation, and cooperative.

Sole proprietorship is the simplest and most common business structure. As a sole proprietor, you are the sole owner of the business and are personally liable for its debts and obligations. This structure is often chosen by entrepreneurs who are just starting out and have a small business with minimal risk.

Partnerships, on the other hand, involve two or more individuals who share ownership and control of the business. Each partner is personally liable for the debts and obligations of the partnership. This structure may be appropriate for Black entrepreneurs who are looking to start a business with one or more partners, but should be aware of the added complexity that comes with having multiple owners.

Limited Liability Company (LLC) is a hybrid business structure that combines the personal liability protection of a corporation with the tax benefits of a partnership or sole proprietorship. This is a popular choice among entrepreneurs because it offers personal liability protection while also allowing for pass-through taxation, meaning that the business itself is not taxed.

Corporations are separate legal entities that are owned by shareholders and managed by a board of directors. They offer personal liability protection to their shareholders, but also have more complex management and reporting requirements.

Cooperatives are a business structure that is owned and controlled by its members. This structure is suitable for Black entrepreneurs looking to start a business that is focused on meeting the needs of its members.

It's also important to note that there are statistics and reports that highlight the challenges Black entrepreneurs face when starting a business and the unique ways they could benefit from different business structures. Remember that one report by the National Black Chamber of Commerce which found that black-owned businesses have a higher rate of failure than businesses owned by other groups? Well, that is partly due to lack of access to capital and other resources. LLCs and Corporations have more access to capital via equity and debt financing, which could be beneficial for Black entrepreneurs.

Consider this to be free legal advice: each situation is a little different from the next, but, choosing the right business structure for your business is a crucial decision that should be made with careful consideration of your business goals, financial situation, and personal liability. It is important to consult with an attorney or financial advisor to understand the legal and financial implications of each business structure and to choose the one that best fits your needs. My office is located in Downtown Dallas, Texas and we would love to help your business.

PROTECTING YOUR INTELLECTUAL PROPERTY

Protecting your intellectual property (IP) is an important step in the success of any business, especially for Black entrepreneurs who may face additional barriers and challenges in the business world. Intellectual property refers to creations of the mind, such as inventions, literary and artistic works, symbols, names, images, and designs used in commerce.

There are several types of IP that Black entrepreneurs may need to consider protecting, including:

- Patents, which protect new and useful inventions
- Trademarks, which protect brand names, logos, and other distinctive marks
- Copyrights, which protect original literary, musical, and artistic works
- Trade secrets, which protect confidential business information

For example, a black-owned fashion designer who creates unique clothing designs may want to obtain a design patent to protect their creations from being copied. A black-owned restaurant that has created a unique recipe may want to protect it as a trade secret. Additionally, a black-owned technology company with a unique software application may want to obtain a patent for the invention and a trademark for the company name and logo.

Statistics from the US Patent and Trademark office (USPTO) shows that the number of patent applications by black inventors has increased over the years, but it is still underrepresented, Black inventors represented only 2.6% of all patent applications filed with USPTO in 2020. However, it is still important to note that the process of protecting IP rights can be complex, time-consuming, and costly, and the lack of resources, knowledge, and access to capital may be an obstacle for many Black entrepreneurs.

There are several steps that Black entrepreneurs can take to protect their IP, including:

- Conducting a search to ensure that your IP is unique and not already protected by someone else
- Documenting the creation and development of your IP
- Registering your IP with the appropriate government agency
- Establishing an IP management plan and strategy to enforce your rights and prevent infringement
- Considering licensing or franchising agreements as a way to monetize your IP

It is important to consult with an attorney or other IP professional to understand the legal and financial implications of protecting your IP and to develop a plan that is tailored to your business needs.

Read this section a few times if needed. Protecting your intellectual property is a crucial step for any business, and for Black entrepreneurs who may face additional barriers and challenges. By taking the necessary steps to protect their IP, Black entrepreneurs can secure their creations, prevent infringement and monetize their ideas, which will ultimately contribute to the success and growth of their businesses.

COMPLYING WITH REGULATIONS

Complying with legal regulations is a critical aspect of starting and running a business, and this applies to Black entrepreneurs as well. Legal regulations can come in many forms, including those related to taxes, employment, and industry-specific laws.

One important area of legal compliance for Black entrepreneurs is tax regulations. Black entrepreneurs, like all other business owners, must comply with federal, state, and local tax laws. This includes registering for and obtaining the necessary licenses and permits, as well as filing and paying taxes on time. Failure to comply with tax regulations can result in penalties, fines, and even criminal prosecution.

Another important area of legal compliance is employment regulations. This includes complying with laws related to minimum wage, overtime pay, and anti-discrimination and harassment laws. For example, Black entrepreneurs must comply with federal and state laws related to equal employment opportunities and non-discrimination, and must avoid discrimination against employees on the basis of race, ethnicity, gender, age, and other protected characteristics.

In addition, Black entrepreneurs may also need to comply with industry-specific regulations and laws. For example, if an entrepreneur is operating a business in the healthcare industry, they must comply with laws and regulations related to patient privacy and healthcare standards. A black entrepreneur operating in the food industry must comply with regulations related to food safety and sanitation.

It's important to note that studies have shown that black-owned businesses are disproportionately affected by the burden of compliance and regulatory costs. A report by the National Black Chamber of Commerce found that compliance costs disproportionately affect small businesses, and black-owned firms are disproportionately represented among small firms. According to the same report, between 2001 and 2018, the number of black-owned businesses increased by 43.9%, compared to 51.1% for all firms. As a result, Black entrepreneurs may find it harder to comply with legal regulations and as a result, could face a greater risk of penalties and fines.

To comply with legal regulations, Black entrepreneurs should take the following steps:

- Seek the advice of an attorney or other legal professional
- Research and understand the laws and regulations that apply to their business
- Develop and implement policies and procedures to ensure compliance
- Monitor and review compliance on an ongoing basis
- Stay informed and adapt to changing regulations

Summarily, complying with legal regulations is a critical aspect of starting and running a business for Black entrepreneurs, as well as any other entrepreneur. While it may be a challenging task, Black entrepreneurs must understand and comply with the laws and regulations that apply to their business to minimize the risk of penalties, fines, and other legal issues. By proactively addressing legal compliance, Black entrepreneurs can set their business up for success and protect themselves from potential liabilities.

DRAFTING LEGAL DOCUMENTS

Drafting legal documents can be a fundamental aspect of conducting business in certain businesses, and those owned by Black entrepreneurs are no exception. These documents, such as contracts, non-disclosure agreements (NDAs), and terms of service, can play a critical role in protecting the interests of both the business and its clients or partners.

One example of a legal document that Black entrepreneurs may need to draft is a contract. Contracts are legally binding agreements between two or more parties, outlining the terms and conditions of a business relationship. Black entrepreneurs may need to draft contracts for various reasons, such as hiring employees, leasing office space, or partnering with another business. These contracts must be clear, specific, and enforceable in order to protect the interests of all parties involved. I frequently draft contracts for my entertainment business clients, and would be happy to help you out if you need legal assistance.

Another example of a legal document that Black entrepreneurs may need to draft is an NDA. NDAs are agreements that prohibit one party from disclosing confidential information to a third party without permission. Black entrepreneurs may need to draft NDAs in order to protect their confidential business information or to maintain the confidentiality of their clients or partners.

Additionally, Black entrepreneurs may need to draft terms of service agreements when they are launching digital products, such as an app or a website. These agreements outline the rules, responsibilities, and limitations of using their services and products. This can be important to protect the rights and interests of the Black entrepreneurs, and also to make sure users are aware of any conditions before using the service.

However, it's important to note that despite the importance of drafting legal documents, Black entrepreneurs may face significant barriers to obtaining legal services. According to a study, Black entrepreneurs face greater challenges than non-Black entrepreneurs in accessing legal services, and are more likely to rely on non-lawyers for legal assistance. In this sense, it's important to consider hiring a lawyer or legal professional to review or draft legal documents. Failing to properly draft and execute legal documents can result in legal disputes, liability and loss of money, which may be detrimental for the future of their business.

A cautionary tale that serves as an example of the importance of drafting legal documents is the case of "Jane", a black entrepreneur who had an idea for a new product and started working on it with a friend. She and her friend verbally agreed on how to split the profits and how to handle the product. But after spending a significant amount of money, time and effort in the development of the product, her friend decided to take the product and start selling it on their own, leaving Jane with nothing. If they had taken the time to draft a legally binding contract outlining their business relationship and the ownership of the product, this unfortunate outcome could have been avoided.

Drafting legal documents is a crucial task that Black entrepreneurs need to perform in order to conduct business and protect their interests. These documents can include contracts, non-disclosure agreements, and terms of service agreements. The challenges Black entrepreneurs face in obtaining legal services and the potential consequences of failing to properly draft legal documents make it even more important to seek professional legal help. By taking the necessary steps to draft and execute legally binding documents, Black entrepreneurs can minimize the risk of legal disputes, protect their interests and assets, and set their business up for success.

SEEKING PROFESSIONAL ADVICE

Seeking professional advice is an important step for any entrepreneur, and again, for Black entrepreneurs, it is no different. Black entrepreneurs may face additional barriers and challenges in the business world and seeking the advice of a lawyer or legal professional can help them navigate the legal considerations of running a business.

A lawyer or legal professional can provide guidance and advice on the variety of legal matters mentioned previously, including:

- Choosing the right business structure
- Protecting intellectual property
- Complying with legal regulations
- Drafting and executing legal documents
- Managing legal disputes
- Advising on tax and employment laws.

Additionally, a lawyer or legal professional can provide advice on ways to mitigate legal risks and potential liabilities. They can also help Black entrepreneurs understand the legal implications of their business decisions and provide strategies to minimize risk and protect assets.

It is important to note that according to some studies, Black entrepreneurs face significant barriers to obtaining legal services. For example, a study found that Black entrepreneurs are less likely than white entrepreneurs to have access to legal advice, which could be due to a variety of factors such as lack of knowledge, access to capital, and cultural barriers. However, it's important to recognize that seeking professional legal advice can play a crucial role in the success and longevity of a business. I can't stress how important it is that you reach out to a good business lawyer if you're just getting going in business.

A cautionary tale that serves as an example of the importance of seeking professional legal advice is the case of "John", a black entrepreneur who started a small retail business. He thought that he could handle all the legal matters on his own and did not seek professional legal advice. He ended up signing a lease for a store location that had hidden and unexpected fees and clauses that ended up costing him a lot of money and almost causing him to lose his business. If he had sought the advice of a lawyer before signing the lease, he would have been able to avoid those issues and potential losses.

Another example is a case where a young black entrepreneur with a vending machine business was denied a contract from a government institution because she was Black. SHe retained counsel and in a short time, she had a contract with the county with even better terms than she originally asked for. Hiring an attorney can go a long way when things go wrong in business.

In conclusion, seeking professional advice from a lawyer or legal professional can be a valuable asset for Black entrepreneurs. Lawyers and legal professionals can provide guidance and advice on legal matters and help entrepreneurs navigate the legal considerations of running a business. The potential barriers Black entrepreneurs face to obtaining legal services highlights the importance of seeking professional legal advice, which can be crucial to the success and longevity of their businesses. By taking the necessary steps to seek professional legal advice, Black entrepreneurs can protect their interests, minimize risk, and set their business up for success.

MANAGING LEGAL DISPUTES

Managing legal disputes is an inevitable aspect of running a business, and–say it with me–Black entrepreneurs are no exception. Legal disputes can arise from a variety of situations, such as contract disputes, intellectual property disputes, and discrimination claims. It's important for Black entrepreneurs to be prepared to handle these disputes in a timely and effective manner, and seek professional advice as needed.

One strategy that Black entrepreneurs can use to manage legal disputes is to have a policy in place before a dispute arises. This policy should include identifying potential sources of disputes, creating policies and procedures to prevent disputes, and identifying the right professionals to handle disputes. By having a contingency plan in place, entrepreneurs can be better prepared to handle disputes when they arise.

I will expand a little more on why you need to seek professional advice from a lawyer or legal professional. Lawyers can provide guidance and advice on the legal issues involved in a dispute, and can help Black entrepreneurs understand their rights and options. They can also represent Black entrepreneurs in court or mediation, and help them to negotiate a settlement. Oftentimes, hiring a lawyer at the outset of a dispute is the best policy, because lawyers can come in and objectively analyze an emotionally-charged or hostile situation and render rational legal advice.

It's important to note that according to some studies, Black entrepreneurs may face additional barriers and challenges in the context of legal disputes. For example, a study found that black-owned businesses are more likely than white-owned businesses to face discrimination claims, and that Black entrepreneurs may be more likely to face discrimination in the court system. It's important for Black entrepreneurs to be aware of these potential challenges and to seek professional legal advice early on in the process in order to protect their interests.

A cautionary tale that serves as an example of the importance of managing legal disputes and seeking professional advice is the case of "Rachel", a black entrepreneur who runs an e-commerce business. She received an email from a customer claiming that they had received a damaged product. She did not take the complaint seriously and did not reply to the email, thinking that it would not turn into a big issue. But soon after, the customer filed a lawsuit for compensation, which ended up being costly for Rachel's business and her reputation. If she had handled the complaint properly, sought professional legal advice and had a plan in place to handle customer complaints, she could have avoided the lawsuit, and the negative consequences that came with it.

In conclusion, managing legal disputes is an inevitable aspect of running a business for Black entrepreneurs, as for any other entrepreneur. Black entrepreneurs should be prepared to handle legal disputes that may arise, and seek professional advice as needed. By having a plan in place, seeking professional advice early on, and being aware of the potential challenges, Black entrepreneurs can better protect their interests and minimize the impact of legal disputes on their businesses.

Chapter Thirteen:
Building A Diverse And Inclusive Workplace

As Black entrepreneurs, creating a diverse and inclusive workplace can be a vital part of building a successful business. A diverse workforce not only brings different perspectives and ideas to the table, but it also helps to create an environment where everyone feels valued and respected. Inclusivity, on the other hand, means creating a culture in which all employees feel welcome and supported, regardless of their background. This chapter will delve into the various ways that Black entrepreneurs can create a more diverse and inclusive workplace, from recruiting and hiring practices to fostering a positive and welcoming company culture. The chapter will also discuss some of the benefits and challenges that come with building a more diverse and inclusive workplace, and how to deal with them. By understanding the importance of diversity and inclusivity, and taking steps to create a more inclusive environment, Black entrepreneurs can not only help their employees to thrive, but also increase the competitiveness, innovation and success of their businesses.

COMMITTING TO DIVERSITY AND INCLUSION

As Black entrepreneurs, committing to diversity and inclusion is a crucial step in building a successful business. A diverse and inclusive workplace can bring a variety of benefits, including improved innovation, better decision-making, and increased competitiveness. However, building a diverse and inclusive workplace requires a sustained effort and a clear commitment from leadership.

One of the first steps in committing to diversity and inclusion is to establish clear goals and objectives. This may include setting targets for the representation of underrepresented groups within the organization, implementing training and development programs to support diversity and inclusion, and regularly monitoring progress towards these goals. Additionally, Black entrepreneurs should be aware of and implement policies and procedures that help to promote diversity and inclusion in the workplace, including anti-discrimination and anti-harassment policies, and recruitment and retention initiatives.

It's also essential to communicate the company's commitment to diversity and inclusion to all employees, and ensure that this message is embedded in all aspects of the business, from recruitment to day-to-day operations. This can be done by:

- Clearly communicating the importance of diversity and inclusion through regular internal communications and training
- Encouraging open dialogue and feedback from employees on diversity and inclusion issues
- Leading by example and promoting a culture of inclusivity and mutual respect

- Making sure that the company's actions and decisions align with their commitment to diversity and inclusivity.

It's important to note that despite good intentions, committing to diversity and inclusion may not always be easy. Some of the common challenges Black entrepreneurs may encounter include resistance to change, lack of employee buy-in, and difficulties in measuring progress. However, by having clear goals and objectives, consistent messaging, and open dialogue and feedback, Black entrepreneurs can overcome these challenges and create a more inclusive workplace.

Additionally, Black entrepreneurs may face additional barriers to building a diverse and inclusive workplace, such as lack of access to resources and networks, and unconscious bias. It's important to acknowledge these challenges and actively work to address them.

In conclusion, committing to diversity and inclusion is a crucial step in building a successful business for Black entrepreneurs. By setting clear goals and objectives, implementing policies and procedures, communicating the commitment to the entire team, and actively addressing challenges, Black entrepreneurs can create a more inclusive workplace, which can ultimately lead to better innovation and competitiveness. By making a concerted effort to build a more diverse and inclusive workplace, Black entrepreneurs can help create a more equitable society and a business that is more reflective of the communities it serves.

DEVELOPING A DIVERSITY AND INCLUSION PLAN

As a Black entrepreneur, it is important to recognize the value of diversity and inclusion within your business. A diverse and inclusive workforce not only promotes equity and fairness, but it also leads to increased creativity and innovation, improved decision-making, and ultimately, greater success for your business. However, diversity and inclusion do not happen naturally and must be actively promoted. One way to do this is by developing a diversity and inclusion plan.

A diversity and inclusion plan should include specific goals and strategies for promoting diversity and inclusion within your business. Some goals that you may want to include are:

- Increasing the representation of underrepresented groups, such as people from different cultures and women, within your workforce.
- Creating a culture of equity, inclusion, and belonging within your company.
- Ensuring that all employees have equal opportunities for career development and advancement.

To achieve these goals, you will need to implement specific strategies. Some strategies that you may want to include in your plan are:

- Recruiting and hiring diverse candidates through a variety of channels, such as diversity job fairs, employee referrals, and online job boards.

- Offering training and development opportunities that promote an understanding of diversity and inclusion, and provide employees with the skills they need to work effectively in a diverse environment.
- Establishing mentoring programs that connect employees from underrepresented groups with experienced mentors who can help guide their career development.
- Implementing policies and practices that promote equal opportunities for all employees, such as equal pay for equal work, flexible work arrangements, and family-friendly policies.
- Regularly monitoring and assessing the progress of the diversity and inclusion plan, and making adjustments as necessary.

Finally, it is important to remember that promoting diversity and inclusion is an ongoing process, and you should regularly review and update your plan as your business evolves. A comprehensive and well-implemented diversity and inclusion plan can make a positive impact on your business and its success in the long run.

Please note that this is a general approach and you should consult legal, HR and any other professional as per need.

RECRUITING A DIVERSE TEAM

Recruiting a diverse team is an essential aspect of creating a successful business. Having a team that represents a range of backgrounds and perspectives can lead to increased creativity, innovation, and problem-solving abilities, as well as a better understanding of and ability to serve a diverse customer base.

For Black entrepreneurs, it can be particularly challenging to recruit a diverse team, as the tech and startup industries in particular have been historically lacking in diversity. However, there are a number of practical methods that can be used to increase the diversity of your team.

1. Be proactive in your recruiting efforts. This can involve reaching out to individuals and organizations that support and promote diversity in the workplace, such as historically black colleges and universities, women in tech groups, and organizations for people of color in tech. You can also attend diversity-focused career fairs and networking events.
2. Use inclusive language in job postings and during the interview process. This can involve avoiding language that may exclude certain groups of people and instead focusing on the skills and qualifications that are truly necessary for the job.
3. Leverage your networks to reach diverse candidates. This can involve asking friends, colleagues, and business contacts if they know of any qualified candidates from underrepresented groups, and also utilize referral bonuses to incentivize employees to refer diverse candidates.
4. Be transparent in the hiring process. Be open and honest about the steps involved in the hiring process, the qualifications required for the position, and the company's commitment to diversity and inclusion. This can help build trust with potential candidates from underrepresented groups.

5. Use blind hiring techniques. This can involve not including personal information such as name, age, or education in resumes or applications to avoid bias. And also consider using standardized tests or skill assessments to evaluate candidates.
6. Start an Employee Resource Group. Employee Resource Groups (ERGs) can support a diverse workplace culture and create a sense of belonging for employees of different backgrounds. This can include groups for Black or African American employees or people of color in general.
7. Once you successfully recruit diverse candidates, make sure they feel comfortable and included in the workplace, this includes providing cultural sensitivity training and actively seeking out their perspectives, ideas and feedback.
8. Finally, regularly review the progress you are making and make changes as necessary. Hold managers accountable for diversity numbers and progress in the workplace, and track and publish diversity data.

By implementing these practical methods, Black entrepreneurs can increase the diversity of their teams, creating a more inclusive and innovative workplace for everyone.

PROVIDING INCLUSIVE LEADERSHIP

Providing inclusive leadership is a critical aspect of creating a successful and sustainable business. Inclusive leaders understand and value the unique perspectives and contributions that each team member brings to the table, and actively work to create an environment where all team members feel valued, respected, and supported, regardless of their background.

For Black entrepreneurs, creating an inclusive culture is particularly important, as the tech and startup industries in particular have been historically lacking in diversity. However, there are a number of steps that Black entrepreneurs can take to provide inclusive leadership and create a more inclusive culture within their organizations.

1. *Start by examining your own biases*. Everyone has unconscious biases, and it's important to be aware of them and take steps to mitigate them. This can involve taking an implicit bias test, seeking out feedback from team members, and seeking training and education on diversity and inclusion.
2. *Actively seek out diverse perspectives*. Inclusive leaders actively seek out and value the unique perspectives that each team member brings to the table. This can involve creating opportunities for team members from underrepresented groups to share their ideas and experiences, and actively seeking out feedback and input from all team members.
3. *Lead by example*. As a leader, your actions and words have a big impact on the culture of your organization. Make sure that you are modeling the behaviors and attitudes that you want to see in others.
4. *Encourage open and honest communication*. Creating an inclusive culture requires open and honest communication. Encourage team members to share

their thoughts and feelings, and create an environment where people feel comfortable discussing their differences and similarities.
5. *Create an action plan and hold yourself accountable*. Having a plan is great, but it is important to monitor the progress and make adjustments as necessary. Set goals and targets, and hold yourself and your leadership team accountable for achieving them.
6. *Promote diversity and inclusion throughout the company*. Inclusive leaders should work to promote diversity and inclusion throughout the entire company, not just within their own teams. This can involve creating a diverse and inclusive hiring process, developing diversity and inclusion training programs, and implementing policies that support a diverse and inclusive workplace.
7. Implement policies and programs that support the well-being and development of all employees. Ensure that all employees have access to the same resources, development opportunities, and benefits, regardless of their background. Remember, don't hold anyone back in any way.
8. *Regularly review progress and make changes as needed*. This includes tracking and publishing diversity data and holding managers accountable for progress in creating a more inclusive culture.

By providing inclusive leadership, Black entrepreneurs can create a more inclusive culture that values and supports all team members, regardless of their background. This can lead to increased creativity, innovation, and problem-solving abilities, as well as a better understanding of and ability to serve a diverse customer base.

PROMOTING DIVERSITY AND INCLUSION

Providing diversity and inclusion training is an important step that Black entrepreneurs can take to promote a more inclusive workplace. A comprehensive and well-executed training program can help employees understand the importance of diversity and inclusion, identify and address their own biases, and develop the skills and knowledge needed to create a more inclusive environment. Don't assume that because you're a black entrepreneur that you can't be guilty of unfair bias and prejudice.

There are a number of resources that Black entrepreneurs can use to provide diversity and inclusion training to their teams. Some of these include:

1. *Online training courses and tutorials*. A number of organizations and universities offer online training courses on diversity and inclusion. Some examples include:
    a. Micro-affirmations: The Power of Small Recognitions by the Harvard Business Review.
    b. Unconscious Bias Training by Google's ATD team
    c. The Intersectionality Training Curriculum from the Center for Talent Innovation
    d. Developing Cultural Intelligence from the University of California, Berkeley

2. *In-person training sessions and workshops*. Many organizations and consulting firms offer in-person training sessions and workshops on diversity and inclusion.
    a. The Kaleidoscope Group, which specializes in providing diversity and inclusion training and consulting services to organizations
    b. The Diversity, Equity, and Inclusion Group of Catalyst
    c. The Conscious Inclusion Institute
3. *Books, articles, and other written materials*. There are a wide variety of books, articles, and other written materials available on the topic of diversity and inclusion. Some examples include:
    a. The Diversity Bonus: How Great Teams Pay Off in the Knowledge Economy by Scott E. Page
    b. Whistling Vivaldi: How Stereotypes Affect Us and What We Can Do by Claude M. Steele
    c. Inclusion: Diversity, The New Workplace & The Will To Change by Jennifer Brown
    d. The Inclusion Dividend: Why Investing in Diversity & Inclusion Pays Off by Mark Kaplan and Mason Donovan

In addition to providing training resources, Black entrepreneurs should also work to create a culture of continuous learning and development. This can involve providing ongoing opportunities for employees to learn and grow, and encouraging them to take advantage of training and development opportunities both within and outside the company.

It's important to note that providing diversity and inclusion training is just one step in creating a more inclusive workplace. Black entrepreneurs should also work to create an inclusive culture, set clear diversity goals, hold managers accountable for progress, and be transparent about progress. Also, it's a continuous journey, and adjustments and improvements should be made when necessary.

Besides making the workplace more interesting, by providing diversity and inclusion training to their teams, Black entrepreneurs can help their employees develop the knowledge and skills needed to create a more inclusive environment, foster greater understanding and respect among team members, and ultimately lead to increased creativity, innovation, and problem-solving abilities.

96

Chapter Fourteen:
Managing Work-Life Balance

Work-life balance is a crucial aspect of maintaining a healthy and productive life as an entrepreneur. For Black entrepreneurs, it can be particularly challenging to achieve a balance between work and personal life. This can be due to a number of factors, including systemic racism, bias, and discrimination in the workplace, as well as the additional challenges and responsibilities that come with being a business owner. The pressure to "prove" oneself and to be seen as successful can make it difficult for Black entrepreneurs to set boundaries, leading to burnout and poor work-life balance.

In this chapter, we will explore the challenges and benefits of maintaining a healthy work-life balance as a black entrepreneur. We will discuss practical strategies and tactics that can be used to create a balance between work and personal life. We will also look at how to set realistic boundaries, how to manage stress and prioritize self-care, and how to create a supportive work environment that encourages balance. Additionally, this chapter will cover the role that personal development plays in achieving work-life balance, and how to develop the right mindset and habits to stay productive and fulfilled.

Throughout this chapter, we will explore the unique challenges and perspectives of Black entrepreneurs, and how they can best navigate the complex demands of running a business while also maintaining a healthy and fulfilling personal life. Whether you're just starting out as an entrepreneur or you've been running your own business for years, this chapter will provide valuable insights and strategies for managing work-life balance.

SETTING BOUNDARIES

"Boundaries are a form of respect: they show that you care enough about yourself to stand up for yourself." - Dr. Henry Cloud

As Black entrepreneurs, it can be challenging to set clear boundaries between work and personal time. This can be due to a number of factors, including systemic racism and bias, the pressure to "prove" oneself, and the demands of running a business. However, setting clear boundaries is essential for maintaining a healthy work-life balance and avoiding burnout.

According to a study by the National Business League, 72% of black business owners reported experiencing high levels of stress, as compared to 59% of white business owners. Additionally, a report by the American Psychological Association found that black people are disproportionately affected by stress due to experiences of discrimination, racism, and violence.

Setting boundaries involves clearly communicating our needs and limits to others, and being assertive in upholding them. This can include setting specific times for when work-related activities should be completed, setting limits on availability outside of work hours, and saying "no" to unreasonable demands or expectations.

"Your boundaries are your sacred space, and it is essential that you respect them." - Brené Brown

Boundaries are also important for our personal well-being, as they allow us to make time for activities that bring us joy and fulfillment. This can include engaging in hobbies, spending time with loved ones, and taking care of ourselves physically and emotionally. By setting boundaries and making time for these activities, we can recharge and return to work with renewed energy and focus.

It's important to note that setting boundaries is a continuous process and requires ongoing communication, assertiveness, and self-awareness. This can involve saying "no" when necessary, renegotiating boundaries when they are crossed, and regularly reviewing and adjusting them as needed.

Finally, setting clear boundaries between work and personal time is essential for Black entrepreneurs to maintain a healthy work-life balance. It's important to communicate our needs and limits to others and be assertive in upholding them. By setting boundaries, we can create a sense of balance, respect for ourselves and others, and ensure that we have the energy and focus to sustain ourselves and our businesses in the face of the unique challenges we face.

PRIORITIZING SELF-CARE

"Self-care is not self-indulgence, it is self-preservation" - Audre Lorde

Self-care is defined as "the practice of taking an active role in protecting one's own well-being and happiness, in particular during periods of stress" by the World Health Organization. Self-care practices can include physical activities such as exercise and yoga, relaxation techniques like meditation and deep breathing, and spending time with loved ones and engaging in activities that bring joy and fulfillment.

It's important to note that self-care is not a luxury, but a necessity. Prioritizing self-care means making time for activities that promote physical and mental well-being, and can also mean setting boundaries and saying no to unrealistic expectations, requests, or demands.

Additionally, Black entrepreneurs should also take the time to educate themselves about their mental health and any potential barriers to accessing help, such as financial constraints, stigma or mistrust in the healthcare system and work to overcome them.

"The ultimate form of self-care is self-love" - Iyanla Vanzant

Self-care is not a one-time thing, it should be an ongoing practice. Black entrepreneurs should make a conscious effort to make self-care an integral part of their daily routine. To that end, it's important to establish a consistent self-care routine, this can involve setting aside time each day or week for self-care activities and making it a non-negotiable commitment.

As Black entrepreneurs, it is vital that we prioritize self-care and make time for activities that nourish our physical and mental well-being. I like to "get away" to do my self-care. I'll take a spontaneous road trip, or a flight to a random destination for a day or two. Sometimes, I just have to get a change of pace and scenery in order to maintain my mental health. By making self-care a priority, we can ensure that we have the energy and resilience we need to sustain ourselves and our businesses in the face of the unique challenges we face.

SEEKING EMOTIONAL SUPPORT

As Black entrepreneurs, we often face unique challenges and experiences of discrimination, racism, and bias in the workplace. These experiences can take a toll on our emotional well-being and lead to feelings of isolation, stress, and burnout. In such times, it's important for us to seek emotional support from our network of friends, family, and close colleagues.

Having a strong support system can help us navigate the emotional and mental toll of running a business. Studies have shown that black business owners who had a network of supportive friends, family, and colleagues reported higher levels of job satisfaction and were more likely to be successful.

One way to seek emotional support is by talking to someone in your network who you trust and feel safe to share your feelings and thoughts with. They could be family members, friends, or close colleagues who understand your experiences and can provide you with a listening ear, a different perspective and constructive feedback.

Additionally, seeking professional help can also be a valuable source of emotional support. This can include counseling, therapy, or coaching, which can provide a safe space to process our emotions and develop coping strategies. It's also important to be aware of any potential barriers to accessing help such as financial constraints, stigma or mistrust in the healthcare system and work to overcome them.

Another way to seek emotional support is by joining support groups for Black entrepreneurs. This can provide an opportunity to connect with others who understand the unique challenges and experiences you face and offer emotional support, advice, and encouragement.

"No one can do it alone. It's a collective effort." - Dwayne Johnson

It's important to note that seeking emotional support should be an ongoing process, and not just a one-time thing. Black entrepreneurs should make a conscious effort to reach out for support when they need it, and actively work to build and maintain a strong support system.

Seeking emotional support is crucial for Black entrepreneurs to navigate the challenges and emotional toll of running a business. Whether it's through talking to a friend, seeking professional help, joining support groups or other means, building a network of supportive people is important to maintain mental and emotional well-being, foster resilience and ensure success.

MANAGING STRESS

Entrepreneurship can be a rewarding and fulfilling journey, but it can also be stressful. Stress can take a toll on an entrepreneur's mental and physical health, and can even affect their business. Being an entrepreneur can be stressful, and being black only compounds that stress.

One effective strategy for managing stress is practicing relaxation techniques. Relaxation techniques, such as deep breathing, meditation, and yoga, have been shown to reduce stress and improve mental health. In fact, a study found that a mindfulness-based stress reduction program led to a significant reduction in symptoms of depression, anxiety, and stress in adults.

Another effective way to manage stress is by participating in hobbies and activities that bring joy and relaxation. Hobbies such as fishing or hiking can provide a much-needed break from the demands of entrepreneurship and can help entrepreneurs recharge and refocus. A study published in the Journal of Leisure Research found that participants who engaged in outdoor recreation, such as hiking and fishing, reported lower levels of stress and greater levels of well-being. My friend taught me about a relaxation technique known as grounding, which is walking around barefoot on grass or organic soil. If you focus hard enough, this can be a very relaxing practice.

Finally, regular exercise is also a critical aspect of managing stress and maintaining mental health. Exercise can help reduce anxiety and depression and improve overall mental well-being. Moreover, an article published in Biological Psychology highlighted findings that regular exercise is as effective as medication in treating mild to moderate depression[15].

Clearly, managing stress is crucial for the overall well-being of Black entrepreneurs. Strategies such as practicing relaxation techniques, participating in hobbies, and regular exercise can help Black entrepreneurs manage stress and maintain their mental health. It's important to remember to give yourself the time and resources to de-stress, relax, and maintain a healthy mind. My advice is to get out into nature and clear your mind to make room for clear vision.

SEEKING PROFESSIONAL HELP

Entrepreneurship can be a challenging and demanding journey, and it is not uncommon for entrepreneurs to experience stress, anxiety, and depression. For Black entrepreneurs, the added stressors of discrimination and bias can make it even more important for them to seek professional help if they are struggling with their mental health. Unfortunately, many Black entrepreneurs may feel hesitant to seek therapy or counseling, but it is essential to understand that seeking professional help is not a sign of weakness. It is a proactive step towards taking care of oneself, both personally and professionally.

Therapy and counseling can be incredibly beneficial for entrepreneurs who are struggling with their mental health. Unfortunately, black people are less likely to seek medical care when it comes to issues involving mental health than other peoples.[16] Talking with a

---

[15] Paolucci, Emily M., Dessi Loukov, Dawn ME Bowdish, and Jennifer J. Heisz. "Exercise reduces depression and inflammation but intensity matters." Biological psychology 133 (2018): 79-84.

[16] Turner, Natalie, Julia F. Hastings, and Harold W. Neighbors. "Mental health care treatment seeking among African Americans and Caribbean Blacks: what is the role of religiosity/spirituality?." Aging & mental health 23, no. 7 (2019): 905-911.

therapist or counselor can help entrepreneurs understand and manage their feelings, set realistic goals, and develop coping mechanisms for stress. Additionally, therapy and counseling can also help entrepreneurs identify and address any underlying issues that may be contributing to their mental health struggles.

There are many resources available to Black entrepreneurs who are seeking professional help. One of them is the National Alliance on Mental Illness (NAMI) which offers a variety of resources, including support groups, education programs, and referral services. There is also the Black Emotional and Mental Health Collective (BEAM) which aims to center and advocate for the mental health and emotional well-being of Black communities. They also offer mental health resources, therapy and counseling services, and professional development training for clinicians and advocates. The American Psychological Association (APA) also offers a database of psychologists and mental health providers that includes providers who specialize in working with Black and African American clients.

It's also worth noting that some insurance plans may cover the cost of therapy or counseling, and there are also sliding scale fee options that might be available from certain providers or community clinics. For Black entrepreneurs who are struggling to afford therapy, organizations like Therapy for Black Girls or The Loveland Foundation also provide financial assistance for therapy and counseling.

Bottom line is, seeking professional help should not be stigmatized, and seeking therapy or counseling can be an essential step for Black entrepreneurs who are struggling with their mental health. Black entrepreneurs should know that there are many resources available to them that can help them take care of their mental well-being and continue to thrive both personally and professionally.

FREE YOUR MIND

Entrepreneurship is a challenging and demanding journey, and it is not uncommon for entrepreneurs to experience stress, anxiety, and depression. These feelings can be compounded by the added stressors of discrimination and bias faced by Black entrepreneurs. One way to improve mental health and cope with the demands of entrepreneurship is by striving to become a free-thinker.

Being a free-thinker means being able to think for yourself, question assumptions and societal norms, and make decisions based on your own beliefs and values. It also means being able to critically examine the information and influences that are present in one's life, and not getting caught up in societal pressures or biases. Social media and the American news media can be a huge distraction and source of self-doubt and negative energy. Stay away from social media if you can, and only use it to further your business goals if needs be.

As the African-American author and philosopher, James Baldwin, famously said, "Not everything that is faced can be changed, but nothing can be changed until it is faced." By being a free-thinker, Black entrepreneurs can face their mental health struggles and not let societal pressures or biases prevent them from seeking help and making positive changes.

If you look around and find yourself doing what mostly everyone else is doing as far as latest trends in fashion, political views, and so on, then odds are that you are not that much of a free-thinker. Free-thinkers usually stand out. Not always in a loud and boisterous way, but they always stand out for being different. Only dead fish go with the flow. We're not trying to go with the flow here, or you wouldn't be reading this book. You want to swim with the sharks or become a whale. You want big ideas to change the world? Free your mind from the world first.

Free-thinking can also help entrepreneurs to find their own unique path and approach to entrepreneurship. As the great Nelson Mandela once said, "I learned that courage was not the absence of fear, but the triumph over it. The brave man is not he who does not feel afraid, but he who conquers that fear." Through free-thinking, Black entrepreneurs can learn to recognize and address their fears, and channel them into their entrepreneurial pursuits.

Furthermore, free-thinking can also help Black entrepreneurs to develop a strong sense of self-awareness, which is essential for mental health. As the business leader and author, Dr. Travis Bradberry said, "The most successful people are those who have a strong sense of self-awareness. They understand their strengths and weaknesses, and they work on the latter." By developing a strong sense of self-awareness, Black entrepreneurs can understand their unique strengths and limitations, and use them to their advantage in their business pursuits.

Again, striving to become a free-thinker can be an essential step for Black entrepreneurs who are struggling with their mental health. By being able to think for themselves, question assumptions and societal norms, and make decisions based on their own beliefs and values, Black entrepreneurs can improve their mental health and achieve success in their entrepreneurial pursuits.

Chapter Fifteen:
Leveraging Your Personal Brand

In today's competitive business environment, it is essential for entrepreneurs to establish a strong personal brand. A personal brand is the reputation that precedes you and is the perception of you in the mind of others. It is how you are seen, known and remembered by your target audience. For Black entrepreneurs, the ability to leverage their personal brand can be especially important, as they may face additional obstacles in the business world due to discrimination and bias.

In this chapter, we will explore the importance of personal branding for Black entrepreneurs and how it can be leveraged to achieve success. We will discuss the elements that make up a personal brand and how to create a brand that truly represents you and your business. We will also look at how personal branding can be used to build credibility and establish trust with potential clients and investors.

In addition to these concepts, we will discuss some of the ways to promote and maintain a personal brand, such as the use of social media and networking events. Furthermore, we will also explore the importance of being authentic and true to yourself when building your personal brand.

As Black entrepreneurs, it's vital to have a clear understanding of your personal brand, as it will be a key asset to gaining traction and attracting customers, as well as investors. By the end of this chapter, you will have a better understanding of how to create, promote, and leverage your personal brand to achieve success as a Black entrepreneur.

DEFINING YOUR PERSONAL BRAND

In today's business landscape, establishing a strong personal brand is essential for success as an entrepreneur. A personal brand is the perception of you in the minds of others and it's what sets you apart from the competition. For Black entrepreneurs, the ability to define and leverage their personal brand can be especially important, as they may face additional obstacles in the business world due to discrimination and bias.

One way for Black entrepreneurs to define their personal brand is by identifying their unique strengths, values, and purpose. Your unique strengths are the talents and abilities that make you stand out from the crowd. Your values are the principles and beliefs that guide your actions and decisions. Your purpose is the reason why you do what you do and the impact you want to make in the world.

By identifying and understanding these elements, Black entrepreneurs can create a brand that truly represents who they are and what they stand for. A relevant case study of this is Daymond John, the Founder and CEO of FUBU and Shark Tank investor, who defined his personal brand by highlighting his unique strengths, values, and purpose. Daymond leveraged his ability to recognize and capitalize on fashion trends, his belief in the power of hard work and perseverance, and his purpose of empowering and mentoring young entrepreneurs of color to create a brand that resonated with consumers and investors alike.

Once these elements are identified, Black entrepreneurs can communicate their personal brand effectively through their interactions, marketing materials, and online presence. Being consistent and authentic in these interactions and materials will help ensure that their personal brand stays true to their strengths, values, and purpose.

In conclusion, defining your personal brand as a Black entrepreneur is crucial for standing out in a competitive market, building credibility and trust with customers, and attracting investors. By identifying and understanding their unique strengths, values, and purpose, Black entrepreneurs can create a personal brand that truly represents who they are and what they stand for.

BUILDING YOUR ONLINE PRESENCE

In today's digital age, building a strong online presence is crucial for entrepreneurs looking to establish their personal brand and reach their target audience. For Black entrepreneurs, building a strong online presence can be especially important, as it can help counteract discrimination and bias they may face in the offline world.

One way for Black entrepreneurs to build a strong online presence is by being consistent and authentic in their online interactions and materials. This means using a consistent tone, aesthetic, and messaging across all online platforms, such as social media, websites, and blogs. It also means being true to their personal brand and values, rather than trying to be something they're not.

A relevant case study of this approach is Gary Vaynerchuk, the CEO of VaynerMedia and a well-known angel investor and internet personality. Gary has built a strong personal brand and online presence by being consistently authentic and transparent on social media and other online platforms. He uses these platforms to share his personal and professional journey, his insights and opinions, and his experiences with his audience. This authenticity and transparency helped Gary to build a strong and loyal following, which in turn helped him grow his personal brand and his business.

Another important aspect of building an online presence is utilizing SEO (Search Engine Optimization) techniques and paid advertising. Through SEO, entrepreneurs can improve the visibility of their website and social media platforms, making it more likely to reach their target audience through organic search results. Paid advertising such as Google Adwords and Facebook Ads can help to increase visibility and reach target audience more directly.

So, building a strong online presence is essential for Black entrepreneurs looking to establish their personal brand and reach their target audience. By being consistent and authentic in their online interactions and materials and utilizing SEO and paid advertising, Black entrepreneurs can showcase their personal brand, build a loyal following, and grow their business.

NETWORKING AND BUILDING RELATIONSHIPS

Networking and building relationships is a crucial aspect of any entrepreneur's journey, regardless of their background. For Black entrepreneurs, networking and building relationships can be especially important, as it can help them connect with like-minded individuals and expand their influence in the internet age.

Networking can take many forms, from attending industry events and joining professional organizations to participating in online communities and networking groups. In-person networking events can provide an opportunity to meet and connect with other entrepreneurs, industry experts, and potential customers or investors in a more traditional, face-to-face setting. Online networking, on the other hand, can be a valuable way to connect with individuals and organizations who share similar interests and goals and to expand one's reach.

One effective way to network and build relationships as a Black entrepreneur is by seeking out and joining communities specifically geared towards people of color. Organizations such as Black Women Talk Tech and Black Tech Unplugged are examples of networks that provide support and resources specifically for Black entrepreneurs and innovators in the tech industry.

Another important aspect of networking and building relationships is utilizing social media platforms to connect with like-minded individuals and influencers in your industry. By following and engaging with individuals who inspire you and align with your personal brand, you can expand your reach, establish yourself as a thought leader, and learn about new opportunities and resources.

Building relationships is not just about the quantity of contacts you make, but also the quality of those connections. As the famous quote from Malcolm Gladwell states "The people you surround yourself with - the relationships you build - are the most important part of your life." By building relationships with individuals who share similar interests and goals, Black entrepreneurs can gain access to valuable resources, advice, and support that can help them grow their business and personal brand.

Again, networking and building relationships is an essential aspect of any entrepreneur's journey. By seeking out and joining communities specifically geared towards people of color, utilizing social media platforms, and focusing on building quality relationships, Black entrepreneurs can connect with like-minded individuals, expand their influence, and gain access to valuable resources and support.

DEVELOPING YOUR PERSONAL BRAND MESSAGE

A personal brand message is the core messaging that communicates an entrepreneur's unique value proposition (UVP), what makes them stand out from the competition, and their target audience. I'll go into more detail about this throughout this book. It is essential for any entrepreneur to have a strong and consistent personal brand message, but, as I said earlier, it can be especially important for Black entrepreneurs as they may face additional obstacles in the business world.

One way for Black entrepreneurs to develop a consistent and compelling personal brand message is by identifying their unique value proposition. A unique value proposition is a statement that describes what makes an entrepreneur different and valuable to their target audience. It is the unique benefit that an entrepreneur provides to their customers or clients that sets them apart from the competition. By identifying their unique value proposition, Black entrepreneurs can create a message that truly reflects who they are and what they stand for.

A notable case study of this approach is Oprah Winfrey, an American media executive, television host, and philanthropist. Oprah's personal brand message is centered around the idea of truth, empowerment, inspiration, and positivity. Her unique value proposition is her ability to empower people through her media platform, her talk shows, and her philanthropy. By consistently communicating this message, Oprah has built a loyal following, and her personal brand is considered to be one of the most influential in the world.

Once the unique value proposition is identified, Black entrepreneurs can craft a message that reflects it, and then communicate it consistently across all of their interactions, marketing materials, and online presence. This consistency helps to build credibility and trust with customers and investors, and it also helps to make it easier for them to identify and remember the entrepreneur.

Therefore, developing a consistent and compelling personal brand message is essential for Black entrepreneurs looking to establish themselves in a competitive market and reach their target audience. By identifying their unique value proposition, Black entrepreneurs can craft a message that reflects who they are and what they stand for, and by consistently communicating that message, they can build credibility, trust, and loyalty with their customers and investors.

COLLABORATING WITH OTHERS

Collaboration is a key aspect of any entrepreneur's journey, and it is a powerful way for Black entrepreneurs to leverage their personal brand by working with other professionals or organizations that share their values and mission. Collaboration can take many forms, from forming partnerships and strategic alliances to participating in mentorship programs and joining industry organizations.

One way for Black entrepreneurs to leverage their personal brand through collaboration is by seeking out and forming partnerships and strategic alliances with other professionals or organizations that share their values and mission. This can help to expand their reach and influence, as well as providing access to new resources and networks.

A notable example of this approach is Stacey Abrams, an American lawyer, voting rights advocate, and politician. Abrams leveraged her personal brand by collaborating with the New Georgia Project, a non-profit organization she founded, which aimed to register, mobilize and empower people of color, low-income and young voters. Through this collaboration, she was able to reach her target audience and expand her influence on a larger scale, as well as increase voter turnout in the state of Georgia.

Another way Black entrepreneurs can leverage their personal brand through collaboration is by participating in mentorship programs. This can help entrepreneurs to gain new knowledge, skills and perspectives. Additionally, it can also provide the opportunity to connect and build relationships with established professionals and leaders in the industry, which can be invaluable for personal and professional development.

Clearly, collaborating with others is an essential aspect of any entrepreneur's journey. By seeking out and forming partnerships and strategic alliances, participating in mentorship programs, and joining industry organizations, Black entrepreneurs can leverage their personal brand by working with others who share their values and mission. Collaboration can provide access to new resources, networks, and opportunities that can help entrepreneurs to grow and achieve success.

Chapter Sixteen:
Using Social Media To Promote Your Business

Social media has become a powerful tool for businesses of all sizes to promote their products and services, and Black entrepreneurs are no exception. According to a 2020 survey by the National Black Chamber of Commerce, more than 75% of black-owned small businesses in the United States use social media to connect with customers and grow their businesses. Additionally, a 2019 report by the Pew Research Center found that a majority of black adults in the US use social media platforms, including Facebook, Instagram, and Twitter.

As the use of social media continues to grow, it's important for Black entrepreneurs to understand how to effectively use these platforms to reach their target audience and drive sales. In this chapter, we'll explore some of the current trends and best practices for using social media to promote your business as a black entrepreneur. We'll discuss the various platforms available and how to choose the ones that are most relevant for your business, as well as strategies for creating and curating content that resonates with your target audience.

IDENTIFY YOUR TARGET AUDIENCE

In today's digital age, social media has become a vital tool for businesses of all sizes to promote their products and services. However, with so many different platforms and options to choose from, it can be difficult for entrepreneurs to know where to focus their efforts. This is especially true for Black entrepreneurs, who may face additional barriers and challenges when it comes to reaching and engaging with their target audience.

In order to effectively use social media to promote their business, Black entrepreneurs must first understand who their target audience is and what their needs and preferences are. In this chapter, we will explore the importance of identifying your target audience and the various strategies and tools available for doing so. We will also discuss how Black entrepreneurs can use this information to create and curate content that resonates with their target audience, ultimately helping them to achieve their business goals.

One of the most critical steps in using social media to promote your business is understanding who your target audience is. This includes identifying their demographics, psychographics, and behavior patterns. By understanding these characteristics, you can tailor your social media efforts to more effectively reach and engage with them.

Additionally, identifying your target audience allows you to understand their pain points, needs and preferences, which is crucial in building an effective marketing strategy.

Once you understand the importance of identifying your target audience, the next step is to actually identify them. There are a variety of different strategies and tools that Black entrepreneurs can use to do this, including:

- Market research: Conducting research on your industry and competitors can provide valuable insights into your target audience.
- Surveys and focus groups: Surveying your current customers and conducting focus groups can provide valuable information about your target audience's needs and preferences.
- Analytics: Using analytics tools to track the performance of your social media accounts can provide valuable insights into who is engaging with your content.
- Audience segmentation: Creating segments of your audience based on demographics, behavior, and interest can make your targeting more effective.

Once you have a solid understanding of who your target audience is, the next step is to use this information to create and curate content that resonates with them. This includes:

- Creating content that addresses their pain points, needs and preferences
- Using language and imagery that appeals to them
- Selecting platforms and posting at times when they are most active
- Offering solutions and products that solve their problems

By effectively using social media to reach and engage with your target audience, Black entrepreneurs can build stronger relationships with their customers and ultimately drive more sales for their business.

Identifying your target audience is a crucial step in effectively using social media to promote your business. By understanding your target audience's demographics, psychographics, and behavior patterns, Black entrepreneurs can create and curate content that resonates with them and addresses their needs and preferences. This will help them to build stronger relationships with their customers and ultimately drive more sales for their business. As a result, the more you understand your target audience, the more successful your social media strategy will be.

CHOOSING THE RIGHT PLATFORM

As a black entrepreneur, social media can be a powerful tool for promoting your business and connecting with customers. However, with so many different platforms to choose from, it can be difficult to know which ones will be most effective for your business. In this chapter, we will explore the importance of choosing the right social media platforms and the various strategies and tools available for doing so. By understanding how to choose the platforms that are most relevant to your target audience and business goals, you can ensure that your social media efforts are as effective as possible.

One of the most critical steps in using social media to promote your business is choosing the platforms that are most relevant to your target audience and business goals. This includes understanding which platforms your target audience is most active on, as well as which platforms are most effective for promoting different types of products and services.

Additionally, choosing the right platforms is important for building an effective marketing strategy. Platforms like Facebook, Instagram, Twitter, and LinkedIn have different audience demographics, content type, and audience behavior, and thus choosing the right one can make all the difference.

Once you understand the importance of choosing the right social media platforms, the next step is to actually choose them. There are a variety of different strategies and tools that Black entrepreneurs can use to do this, including:

- Audience research: Understanding your target audience's demographics, psychographics, and behavior patterns can help you identify which platforms they are most active on.
- Platform research: Researching the different platforms and their audience demographics, features, and content policies can help you identify which platforms will be most effective for your business.
- Competitive research: Examining the social media efforts of your competitors can provide valuable insights into which platforms they are using and how they are using them.

Once you have chosen the social media platforms that are most relevant to your target audience and business goals, the next step is to effectively use them. This includes:

- Creating a content strategy that aligns with the platform's features and audience behavior.
- Consistently and regularly post content to keep your audience engaged.
- Utilize features like Facebook's Shop, Instagram's IGTV, Tiktok's Reel feature to gain the most benefits from the chosen platform
- Measuring the performance of your content and using analytics to track your progress

By effectively using the right social media platforms, Black entrepreneurs can connect with their target audience and promote their business more effectively.

Choosing the right social media platforms is crucial for Black entrepreneurs looking to effectively promote their business. By understanding your target audience's demographics, psychographics, and behavior patterns and researching the different platforms, you can identify which platforms will be most effective for your business. Additionally, by utilizing the platforms' features, creating a content strategy, and regularly posting content, Black entrepreneurs can connect with their target audience and promote their business more effectively. Ultimately, the key is to choose the platforms that align with your audience and business goals, as it will help you to reach your target audience and achieve your business objectives.

DEVELOPING A SOCIAL MEDIA STRATEGY

In today's digital age, social media has become a vital tool for businesses of all sizes to promote their products and services. However, creating a social media strategy that outlines your goals, target audience, and content plans can be challenging. It's particularly important for Black entrepreneurs to have a solid social media strategy in place, as they may face additional barriers and challenges when it comes to reaching and engaging with their target audience. In this chapter, we will explore the importance of developing a social media strategy and the various steps and considerations that Black entrepreneurs can take when creating one.

One of the most critical steps in using social media to promote your business is developing a strategy that outlines your goals, target audience, and content plans. This includes setting specific, measurable, and achievable goals, identifying your target audience, and creating a content plan that addresses their needs and preferences. Having a solid strategy in place allows you to focus your efforts and resources on the most important aspects of your social media efforts, ultimately helping you to achieve your business goals.

Once you understand the importance of developing a social media strategy, the next step is to actually create one. The steps for developing a social media strategy can include:

1. Identifying your business objectives: Define what you want to achieve with social media, it can be increased sales, brand awareness or engagement.
2. Identifying your target audience: Understand who you are trying to reach, their demographics, and behavior patterns.
3. Researching your competition: Analyze what your competition is doing on social media and learn from their strategies.
4. Choosing the right platforms: Identify the platforms your target audience is active on and choose the ones that align with your business objectives
5. Creating a content plan: Develop a content calendar that outlines the type of content you will be posting, when you will post it, and how often.
6. Measuring and analyzing: Use tools to track your social media efforts, analyze your performance and adjust your strategy accordingly.

Implementing a social media strategy can be challenging, but there are a few best practices that can help ensure that your efforts are successful. These include:

- Consistency: To be effective, you need to be consistent in your efforts and stick to your content plan.
- Creativity: Be creative and unique with your content, use visuals and storytelling to engage your target audience
- Engagement: Encourage and respond to engagement, this will help you understand your target audience's preferences and behavior.
- Adaptation: Be flexible and willing to adapt your strategy as needed to align with your goals and target audience.

Developing a social media strategy is a crucial step in effectively using social media to promote your business. By outlining your goals, identifying your target audience, and creating a content plan, Black entrepreneurs can focus their efforts and resources on the most important aspects of their social media efforts. Additionally, by implementing best practices like consistency, creativity, engagement, and adaptation, Black entrepreneurs can ensure that their social media strategy is effective and helps them achieve their business goals. It's important to remember that social media strategy is not a one time task, but rather a continuous effort, thus it should be regularly reviewed and adjusted accordingly.

CREATING ENGAGING CONTENT

One of the most important elements of a successful social media strategy is creating high-quality, engaging content that resonates with your target audience. For Black entrepreneurs, creating content that showcases their unique perspective, culture, and experiences can be especially powerful in connecting with their target audience and building a strong online presence.

There are a number of strategies and best practices that Black entrepreneurs can use to create engaging content that resonates with their target audience. These include:

- Showcasing your unique perspective: Black entrepreneurs can leverage their unique experiences, background and culture to create content that stands out and resonates with their target audience.
- Telling your brand's story: A powerful way to connect with your target audience is by sharing your business story, mission and values.
- Using visuals: Visual content, such as photographs and videos, can be a powerful way to showcase your business and connect with your target audience.
- Using interactive features: Use features like polls, quizzes, and live streaming to engage your target audience and create a sense of community around your business.
- Staying up to date: Stay up to date with current events, trends and cultural moments that may be relevant to your target audience, this can help you create timely and relevant content.
- Keep it authentic: Authenticity is key, avoid trying to be something you are not, show your audience the real you and they will be more likely to connect with you.

As the famous quote goes "Black people are the original trendsetters and the internet has been a powerful tool to amplify our voices and creativity." -Fiona Alan, Founder of Black Girl Fest.

This statement underlines the importance of Black voices and creativity on the internet. The unique perspectives and culture of Black entrepreneurs can be leveraged to create engaging and impactful content that resonates with their target audience. By understanding the importance of creating high-quality, engaging content, and utilizing the above strategies, Black entrepreneurs can create a powerful online presence that showcases their business and connects with their target audience.

BUILDING A COMMUNITY

In addition to creating high-quality, engaging content, another key element of a successful social media strategy is building a community of followers and engaging with them regularly. For Black entrepreneurs, this can be particularly important as building a sense of community and connection can be a powerful way to overcome the barriers and challenges that they may face when trying to reach and engage with their target audience.

There are a number of strategies and best practices that Black entrepreneurs can use to build a community of followers and engage with them regularly. These include:

- Engage with your followers: Regularly responding to comments, messages, and reviews, will show your audience that you are listening to them and that they are important to you.
- Encourage user-generated content: Encourage your followers to share their own content, this can help create a sense of community around your business.
- Host events and webinars: Host events or webinars where your followers can interact with each other and with you, this can help build a sense of community around your business.
- Encourage interaction and feedback: Encourage interaction and feedback from your followers, this can help create a sense of community around your business.
- Collaborate with other businesses and influencers: Collaborating with other businesses and influencers in your industry can help you reach a wider audience and build a sense of community around your business.
- Create a private community: Consider creating a private community (e.g. Facebook group, discord) where your audience can interact, share and learn from each other.

By building a community of followers and engaging with them regularly, Black entrepreneurs can create a sense of community and connection that can be powerful in connecting with their target audience and overcoming barriers and challenges they may face. The community can also act as a source of support and feedback that can lead to better understanding of the target audience and more effective marketing efforts.

Also, it is important to remember that building a community is not a one time task, it requires consistent and active efforts, so it should be included in your social media strategy and consistently executed.

ANALYZING AND IMPROVING PERFORMANCE

One of the key components of a successful social media strategy is being able to track your performance and identify areas for improvement. Black entrepreneurs can use social media analytics to understand how their efforts are impacting their target audience and business goals, and use this information to make data-driven decisions that help improve their social media strategy over time.

There are a number of tools and strategies that Black entrepreneurs can use to analyze and improve their performance on social media, including:

- Social media analytics: Most social media platforms have built-in analytics tools that allow you to track the performance of your accounts, such as reach, engagement, and click-through rates.
- Google Analytics: Google Analytics is a web analytics service that allows you to track the performance of your website and social media accounts. It can provide insights on how your social media efforts are impacting your website traffic, conversions and business goals.

- Setting up goals and tracking them: Setting specific, measurable, and achievable goals for your social media efforts and tracking your progress towards those goals can help you identify areas for improvement and make data-driven decisions.
- Identifying areas for improvement: Once you have a solid understanding of your performance, you can start to identify areas for improvement. This may include adjusting your content strategy, targeting different platforms or audience segments, or adjusting your posting schedule to optimize your reach and engagement.

By using social media analytics to track their performance and identify areas for improvement, Black entrepreneurs can make data-driven decisions that help improve their social media strategy over time. Google Analytics specifically can provide valuable insights on how your social media efforts are impacting your website traffic and conversions, which can help you measure the impact of your social media efforts on your business goals.

Remember, the key is to consistently track your performance, analyze it, and make the necessary changes to improve it. And this should be included in your social media strategy and executed regularly.

Chapter Seventeen:
Finding Mentors And Advisors

As a black entrepreneur, finding quality mentors and advisors can be a challenging task. Black entrepreneurs may face additional barriers and challenges when it comes to finding mentors and advisors who understand their unique experiences and can provide valuable guidance and support. However, building a network of quality mentors and advisors can be crucial for the success of any business. In this chapter, we will explore the importance of finding quality mentors and advisors and the various strategies and resources available for doing so. Organizations such as the 100 Black Men of America and similar organizations can be a great resource for Black entrepreneurs looking to connect with successful and experienced mentors and advisors. I became a member of the Collegiate 100 Black Men while in law school at Texas Southern University's Thurgood Marshall School of Law.

Having a mentor can help Black entrepreneurs with navigating the challenges they may face, gain valuable insight and advice and create a strong support system. This chapter will explore how to find and engage with quality mentors and advisors, how to communicate with them effectively and how to make the most of the mentorship relationship. With the right mentors and advisors, Black entrepreneurs can gain valuable insights, knowledge, and resources that can help them overcome the unique challenges they may face, and ultimately achieve their business goals.

IDENTIFY YOUR NEEDS

One of the most critical steps in finding quality mentors and advisors is identifying your business needs and the areas where you could benefit from mentorship or guidance. As a black entrepreneur, you may face unique challenges and barriers that require specific knowledge and experience to navigate. It's important to be honest with yourself about the areas where you need help, as well as to have a clear understanding of what you hope to achieve with the mentorship or guidance.

There are a number of strategies and tools that Black entrepreneurs can use to assess their business needs and identify areas where they could benefit from mentorship or guidance. These include:

- Self-reflection: Take a step back, and reflect on your business, strengths, weaknesses, and opportunities for growth.
- Seeking feedback: Ask for feedback from colleagues, friends, and family, and analyze the areas where they think you could improve.
- Praying and seeking wisdom: As the Bible says in James 1:5 "If any of you lacks wisdom, you should ask God, who gives generously to all without finding fault, and it will

be given to you." So, pray and ask for guidance from the almighty to lead you to the right mentors.
- Identifying knowledge gaps: Identify areas where you lack knowledge or experience and where you could benefit from mentorship or guidance.
- Reflecting on your goals: Reflect on your long-term and short-term business goals, and identify areas where you could benefit from mentorship or guidance in order to achieve them.

As the famous quote goes "Mentorship is a brain to pick, an ear to listen, and a push in the right direction." -John C. Crosby. This statement highlights the importance of having someone to guide and support you, as you journey through the ups and downs of entrepreneurship.

By assessing your business needs and identifying areas where you could benefit from mentorship or guidance, Black entrepreneurs can more effectively find and connect with quality mentors and advisors who can help them overcome the unique challenges they may face and achieve their business goals.

RESEARCH POTENTIAL MENTORS

As a Black entrepreneur, researching potential mentors and advisors can be a crucial step in the process of developing and growing your business. Mentors and advisors can provide valuable guidance, advice, and connections that can help you navigate the challenges of starting and scaling a business.

Once you identify your needs one of the next steps in finding potential mentors and advisors is to identify the specific areas of expertise or experience that you are looking for. For example, if you are a Black entrepreneur in the technology industry, you may want to find mentors and advisors who have experience in software development, product management, or fundraising. You can also look for mentors and advisors who have experience in specific industries such as healthcare, retail or education. In other words, don't just look for a business mentor. Instead, look for a business mentor that specializes in business-to-business sales if that's what you need.

Once you have a clear idea of the type of expertise or experience that you are looking for, you can begin your research. Here are some ways to research potential mentors and advisors:

- Online resources: There are many online resources available that can help you find potential mentors and advisors. Websites such as LinkedIn, and mentorship platforms like Startups and Founders, can help you identify potential mentors and advisors in your industry.
- Referrals: Ask other entrepreneurs, especially Black entrepreneurs, if they know of any mentors or advisors who might be a good fit for your business. You can also ask your network of friends, family, and colleagues if they know of any experts or advisers in your field of interest.

- Networking events: Attend networking events, such as startup meetups and conferences, to meet potential mentors and advisors in person. This allows you to build a personal connection and gauge their level of interest in mentoring or advising you.
- Research: Research the backgrounds of potential mentors and advisors by reviewing their websites, social media profiles, and publications.
- Asking for introductions: Once you have identified some potential mentors and advisors, you can reach out to them and ask for an introduction.

It's important to keep in mind that finding the right mentor or advisor can take time, so don't be discouraged if it takes a few tries to find someone who is the right fit for you and your business. Additionally, you can always rotate your mentors and advisors as your business evolves, to take advantage of different insights and experiences that they may offer.

BUILDING A RELATIONSHIP

Once you have identified and contacted potential mentors and advisors, the next step is to work on building a strong, mutually beneficial relationship with them. Here are some tips for building a successful relationship with your mentors and advisors:

- Set clear expectations: Make sure that you and your mentors or advisors are on the same page about what you hope to gain from the relationship. Be clear about your goals and what you expect from your mentors or advisors, and ask them what they expect from you in return.
- Communicate regularly: Regular communication is key to a successful mentor-mentee relationship. Establish a regular schedule for check-ins and updates, whether it be in person, via phone or video call. This will help ensure that you stay on track and that your mentors or advisors are aware of any challenges or successes that you are experiencing.
- Be open and honest: Be open and honest with your mentors and advisors about your business and any challenges you are facing. This will help them provide you with the best possible advice and guidance.
- Take their advice: Your mentors and advisors have a wealth of experience and knowledge that can be incredibly valuable to your business. When they offer advice or make suggestions, be sure to consider them carefully and implement them where you can.
- Show appreciation: Show your appreciation for your mentors' and advisors' time, expertise, and support. It can be as simple as sending an email or a handwritten note to express your gratitude. It's also important to be prompt and responsive, take notes during any conversations and to follow up in a timely manner.
- Be respectful: Remember that your mentors and advisors are busy people and they are taking time out of their schedule to help you. Be respectful of their time and try to make the most of the time you have together.
- Pay it forward: As your business grows, consider how you can "pay it forward" and give back to other Black entrepreneurs. Share your own knowledge and experience, and use your network to connect them with other helpful resources.

Building a strong, mutually beneficial relationship with your mentors and advisors takes time and effort, but the rewards can be significant. With the right mentor or advisor, you can gain valuable insights, experience and guidance that can help you take your business to the next level.

MENTORSHIP PROGRAMS

In addition to identifying and building relationships with individual mentors and advisors, Black entrepreneurs can also benefit from seeking out mentorship programs or organizations that can connect them with experienced mentors or advisors. Here are some tips for finding mentorship programs or organizations that can help you grow your business:

- Research: Research mentorship programs or organizations that specifically target Black entrepreneurs. Also look for ones that focus on your industry or business area of interest.
- Network: Ask other Black entrepreneurs if they are aware of any mentorship programs or organizations that they have found helpful. Reach out to industry associations and professional organizations to see if they offer any mentorship programs.
- Look for government-funded programs: Many government-funded programs are available to support small businesses, especially those that are owned by minorities. Research grants or incubators that focus on Black entrepreneurs, like the Minority Business Development Agency (MBDA) or the Small Business Administration (SBA) .
- Check out online platforms: There are many online platforms that offer mentorship programs, such as The Kairos Society, or The Startup Garage. These platforms can provide access to a wide variety of mentors and advisors from a variety of industries.
- Attend events: Attend networking events, conferences and other industry-specific events to learn about mentorship programs or organizations. Many of these events offer mentorship opportunities or have resource fairs where you can learn more about the different programs and organizations available to you.
- Look for local resources: Seek out local resources like Small Business Development Centers (SBDCs), SCORE, or non-profit organizations that offer mentorship programs and services for small businesses.

When considering a mentorship program or organization, it is important to research the program's track record, the credentials of the mentors and how the program is run. Ask for references or testimonials from previous participants, and find out how the program is designed to help entrepreneurs succeed. Many mentorship programs offer a variety of services, like workshops, networking events, and resources to help entrepreneurs at different stages of business development.

Overall, mentorship programs or organizations can be a valuable resource for Black entrepreneurs, providing access to experienced mentors or advisors and a community of like-minded business owners. By seeking out these programs and organizations, Black entrepreneurs can gain the knowledge, skills and networks needed to grow their businesses.

ADVISORY SERVICES

Black entrepreneurs may also want to seek the advice of industry experts or consultants to help them find the right mentors or advisors. These experts and consultants can offer a variety of services, including:

- Matchmaking services: Some consultants or industry experts offer matchmaking services that can help connect Black entrepreneurs with mentors or advisors who have the right experience and expertise. They can help identify potential mentors or advisors based on the entrepreneur's goals and business needs.
- Industry insights: Industry experts and consultants can provide valuable insights into the specific industry or market in which the entrepreneur operates. They can help identify potential mentors or advisors who have experience in that industry and who understand the specific challenges and opportunities that the entrepreneur is facing.
- Referrals: Consultants and industry experts may have a wide network of professionals, including mentors or advisors, in their industry that they can refer Black entrepreneurs to.
- Background research: Professional consultants or industry experts may be able to conduct background research on potential mentors or advisors, looking at their professional and educational experience, as well as current or previous successful ventures or projects.
- Assistance in communication: These consultants or experts can also assist in the initial communication process, helping Black entrepreneurs to make the first contact with potential mentors or advisors, and provide guidance on how to structure the communication and what information to present to the potential mentor.
- Professional development: These experts and consultants can also help Black entrepreneurs develop the necessary skills, such as networking or communication, to successfully build and maintain a mentorship relationship.

To find industry experts or consultants who can help you find the right mentors or advisors, you can start by researching consultants or industry experts that specialize in your area of interest. Ask for referrals from other Black entrepreneurs or business associations. You can also check out professional organizations or consulting firms that offer services for small businesses.

It's important to note that hiring an industry expert or consultant can be an added expense, but the expertise and guidance that they provide can be invaluable in finding the right mentors or advisors for your business.

Chapter Eighteen:
Developing Your Leadership Skills

As a Black entrepreneur, developing strong leadership skills is essential to the success of your business. Leadership skills allow you to effectively manage and motivate your team, navigate challenges and opportunities, and make strategic decisions that can help your business grow and thrive.

Building confidence as a leader is also important for Black entrepreneurs. Black entrepreneurs may face additional challenges in the business world, such as unconscious bias, racial prejudice, and discrimination, which can make it harder to gain the respect and trust of employees, partners, investors, and customers. Developing confidence as a leader can help you overcome these challenges and be taken seriously in the business world.

This chapter will explore various strategies and techniques that Black entrepreneurs can use to develop their leadership skills and build confidence as a leader. It will cover a range of topics including: learning how to make effective decisions, building a strong team, managing and motivating employees, and learning how to communicate effectively and build relationships with partners, investors and customers.

We will also look at how to identify and overcome unconscious bias, and how to create an inclusive and diverse working environment, as well as how to develop a leadership style that authentically reflects who you are and what you stand for.

The chapter will provide practical advice, tips and exercises that you can apply to your business, as well as real-world examples of Black entrepreneurs who have successfully developed their leadership skills and built confidence as a leader. By following the advice and techniques in this chapter, you will be on your way to becoming a more effective, confident and successful leader.

IDENTIFYING YOUR LEADERSHIP STRENGTHS

As a Black entrepreneur, it is important to identify your leadership strengths and areas for improvement in order to become an effective leader and grow your business. There are several methods and techniques that you can use to assess your leadership strengths and identify areas for improvement.

1. Self-assessment: Start by taking a self-assessment of your leadership skills. This can be done through self-reflection, journaling or even taking a leadership assessment test. This will help you identify your current leadership strengths and weaknesses and give you a baseline from which to work.
2. 360-degree feedback: Utilize 360-degree feedback, which is a way of assessing a leader's performance from multiple perspectives. This can include feedback from employees, colleagues, and even customers. This type of feedback is useful in

identifying areas for improvement because it can provide insights that a self-assessment alone might not.
3. Executive coaching: Consider working with an executive coach who can provide you with an objective perspective on your leadership skills and help you identify areas for improvement. A coach can also help you develop a plan to improve your skills and hold you accountable to making progress.
4. Benchmark against industry standards: Take time to research industry standards and best practices for leadership. Look at what other successful leaders in your industry are doing, and benchmark your skills and performance against those standards. This will help you identify areas where you might need to improve to stay competitive.
5. Develop a Learning Plan: Based on your self-assessment, feedback and benchmarking, create a plan that outlines what areas you need to focus on to improve your leadership skills. This plan should include specific goals, action steps and milestones. Schedule regular check-ins and hold yourself accountable for making progress.
6. Embrace lifelong learning: Leadership is a skill that can be developed over time through continuous learning and improvement. Embrace lifelong learning by reading, attending workshops, and seeking out mentorship.
7. Encourage constructive feedback: Encourage feedback from those you work with, whether employees, colleagues, partners, or supervisors. Be open to constructive feedback and actively seek out advice and guidance from those around you. Show your willingness to improve and being receptive to feedback often helps to build trust and respect.

By using these methods and techniques, Black entrepreneurs can assess their leadership strengths and identify areas for improvement. With this understanding, they can take steps to improve their skills, build confidence and become more effective leaders.

IMPLEMENTING CHANGE

As a Black entrepreneur, it is important to apply the lessons learned from feedback in order to implement changes to your leadership style and increase effectiveness. The Harvard Business School has developed several advanced business management techniques that can be used in this process:

1. Action Planning: Develop an action plan that outlines specific goals and steps to take in order to address areas for improvement identified through feedback. Make sure to include clear objectives, timelines, and accountability measures.
2. Prioritization: Prioritize the changes that you need to make based on their potential impact on your leadership style and effectiveness. Focus on the changes that will have the greatest impact and that can be implemented most easily.
3. Implementation: Implement the changes by communicating them clearly to your team and advisors, and providing the necessary resources and support to ensure their success.

4. Communication: Communicate progress to your team and advisors throughout the implementation process, and seek their feedback on how well the changes are working and whether additional adjustments need to be made.
5. Continuous improvement: Continuously monitor the effectiveness of the changes made, and seek feedback on a regular basis to track progress. Use the feedback to adjust your leadership style as necessary and to make additional changes as needed.
6. Reflect and Learn: Reflect on the experience and learn from the feedback and the change process, in order to continuously improve your leadership style and effectiveness.

In summary, by applying the lessons learned from feedback and using advanced business management techniques, you can effectively implement changes to your leadership style, increase your effectiveness and drive success in your business.

SEEKING LEADERSHIP TRAINING

As a Black entrepreneur, seeking leadership training or development opportunities is an essential step in enhancing your skills and building confidence as a leader. There are several leadership training academies and courses available for free or low cost that can help you improve your leadership skills.

Small Business Administration (SBA) offers free resources and training on topics such as leadership, management, and business planning through its Small Business Development Centers (SBDCs) and SCORE offices. The Minority Business Development Agency (MBDA) offers training and resources specifically designed to help minority-owned businesses and entrepreneurs develop their leadership skills.

The Kauffman Foundation offers online courses and resources for entrepreneurs on topics such as leadership and management through its Kauffman FastTrac program. Online platforms like Coursera, edX, and Udemy offer a wide range of leadership development courses, often with reputable universities or business schools as the providers, for a minimal cost.

National Association of Small Business Owners(NASBO) offers training, events, and networking opportunities, as well as publications and research, tailored to the needs of small business owners. Black-owned Business Associations: Many local and regional black-owned business associations offer training, events, and networking opportunities tailored to the specific needs of Black entrepreneurs.

Additionally, many universities and business schools offer leadership development programs and courses, some of which may be available online. These programs and courses can provide a more structured and in-depth approach to leadership development. Some examples are Harvard Business School which offers the "Leadership Development Program" to accelerate the development of leadership skills for current and aspiring leaders. Similarly, the Kellogg School of Management at Northwestern University offers "Leadership Programs" that focuses on developing leadership skills through interactive and hands-on learning. Many other universities have leadership programs that are included as part of their graduate studies program.

The main takeaway is that there are a variety of leadership training and development opportunities available to Black entrepreneurs, many of which are free or low cost. By seeking out these opportunities, Black entrepreneurs can gain the knowledge, skills and networks needed to become effective and confident leaders. This is how you boss up!

BUILDING YOUR CONFIDENCE

As a Black entrepreneur, building confidence as a leader is crucial to the success of your business. Confidence enables you to effectively manage and motivate your team, navigate challenges and opportunities, and make strategic decisions. The US Army Officer Training School has several leadership techniques and methods that can be applied to build confidence as a leader.

- Positive Self-talk: Practice positive self-talk and visualization. This means talking to yourself in a positive and confident manner, and visualizing yourself successfully leading your team. This technique helps to build self-belief and confidence.
- Goal Setting: Set realistic and achievable goals for yourself as a leader. By achieving these goals, you can build confidence in your abilities and in your leadership style.
- Embrace challenges: Embrace challenges and view them as opportunities to grow as a leader and gain confidence. Confronting challenges head-on and coming out victorious will help you to build confidence in your leadership abilities.
- Seek out mentors: Seek out mentors who can provide guidance and support as you develop your leadership skills and build your confidence.
- Build your network: Building a network of trusted colleagues and industry experts can help provide perspective, advice and feedback on your progress, as well as to provide new opportunities and resources.
- Take initiative: Take initiative and be proactive. Showing initiative as a Boss, means being willing to take action, and make decisions even in uncertain situations, by taking initiative, you demonstrate your capability and confidence as a leader.
- Lead by example: Lead by example, model the behavior and actions that you expect from your team. This will inspire trust and respect, and demonstrate that you are a leader who can be followed.
- Develop Emotional Intelligence: Emotional intelligence is a vital component of effective leadership, it helps leaders build trust and strong relationships with their team, which can increase their confidence.

In conclusion, there are several practical methods and techniques that Black entrepreneurs can use to build their confidence as leaders, many of which are used in elite leadership training programs such as officer training schools in the US military. By using these techniques, Black entrepreneurs can gain the confidence they need to inspire and motivate their team, and drive success in their business.

LEADING WITH AUTHENTICITY

Leadership is about more than just managing a team or making strategic decisions; it is about being authentic and true to yourself as a leader. Black entrepreneurs should lead with authenticity and be true to their values and vision as they guide their team.

Leading with authenticity means being honest, transparent, and accountable in your leadership style. It also means being true to your values and beliefs as you make decisions and guide your team. When you lead with authenticity, you create a culture of trust, respect and shared values within your team, which in turn leads to better performance and success.

As the Dalai Lama said, "Leadership cannot just go along to get along. Leadership must meet the moral challenge of the day." This means that leaders have an important responsibility to lead with integrity, and to use their power and influence for the greater good. For Black entrepreneurs, this may mean being an advocate for diversity and inclusion in the workplace, or using their platform to raise awareness about social justice issues.

In order to lead with authenticity, to be a real boss, it is essential for Black entrepreneurs to be aware of their personal values, beliefs and vision, and align their leadership style with them. This means taking the time to reflect on what is important to them, and then incorporating that into their leadership style and decision making. Hopefully, pride in being black and a desire to want to see the uplifting of the black community as a whole are both important to you.

Additionally, being authentic means being open to feedback, learning from your mistakes, and continuously seeking self-improvement. By being open to feedback, Black entrepreneurs can gain insight into how they are perceived by others, and make necessary adjustments to ensure that they are leading in a way that is true to themselves.

Leading with authenticity is an ongoing process, and it requires self-awareness, reflection, and a commitment to personal and professional growth. By being true to themselves and leading with integrity, Black entrepreneurs can build trust and inspire others to follow their lead, which ultimately leads to success for their business.

LEADING BASED ON BEST PRACTICES

As a Black entrepreneur, deploying best practices in leadership policies and techniques is crucial for the success of your business. Best practices are methods and techniques that have been proven to be effective in a particular industry or field. They can provide a framework for decision making, and help to ensure that your leadership style is effective and efficient.

When deploying best practices, it is important for Black entrepreneurs to consider their individual styles and visions as they guide their teams. It is important to find a balance between adhering to industry standards and remaining true to your unique leadership style and values.

One way to deploy best practices is by conducting research on the latest trends and developments in your industry. This can be done by reading industry publications, attending conferences and networking with other industry leaders. This research will provide you with a better understanding of what best practices are being used, and which ones may be most relevant to your business.

Another way to deploy best practices is by seeking guidance from industry experts or consultants. They can provide valuable insight and advice on the most effective leadership policies and techniques, and can help you to tailor them to your business.

Another more direct and obvious way is to merely google terms like "best practices for" and then finish the search with your specific situation. For example, you can search for best practices for things like: social media marketing, microservices, software development, and more.

It is also important to remember that best practices are not a one-size-fits-all solution, they should be adapted to your specific needs and the unique characteristics of your business. It's also important to take a flexible approach when deploying best practices and to be open to making adjustments as needed. Additionally, it is crucial for Black entrepreneurs to actively seek out diverse perspectives and to create an inclusive environment in their businesses. This can be done by implementing those diversity and inclusion policies and by actively recruiting and promoting a diverse workforce. By deploying best practices in leadership, Black entrepreneurs can not only improve the success of their businesses, but also work towards creating a more equitable and inclusive industry.

Chapter Nineteen:
Socializing For Black entrepreneurs

As a Black entrepreneur, developing and maintaining strong relationships is a crucial aspect of success in business. Socializing with colleagues, clients, investors, and industry leaders can help to build trust, establish networks and open up new opportunities. In order to effectively socialize and build these relationships, it is important to have excellent social etiquette.

Social etiquette refers to the set of rules and conventions that govern social interactions and behavior. It encompasses everything from proper manners and protocol, to effective communication and building relationships. Excellent social etiquette can help to create a positive and professional image, and can help to build and maintain strong relationships.

In the business world, social etiquette can be even more important for Black entrepreneurs due to the unconscious bias and discrimination we experience. Having excellent social etiquette can help us to navigate these challenges and showcase their professional capabilities. Moreover, socializing, networking and building relationships can be particularly beneficial for Black entrepreneurs who may face barriers to entry in traditional networks where they have to deal with well-connected people that have little to no experience interacting with those outside their socioeconomic class.

In this chapter, we will explore the various aspects of social etiquette and how they apply to the business world. We will examine different social situations, such as networking events and meetings, and discuss the appropriate social etiquette for each. We will also provide tips and advice on how to improve your social etiquette, and how to use it to build strong relationships and advance your business.

UNDERSTANDING THE PURPOSE OF SOCIAL ETIQUETTE

As a Black entrepreneur, it is important to understand the purpose and benefits of social etiquette when socializing in different public settings. Social etiquette refers to the set of conventions and rules that govern social interactions and behavior. It encompasses everything from manners and protocol, to communication and building relationships.

The purpose of social etiquette is to create a positive and professional image, and to build and maintain strong relationships. Social etiquette can be particularly important for Black entrepreneurs as they may face additional challenges such as unconscious bias and discrimination. By demonstrating excellent social etiquette, they can showcase their professionalism and capability, and navigate these challenges.

Here are some social etiquette tips for different social settings:

- Dinner Parties: RSVP in a timely manner, arrive on time, dress appropriately for the occasion, bring a small gift like a bottle of wine or bouquet of flowers as a token of appreciation, avoid talking about sensitive or controversial topics but be a good conversationalist, mind your cell phone usage as it can appear rude to use it, and thank the host at the end of the night.
- Happy Hours: Don't overstay your welcome, pace yourself with alcohol consumption, be a good listener and try not to oversell your business or yourself as a success, be cool and make good impressions, and keep your phone on silent or vibrate.
- Charity events: Show up on time, dress appropriately for the occasion, be engaged and attentive during the event, show enthusiasm for the charity's mission and goal, be generous with your resources to show support for the cause, and follow the dress code if there is any.
- Office parties: Follow the same conduct you would in the office, avoid discussing sensitive or controversial topics, and respect your colleagues privacy and boundaries. It goes without saying, but you should always be dressed sharp and presentable when you're at the office.

To sum this section up, understanding the purpose and benefits of social etiquette can be a valuable tool for Black entrepreneurs as they socialize in different public settings. By following austere social etiquette in dinner parties, happy hours, charity events, and office parties, they can create a positive and professional image, establish trust, and build strong relationships which in turn can open new business opportunities. It is important to remember that social etiquette can vary depending on the occasion and setting, but by following general guidelines and being mindful of your behavior, Black entrepreneurs can navigate these situations with confidence and grace like a boss.

DEVELOPING GOOD CONVERSATION SKILLS

As a Black entrepreneur, developing good conversation skills is crucial for building and maintaining relationships with colleagues, clients, investors, and industry leaders. Good conversation skills include the ability to listen actively, ask open-ended questions, and effectively communicate ideas. By honing these skills, Black entrepreneurs can establish trust and build strong relationships that can lead to new opportunities and success for their business.

Here are some ways Black entrepreneurs can work to improve their conversation skills:

- Listen actively: This means giving your full attention to the person speaking and showing that you are engaged by nodding, making eye contact and acknowledging what is being said.
- Ask open-ended questions: Instead of asking yes or no questions, ask questions that encourage the other person to open up and share more information. For example, instead of asking "Did you enjoy the event?" ask "What did you think of the event?"

- Practice active listening: This means not just hearing the words, but understanding the message behind them. Listen for both the content and the underlying emotions or concerns of the person speaking.
- Show empathy: By showing empathy, you can build trust, and create a more comfortable conversation. For example, if someone is sharing a personal story, you can respond with phrases like "I understand" or "I can relate" which allows the person to open up and trust you more.
- Share your own experiences: Sharing your own experiences can help to build a rapport and create a sense of shared understanding.
- Show interest in what the other person has to say: This means not interrupting, not talking over them, and showing a willingness to listen actively.
- Be honest and transparent: Honesty and transparency are key in building trust and establishing meaningful conversations, this is even more relevant if you–as a Black entrepreneur–are facing a difficult situation and need to communicate it to your peers.

So, developing good conversation skills is an essential aspect of success as a Black entrepreneur. By listening actively, asking open-ended questions, and effectively communicating ideas, Black entrepreneurs can establish trust, build strong relationships and open new opportunities for their business.

BEING RESPECTFUL AND COURTEOUS

Black entrepreneurs should always aim to be respectful and courteous when socializing with others, both in person and online. This means being mindful of others' feelings and boundaries, and showing consideration for their perspectives and opinions.

One great opportunity to be respectful and courteous is in a networking event. During the event, Black entrepreneurs should make an extra effort to introduce themselves to others, ask about their business or profession, and actively listen to what they have to say. Be fully present in the room both physically and mentally. Work that black magic to gain friends and influence people. Beware of coming across as conceited or arrogant and respect the time limits for conversations being careful to avoid monopolizing the conversation.

Another example of being respectful and courteous can be seen in online communication. When interacting with others on social media, Black entrepreneurs should be mindful of the language they use and avoid making derogatory or offensive statements. They should also be respectful of others' privacy and not share personal information without their consent.

Finally, black bosses should always strive to maintain a positive and professional image, and should avoid getting involved in conflicts or controversies that could damage their reputation. By always being respectful and courteous, you can build strong and lasting relationships with others, and position yourself as a credible and trustworthy individual in your industry.

BEING CONFIDENT

Black entrepreneurs should aim to project confidence in their interactions with others, as it can help them build credibility and establish trust. However, it is important to balance confidence with humility, and not come across as arrogant or dismissive.

One situation in which you should show confidence is in a business meeting. When presenting ideas or proposals, Black entrepreneurs should speak clearly, make eye contact, and use confident body language. Additionally, they should be prepared with supporting data and be able to answer any questions or objections that may come up. Do a few practice runs at home or at the bar with your friends and have them play devil's advocate to prepare you for your meeting. Nothing propels you faster and further than confidence and preparedness. There is nothing more fascinating than a confident and prepared black entrepreneur with tunnel vision on accomplishing their goals.

Another opportunity to exhibit confidence is while serving on board meetings. When answering questions, Black entrepreneurs should give specific examples of their accomplishments and qualifications, and speak with conviction about their ability to perform the job. They should also ask questions about the mission and the company, which shows interest and determination.

It's also important to be aware of unconscious bias, sometimes Black entrepreneurs might not be given the same chance as others, or be doubted on their capabilities, so it's important to not let that discourage you and to maintain a minimum level of confidence.

By being confident, but not arrogant, Black entrepreneurs can effectively communicate their value and capabilities, and increase their chances of success in business and networking opportunities.

BEING AUTHENTIC

Black entrepreneurs should strive to be authentic and genuine when interacting with others, as this can help them build trust and establish strong relationships. Being authentic means being true to oneself and not trying to be someone else or hiding one's true feelings and beliefs.

For example, when meeting new people at networking events, Black entrepreneurs should be honest about their background, experiences, and goals, and not try to present themselves as something they are not. They should also be open to feedback and willing to share their own vulnerabilities and challenges.

Another chance to show authenticity is in normal business interactions. When working with colleagues, partners, or clients, Black entrepreneurs should be clear and direct in their communication, and not sugarcoat or hide their opinions. Additionally, they should be willing to admit their mistakes and take responsibility for their actions.

Being true to oneself also means to embrace their unique qualities, talents and cultural background, and use it to their advantage. Using their own unique experiences, knowledge, and background can make their business or brand more relatable and authentic to their target audience.

By being authentic and genuine, Black entrepreneurs can build stronger and more meaningful connections with others, and–hopefully–that translates into success in both their personal and professional endeavors.

FOLLOWING SOCIAL NORMS

Black entrepreneurs should be aware and respectful of local social norms and etiquette when socializing, considering the specific cultural expectations in a given situation. This means being mindful of customs, traditions, and expectations that are particular to a certain place, community or context. Be true to yourself, but show that you can be open minded to others' way of doing things as well. This is the boss' way.

For example, when doing business in a foreign country, Black entrepreneurs should take the time to research the local customs and etiquette. They should understand the expectations around dress, gift-giving, and the appropriate way to address others. They should also be aware of the local business culture and practices, and adjust their communication style accordingly. Research local history and culture, and maybe visit a local news site to gather information regarding what is going on in that locale before you arrive. This will also give you a few talking points and show that you will go the extra mile to get to know the people and businesses you deal with.

Another opportunity is when socializing within a specific community. Black entrepreneurs should be aware of the cultural expectations and norms of that community, and respect them accordingly. For example, they should be aware of and respect religious and dietary restrictions, and also be aware of customs around gender and social interactions. This is especially important when doing business in the middle east, China, and north Africa.

By following local social norms and etiquette, Black entrepreneurs can show respect and consideration for the people and places in which they are operating, and establish trust and positive relationships. They can also avoid misunderstandings and cultural faux pas that could damage their reputation or harm their business interests.

Chapter Twenty:
Staying Up-To-Date On Industry Trends

As a black entrepreneur, it is essential to stay current and informed about the latest industry trends and developments. Being aware of these trends can help you identify new opportunities, stay competitive, and make better-informed decisions for your business. In this chapter, I will discuss the importance of staying abreast of industry trends and provide strategies and techniques for keeping informed and up-to-date.

I will explore how to conduct market research, identify and track key industry indicators, and how to network and connect with other professionals and experts in your field. Additionally, I will discuss how to stay informed about the latest technologies, regulatory changes, and other factors that can impact your business.

The journey of entrepreneurship is full of challenges and opportunities and staying informed is crucial to make strategic decisions. This chapter will provide you with practical and actionable advice on how to stay ahead of the curve, capitalize on new opportunities, and minimize risks. Being aware of industry trends will make you an informed and effective leader, and give you the tools you need to create a thriving business and become a boss.

IDENTIFYING RELEVANT INDUSTRY TRENDS

As a Black entrepreneur, it is important to stay informed about industry trends that may affect your business and target audience. Identifying relevant industry trends can help you make strategic decisions, such as developing new products or services, adjusting your marketing strategies, or expanding into new markets.

One way to identify relevant industry trends is to conduct market research. This can include surveys, focus groups, and interviews with your target audience, as well as analyzing data from industry reports and trade publications. For example, a Black entrepreneur in the fashion industry might conduct market research to identify the latest trends in clothing styles, colors, and fabrics that are popular among their target audience.

Another way to stay informed about industry trends is to network and connect with other Black entrepreneurs and industry experts. Joining professional associations or attending industry conferences and events can provide valuable insights and connections that can help you stay informed about the latest trends and developments in your industry.

An example of this in practice is a Black entrepreneur who owns a natural hair care product line. They can conduct market research by surveying their target audience to learn about the specific hair care needs and preferences of Black women, and they can also attend natural hair care trade shows and events to connect with other Black entrepreneurs and industry experts in the natural hair care industry.

Thus, identifying relevant industry trends is crucial for Black entrepreneurs to make strategic decisions and stay competitive in their industry. By conducting market research, networking, and staying informed about the latest trends and developments, Black entrepreneurs can better understand the needs and preferences of their target audience and make informed decisions to grow their business.

STAYING CONNECTED TO YOUR INDUSTRY

As a Black entrepreneur, staying connected to your industry is vital for staying informed about the latest trends and developments, as well as for networking and building relationships with other professionals in your field. One way to stay connected to your industry is by joining professional organizations and attending conferences and events.

Professional organizations provide a platform for Black entrepreneurs to connect with other industry professionals, share knowledge and resources, and stay informed about the latest trends and developments in their field. Some notable professional organizations for Black entrepreneurs include the National Black MBA Association, the National Minority Supplier Development Council, and the National Bar Association.

Attending conferences and events is another great way for Black entrepreneurs to stay connected to their industry. These events provide opportunities to network with other professionals, attend keynote speeches and panel discussions, and learn about the latest trends and developments in your field. Some notable conferences and events for Black entrepreneurs include the Black Enterprise Entrepreneurs Summit, the National Black Chamber of Commerce Annual Convention, and the National Black MBA Association Conference & Exposition.

As Oprah Winfrey once said, "Surround yourself with only people who are going to lift you higher." By staying connected to your industry, you can surround yourself with like-minded individuals who can lift you higher and help you achieve your goals.

Therefore, staying connected to your industry is important for Black entrepreneurs to stay informed about the latest trends and developments, as well as for networking and building relationships with other professionals in their field. Joining professional organizations and attending conferences and events are two effective ways for Black entrepreneurs to stay connected to their industry and to stay informed about the latest trends and developments in their field.

READING INDUSTRY PUBLICATIONS

As a Black entrepreneur, staying informed about the latest news and trends in your industry is essential for making strategic decisions, staying competitive, and ultimately growing your business. One way to stay informed is by reading industry publications, which provide valuable insights and information about the latest developments, trends, and best practices in your field.

Reading industry publications can help you stay informed about the latest developments in your field, including new products, services, and technologies, as well as changes in laws and regulations that may impact your business. It can also provide a platform to learn from other successful Black entrepreneurs in your field, and to gain insights and inspiration for your own business.

As Robert L. Johnson, Founder of BET said, "Stay informed, stay engaged, and stay involved in the industry." Reading industry publications is a great way to stay informed, engaged and involved in your industry.

Some examples of industry publications for Black entrepreneurs include Black Enterprise, The Network Journal, and The National Black Chamber of Commerce's Business Advocate. Black entrepreneurs can also get published in these publications by submitting articles, op-eds, or thought-leadership pieces on relevant industry topics. They can also participate in surveys or interviews, as well as pitch their businesses to be featured in the publications.

Thus, reading industry publications is an important way for Black entrepreneurs to stay informed about the latest news and trends in their field. It can help them make strategic decisions, stay competitive, and ultimately grow their business. Black entrepreneurs should make a habit of reading industry publications, and also consider submitting their own writing or pitching their business for feature coverage to gain exposure and establish themselves as thought leaders in their industry.

FOLLOWING INDUSTRY INFLUENCERS

As a Black entrepreneur, staying informed about the latest news and trends in your industry is essential for making strategic decisions, staying competitive, and ultimately growing your business. One way to stay informed is by following industry influencers and thought leaders on social media and other platforms.

Industry influencers are individuals who are well-respected and have a significant following in their respective fields. They often share valuable insights, strategies, and information about the latest developments, trends, and best practices in their field. By following them on social media and other platforms, Black entrepreneurs can stay informed about the latest industry developments and gain valuable insights and inspiration for their own business.

For example, Elon Musk is a well-known industry influencer in the technology and innovation space. He is the CEO of Twitter, SpaceX and Tesla, and is known for his innovation in online payment systems, electric cars, and space exploration. By following him on social media and other platforms, Black entrepreneurs in technology and innovation can stay informed about the latest developments in the industry and gain valuable insights and inspiration for their own business. Plus, Elon Musk is just a really interesting human being in general. The guy currently sits as the wealthiest person on Earth, yet he cares about the everyday human, which is unheard of in modern times. Why do I use Elon Musk as an inspiration in a book about Black entrepreneurship? Well, you may be surprised to know that Elon was born in South Africa, which technically makes him African. And, since he obtained his American citizenship as a young boy, he is technically an African-American.

Other examples of industry influencers include:

@DaymondJohn, Founder of FUBU and Shark on Shark Tank
@GaryVee, Author and Entrepreneur
@MarshawnLynch, Entrepreneur and NFL player

@YvonneOrji, Actor and Entrepreneur

Accordingly, following industry influencers and thought leaders on social media and other platforms is an important way for Black entrepreneurs to stay informed about the latest news and trends in their field. It can help them make strategic decisions, stay competitive, and ultimately grow their business. You should make a habit of following industry influencers and thought leaders on social media and other platforms in order to stay informed and gain valuable insights and inspiration for your own business.

PARTICIPATING IN PROFESSIONAL DEVELOPMENT OPPORTUNITIES

Participating in professional development opportunities, such as training or workshops, can be an effective way to stay current on industry trends and best practices, as well as to gain new skills and knowledge to help grow your business. Professional development opportunities can take many forms, including workshops, seminars, webinars, and mentorship programs, and can cover a wide range of topics, such as marketing, sales, finance, and management.

When considering professional development opportunities, Black entrepreneurs can expect to gain a deeper understanding of the trends and best practices in their industry, as well as to learn new skills and strategies that can help them grow their business. Many professional development opportunities also provide an opportunity to network with other Black entrepreneurs and industry experts, which can be valuable for building relationships and gaining insights into the industry.

In the United States, there are many professional development opportunities available for Black entrepreneurs across the country. Here are some examples of annual opportunities organized by US regions:

- North: The National Black MBA Association Conference & Exposition is held annually in various cities across the North. It provides a platform for Black entrepreneurs to connect with other industry professionals, learn about the latest trends and best practices, and gain valuable insights and inspiration for their own business.
- South: The Black Enterprise Entrepreneurs Summit is held annually in various cities across the South. This event provides Black entrepreneurs with the opportunity to learn from industry experts, connect with other entrepreneurs and gain insights on how to grow their businesses.
- East: The National Minority Supplier Development Council's Business Opportunity Exchange is held annually in the East. This event provides Black entrepreneurs with access to corporate buyers, government agencies and other organizations looking to do business with minority-owned firms.
- West: The National Black Chamber of Commerce Annual Convention is held annually in the West. This event provides Black entrepreneurs with the opportunity to connect with other industry professionals, learn about the latest trends and best practices, and gain valuable insights and inspiration for their own business.

Ultimately, participating in professional development opportunities, such as training or workshops, can be an effective way for Black entrepreneurs to stay current on industry trends and best practices and gain new skills and knowledge to help grow their business. There are many professional development opportunities available for Black entrepreneurs across the US, and by participating in them, Black entrepreneurs can gain a deeper understanding of the trends and best practices in their industry, as well as to learn new skills and strategies that can help them grow their business.

SEEKING PROFESSIONAL ADVICE

As a Black entrepreneur, seeking professional advice can be an effective way to stay up-to-date on the latest trends and developments in your industry, and to gain valuable insights and strategies for growing your business. There are many resources available where Black entrepreneurs can seek advice from industry experts or consultants, including:

- Professional associations: Many professional associations have a network of industry experts and professionals who can provide valuable advice and guidance to Black entrepreneurs. Joining a professional association in your industry can provide access to these resources and connections.
- Mentors and coaching programs: Many organizations and programs offer mentorship and coaching for Black entrepreneurs. These programs match Black entrepreneurs with experienced industry professionals who can provide guidance and advice on a variety of topics, such as business development, marketing, and financial management.
- Online resources: There are a number of online resources that provide advice and guidance for Black entrepreneurs. Websites such as blackbusiness.org, blackenterprise.com, and mentorme.net, offer a wealth of information on topics such as business development, marketing, and financial management.
- Social media platforms: Platforms like LinkedIn and Twitter, are also great resources for connecting with industry experts, thought leaders and entrepreneurs. Through these platforms, Black entrepreneurs can join groups and communities related to their industry and connect with experts who can provide valuable advice and guidance.
- Consultants: Black entrepreneurs can also seek advice from consultants who specialize in their industry. They can provide valuable insights and guidance on topics such as market research, business strategy, and financial management.

Therefore, seeking professional advice is an effective way for entrepreneurs to stay up-to-date on the latest trends and developments in their industry, and to gain valuable insights and strategies for growing their business. There are so many resources available, such as professional associations, mentorship programs, online resources, social media platforms and consultants that Black entrepreneurs can utilize to connect with industry experts and to seek valuable advice and guidance for their business. There are no excuses in 2023.

Chapter Twenty-One:
Crafting A Compelling Elevator Pitch

As a Black entrepreneur, it's essential to be able to effectively communicate your business idea and value proposition in a short amount of time. This is where the elevator pitch comes in. An elevator pitch is a brief, persuasive speech that you can use to spark interest in your business or idea. It's called an elevator pitch because it should be short enough to deliver during a brief elevator ride.

The purpose of an elevator pitch is to capture the attention of potential investors, customers, partners, or other stakeholders in a clear and compelling way. It's a tool that can be used to introduce your business, explain what it does and why it's unique, and convey the value it can provide.

In this chapter, we will explore the key elements of crafting a compelling elevator pitch. We will cover the following topics:

- Understanding the Purpose of an Elevator Pitch
- Identifying Your Unique Value Proposition
- Keeping it Short and Sweet
- Being Clear and Concise
- Practicing Your Pitch
- Being Authentic

Through this section, we will provide tips, strategies, and examples to help you craft an effective elevator pitch that can help you communicate the value of your business and build relationships with potential stakeholders. By the end of this chapter, you will be able to craft a compelling elevator pitch that can help you effectively communicate your business idea and value proposition in a short amount of time.

UNDERSTANDING THE PURPOSE OF AN ELEVATOR PITCH

An elevator pitch is a brief, persuasive speech that you can use to spark interest in your business or idea. It's called an elevator pitch because it should be short enough to deliver during a brief elevator ride. The purpose of an elevator pitch is to capture the attention of potential investors, customers, partners, or other stakeholders in a clear and compelling way.

The main purpose of an elevator pitch is to introduce your business, explain what it does and why it's unique, and convey the value it can provide. It's an effective tool for Black entrepreneurs to communicate their business idea and value proposition in a short amount of time and to capture the attention of potential stakeholders.

To create an effective elevator pitch, Black entrepreneurs should focus on their unique value proposition, what sets their business apart from the competition. They should also keep it short and sweet, ensuring that the pitch is concise and easy to understand. Being clear and concise is key in making sure that the message is received by the listener.

Black entrepreneurs should also practice their pitch, to make sure it flows smoothly and to be able to deliver it confidently. They should also be authentic, making sure that the pitch reflects the personality and values of the business.

Having an elevator pitch on deck, Black entrepreneurs can be ready to introduce their business in any situation. It can be used in networking events, meetings, or even in casual conversations. An elevator pitch can be the first step in building relationships with potential stakeholders and can help Black entrepreneurs effectively communicate their business idea and value proposition.

So, an elevator pitch is a powerful tool for Black entrepreneurs to effectively introduce their business and convey the value it can provide to potential investors, customers, partners, or other stakeholders. By focusing on their unique value proposition, keeping it short and sweet, being clear and concise, practicing their pitch, and being authentic, Black entrepreneurs can craft an effective elevator pitch that can capture the attention of potential stakeholders and help them build relationships with them. Having an elevator pitch on deck, Black entrepreneurs can be ready to introduce their business in any situation and can take the first step in growing their business.

IDENTIFYING YOUR UNIQUE VALUE PROPOSITION

A unique value proposition (UVP) is a statement that clearly communicates the unique benefits and value that a business offers to its customers. It's a critical element of an effective elevator pitch, as it helps to convey what sets a business apart from its competitors and why customers should choose it over others. For Black entrepreneurs, articulating their UVP can be especially important. It can help to communicate the unique perspective and value that their business can bring to a diverse customer base.

For example, consider a solo criminal defense attorney who serves a rural area with no other Black lawyers in the market. This attorney's UVP could be:

"As the only Black criminal defense attorney in the area, I offer a unique perspective and understanding of the community I serve. My clients can trust that I will fiercely advocate for their rights and provide personalized, culturally sensitive representation."

This UVP clearly communicates the unique value that the attorney's business offers to customers. It highlights the attorney's unique perspective and understanding of the community they serve, and the personalized and culturally sensitive representation that they provide. It also emphasizes the attorney's ability to fiercely advocate for the rights of their clients which can be a critical aspect for many customers.

Therefore, Black entrepreneurs should focus on articulating their unique value proposition by highlighting the unique benefits and value that their business offers to customers. This can be especially important for Black entrepreneurs who can communicate the unique perspective and value that their business can bring to a diverse customer base. By clearly communicating their UVP, Black entrepreneurs can help to differentiate their business from competitors and attract customers who are looking for the specific benefits and value that their business offers.

KEEPING IT SHORT AND SWEET

An effective elevator pitch should be short and to the point, ideally no longer than 30 seconds. This is because the purpose of an elevator pitch is to capture the attention of potential investors, customers, partners, or other stakeholders in a clear and compelling way, and a long-winded pitch can lose their attention.

For Black entrepreneurs, keeping their elevator pitch short and sweet can be especially important as it allows them to effectively communicate their business idea and value proposition in a brief amount of time.

For example, in 2014, when I first opened up my law firm in my hometown–located in a rural part of north Texas where no other Black lawyers were available to be retained–my 30-second elevator pitch went something like this:

"I am the only Black criminal defense attorney in the area and I offer a unique perspective and understanding of the community I serve. I provide personalized and culturally sensitive representation for my clients and I fiercely advocate for their rights. If you or someone you know needs a strong defender in court, I'm here to help. Here's my card."

This pitch effectively communicated the unique value proposition of my business, highlighted my unique perspective and understanding of the community I serve, and emphasized the personalized and culturally sensitive representation I provide. It also emphasized my ability to fiercely advocate for my clients. All of this is done in a brief and easy to understand way.

So, Black entrepreneurs should aim to keep their elevator pitch short and sweet, aiming for 30 seconds or less. This allows them to effectively communicate their business idea and value proposition in a brief amount of time and captures the attention of potential stakeholders. By keeping their pitch concise and easy to understand, Black entrepreneurs can effectively convey the unique value of their business and build relationships with potential stakeholders efficiently.

BEING CLEAR AND CONCISE

For Black entrepreneurs, being clear and concise in their elevator pitch can be especially important as it allows them to effectively communicate their business idea and value proposition to a diverse audience.

For example, I also practice entertainment law. But, when I first started my business, I was practicing in an area with no strong entertainment industry infrastructure available. But I knew the power I had to help change that if I were just able to sign a few great clients and help get some infrastructure established. BUt in order to sign those clients, I needed to be able to get them to understand what I did, what my vision was, and how I could help them. So, I would use the following clear and concise elevator pitch:

> *"I am an entertainment attorney with extensive experience in music, film, and television. I understand the unique challenges facing creatives in the local entertainment industry, and I can help navigate the legal and business side of the industry to help you get where you're trying to go professionally. I am committed to helping my clients succeed in an industry where they are underrepresented, and I am dedicated to creating opportunities for them to succeed."*

This pitch effectively communicates the unique value proposition of my business, highlights my understanding of the challenges facing creatives in the local entertainment industry, and emphasizes my ability to help navigate the legal and business side of the industry. It also emphasizes my commitment to helping clients succeed in an industry where they are underrepresented by creating opportunities for them. All of this is done in a clear and easy to understand way.

So, Black entrepreneurs should aim to be clear and concise in their elevator pitch, avoiding the use of jargon or complex language. This allows them to effectively communicate their business idea and value proposition to a diverse audience and captures the attention of potential stakeholders. By being clear and concise, Black entrepreneurs can effectively convey the unique value of their business and build relationships with potential stakeholders. This can be especially important in industries where Black entrepreneurs may be underrepresented, as it allows them to communicate their value proposition in a way that is easily understood and can help them stand out among their competitors.

PRACTICING YOUR PITCH

As the famous lawyer, Johnny Cochran said, "If you don't know your rights, you don't have any." The same applies to an elevator pitch, if you don't practice it, you won't have a successful one.

Practicing your elevator pitch is essential for Black entrepreneurs to be able to effectively communicate their business idea and value proposition in a short amount of time. It allows them to refine their pitch, iron out any kinks, and become comfortable and confident delivering it.

The best way to practice your elevator pitch is by delivering it to a variety of audiences, including friends, family, and potential stakeholders. This will help you get feedback on your pitch and make adjustments as needed. You can also practice delivering your pitch in front of a mirror, or record yourself and play it back to see how it sounds.

Additionally, Black entrepreneurs should also practice adapting their pitch to different situations and audiences. This will help them to be able to deliver their pitch in a variety of settings and to a variety of people.

Again, practicing your elevator pitch is essential for Black entrepreneurs to be able to effectively communicate their business idea and value proposition in a short amount of time. By practicing their pitch and adapting it to different situations and audiences, Black entrepreneurs can become comfortable and confident delivering it, which can help them to build relationships with potential stakeholders and grow their business.

BEING AUTHENTIC

As a Black entrepreneur, it is important to be authentic and genuine when delivering your elevator pitch. This means being true to your values, vision, and mission, and conveying them in a sincere and honest way. When you are authentic, your pitch will resonate with potential investors, customers, partners, or other stakeholders, and they will be more likely to trust and believe in your business.

However, it is important to note that being authentic does not mean conflating or exaggerating the truth. It's important to avoid this tendency as it can be detrimental to the entire business. When you exaggerate or conflate the truth, it can come across as insincere and inauthentic, making it difficult for potential stakeholders to trust and believe in your business. This can lead to a lack of interest in your business and ultimately, a lack of success.

Authenticity is especially important for Black entrepreneurs, as it allows them to communicate the unique perspective and value that their business can bring to a diverse customer base. By being true to themselves and their values, Black entrepreneurs can effectively convey the unique value of their business and build relationships with potential stakeholders.

So, now you know being authentic and genuine when delivering an elevator pitch is essential for Black entrepreneurs. It means being true to your values, vision, and mission and conveying them in a sincere and honest way. Failure to do this can be detrimental to an entire business and it can lead to a lack of interest in your business, making it difficult for potential stakeholders to trust and believe in your business. It is also important to avoid the tendency to conflate or exaggerate the truth as it can come across as tacky and insincere. By staying true to their values and vision, and being authentic in their pitch, Black entrepreneurs can effectively convey the unique value of their business and build relationships with potential stakeholders. This can help them to stand out among their competitors and ultimately, succeed in their business ventures.

Chapter Twenty Two:
Negotiating And Closing Deals

In this chapter, we will delve into the art of negotiation and how it plays a vital role in the success of any business venture. From preparing for negotiations to communicating clearly, building trust and rapport, being flexible and utilizing advanced negotiating tactics, this chapter will provide practical tips and strategies for Black entrepreneurs to successfully navigate the negotiation process and close deals.

Negotiations are an integral part of business, whether it's securing funding, closing a sale, or forming a partnership. Black entrepreneurs often face unique challenges in the business world, and it's important for them to have a solid understanding of the negotiation process. This chapter will cover the key elements of preparing for negotiations, including researching and understanding the other party's interests, setting clear goals and objectives, and developing a solid strategy.

In addition to preparing for negotiations, this chapter will also cover the importance of communicating clearly, building trust and rapport, and being flexible in the negotiation process. We will also delve into advanced negotiating tactics, such as using psychological and emotional tactics, and how to close the deal.

This chapter is designed to provide you with some knowledge, skills, and tools you need to successfully navigate the negotiation process and close deals. Whether you're a seasoned entrepreneur or just starting out, the strategies outlined in this chapter will help you to achieve your business goals and succeed in the competitive world of business.

PREPARING FOR NEGOTIATIONS

Negotiations are an essential part of business and Black entrepreneurs should be well prepared for them. Preparation is key to the success of any negotiation, and it is important for Black entrepreneurs to identify their goals, understand the other party's needs and interests, and research market rates and industry standards.

To start, Black entrepreneurs should identify their goals and objectives for the negotiation. This includes determining what they hope to achieve and what they are willing to give up in exchange. Once their goals are clear, they should research and understand the other party's needs and interests. This includes understanding their priorities, pain points, and what is important to them. This knowledge will help Black entrepreneurs to tailor their approach and make proposals that are more likely to be accepted.

Another important aspect of preparation is researching market rates and industry standards. This means understanding the typical rates and terms for products or services in your industry, as well as the typical terms and conditions of agreements. This knowledge can help Black entrepreneurs to negotiate better deals and avoid making proposals that are unrealistic or out of line with industry standards.

Finally, Black entrepreneurs can also consider using software products designed to assist with negotiations and closing deals. One such product is DealHub. This product provides negotiation management tools that help Black entrepreneurs to prepare, track, and close deals more efficiently. It also offers a secure platform for storing and sharing documents, and it helps to streamline the negotiation process and automate workflows.

Thus, Black entrepreneurs should prepare for negotiations by identifying their goals, understanding the other party's needs and interests, and researching market rates and industry standards. By doing so, they can better position themselves to make proposals that are more likely to be accepted and achieve their desired outcomes. Additionally, using software products such as DealHub can help Black entrepreneurs to streamline the negotiation process and automate workflows, making it more efficient and effective.

COMMUNICATING CLEARLY

Effective communication is a key component of successful negotiations, and Black entrepreneurs should communicate clearly and concisely during negotiations to avoid misunderstandings and build trust with the other party. Clear communication helps to establish a positive and productive negotiation atmosphere.

One important aspect of clear communication is avoiding the use of aggressive or confrontational language. This includes using language that is hostile, dismissive, or disrespectful. Such language can damage the relationship with the other party and can lead to a breakdown in communication and ultimately, a failure to reach an agreement.

Instead, Black entrepreneurs should use language that is respectful, professional, and focused on the issues at hand. This includes using active listening skills, asking questions, and paraphrasing the other party's position to ensure that they understand it. By communicating in a clear, concise and respectful way, Black entrepreneurs can create an environment of trust and cooperation that is more likely to lead to a successful outcome.

For example, a Black entrepreneur negotiating with a potential investor should avoid using confrontational language such as "I refuse to lower my asking price" or "I will not compromise on this issue." Instead, they should communicate their position clearly and concisely, using language such as "I understand your concerns and I am willing to consider alternative options to meet our mutual goals."

So, Black entrepreneurs should communicate clearly and concisely during negotiations, and avoid using aggressive or confrontational language. Clear and respectful communication helps to establish a positive and productive negotiation atmosphere and is more likely to lead to a successful outcome. By using active listening skills, asking questions and communicating in a respectful and professional way, Black entrepreneurs can build trust and cooperation with the other party and achieve their desired outcomes.

BUILDING TRUST AND RAPPORT

Building trust and rapport with the other party is an essential aspect of successful negotiations. When trust and rapport are present, both parties are more likely to be open to compromise and to reach a mutually beneficial agreement.

One way to build trust and rapport is by being reliable and consistent in your actions and words. This means following through on commitments, being honest and transparent, and keeping your promises. Black entrepreneurs should also make an effort to understand the other party's perspective and to show that they are willing to listen and consider their concerns.

Another way to build trust and rapport is by building a personal connection with the other party. This can be done by sharing personal stories or experiences, finding common ground, or building a relationship outside of the negotiation. Building a personal connection can help to establish a sense of trust and understanding between the parties, which can make the negotiation process smoother and more successful.

For example, an entrepreneur negotiating with a new supplier could build trust and rapport by visiting the supplier's facility, learning about their operations and showing genuine interest in their business. By taking the time to understand the supplier's perspective and building a personal connection, the Black entrepreneur is more likely to establish a mutually beneficial agreement.

So, building trust and rapport with the other party is an essential aspect of successful negotiations. Black entrepreneurs should work to establish trust and rapport by being reliable and consistent, understanding the other party's perspective, and building a personal connection. By doing so, they can create an environment of trust and cooperation that is more likely to lead to a mutually beneficial agreement.

BEING FLEXIBLE

Being flexible is a key component of successful negotiations, and Black entrepreneurs should be open to finding creative solutions that meet the needs of both parties. This means being willing to consider alternative options, to compromise and to think outside the box. As the famous quote goes, "Flexibility is the key to stability" - Confucius.

One way to be flexible is by being willing to consider alternative options. This means being open to different ways of achieving your goals and being willing to compromise. Black entrepreneurs should be willing to listen to the other party's perspective and to consider options that they may not have initially considered. This can lead to a more mutually beneficial agreement.

Another way to be flexible is by thinking outside the box. This means being willing to consider unconventional solutions and to take a creative approach to problem-solving. By thinking creatively, Black entrepreneurs can come up with solutions that meet the needs of both parties and that are more likely to be accepted.

For example, a Black entrepreneur negotiating with a landlord to lease a commercial space could be flexible by considering alternative options such as a flexible lease term or a co-working arrangement. By being open to alternative options and thinking creatively, the Black entrepreneur can come to an agreement that meets the needs of both parties.

Again, being flexible is a key component of successful negotiations and Black entrepreneurs should be open to finding creative solutions that meet the needs of both parties. By considering alternative options, being willing to compromise, and thinking creatively, Black entrepreneurs can come to mutually beneficial agreements. Flexibility is the key to stability, and it can lead to a more successful outcome for both parties.

ADVANCED NEGOTIATING TACTICS

As a Black entrepreneur, it is important to have a solid understanding of advanced negotiating tactics in order to obtain the outcomes you desire. As the famous quote goes, "The best deal is the one where both sides walk away happy." - Neil Rackham. In this section, we will discuss advanced tactics that can be used to find creative solutions and achieve mutually beneficial agreements.

1. Identifying and Leveraging Your BATNA (Best Alternative to a Negotiated Agreement): Knowing your BATNA is a powerful tool that can be used to identify your walk-away point and to increase your leverage in negotiations.
2. Using Anchoring: Anchoring is a tactic that involves establishing an initial position that is used as a reference point for future negotiations. By establishing an anchor, you can influence the other party's perception of what is fair and reasonable.
3. Building a coalition: Building a coalition involves enlisting the support of other parties who have a vested interest in the outcome of the negotiation. This can increase your leverage and improve your chances of reaching a mutually beneficial agreement.
4. Using the "ZOPA" (Zone of Possible Agreement): The ZOPA is the range of possible agreements that can be reached in a negotiation. By identifying the ZOPA, Black entrepreneurs can identify areas of compromise and find creative solutions that meet the needs of both parties.
5. Using the "Win-Win" approach: The win-win approach is a collaborative negotiation strategy that focuses on finding solutions that meet the needs of both parties. By using a win-win approach, Black entrepreneurs can achieve mutually beneficial agreements that lead to profitable outcomes.

So, advanced negotiating tactics can be used to find creative solutions that lead to profitable outcomes. Black entrepreneurs should familiarize themselves with techniques such as identifying and leveraging their BATNA, using anchoring, building a coalition, using the ZOPA, and using the win-win approach. By doing so, they can achieve mutually beneficial agreements

CLOSING THE DEAL

Closing a deal is the final step in the negotiation process, and it is important for Black entrepreneurs to be confident and decisive when closing a deal. By following through on any agreed upon terms and being able to close the deal quickly and efficiently, Black entrepreneurs can increase the chances of success and profitability.

1. Be Confident: When closing a deal, it is important to project confidence and to be decisive. This means being able to articulate your position clearly, being willing to make concessions, and being able to close the deal quickly and efficiently.

2. Follow Through on Agreed Upon Terms: Once a deal is reached, it is important for Black entrepreneurs to follow through on any agreed upon terms. This means being timely in delivering on any commitments, being responsive to the other party's needs, and being willing to negotiate any issues that may arise.
    a. Bonus Tip: Use a Closing Script: Having a closing script can be helpful when closing a deal. This script should include key points such as the benefits of the deal, any contingencies, and any next steps.
3. Use a Closing Checklist: Having a closing checklist can be helpful in ensuring that all necessary steps are taken to close the deal. This can include tasks such as finalizing the contract, obtaining necessary approvals, and scheduling follow-up meetings.
4. Conduct Independent Research: Before closing a deal, Black entrepreneurs should conduct independent research as due diligence to ensure that they have a good understanding of the other party's interests, and that they have considered all possible alternatives. This research can include reviewing financial statements, talking to industry experts, and gathering market data. This research can help to identify any potential risks or opportunities, and can help Black entrepreneurs to make informed decisions.

So, closing a deal is the final step in the negotiation process, and it is important for Black entrepreneurs to be confident and decisive when closing a deal. By following through on any agreed upon terms, and by being able to close the deal quickly and efficiently, Black entrepreneurs can increase the chances of success and profitability. Additionally, by using a closing script, a closing checklist, and conducting independent research, Black entrepreneurs can ensure that they have considered all necessary steps to close a deal.

Chapter Twenty-Three:
Protecting Your Intellectual Property

As a Black entrepreneur in the 2020's, it is important to understand the importance of protecting your intellectual property. This includes understanding the different types of intellectual property, such as trademarks, copyrights, and patents, and knowing how to properly secure and protect them. In this chapter, we will cover the following topics: understanding intellectual property, conducting a trademark search, filing for trademarks, protecting copyrights, filing for patents, and seeking professional advice.

Intellectual property refers to the creations of the mind, such as inventions, literary and artistic works, and symbols, names, images, and designs used in commerce. These creations can be protected by legal means, such as patents, trademarks, and copyrights. As an entrepreneur, it is important to understand the different types of intellectual property and how to secure and protect them.

Conducting a trademark search is an important step in protecting your intellectual property. A trademark search can help you to determine if a similar trademark is already in use and can help you to avoid potential legal issues.

Filing for trademarks is another important step in protecting your intellectual property. A trademark can help to protect the name, logo, or slogan of your business, and it can be used to prevent others from using a similar trademark. Be sure to complete the step of registering your trademarks with Customs and Border Patrol for enforcement purposes. You can have a trademark, but if you fail to register your trademark with the CBP, then you risk the threat of counterfeit goods flooding your market. Contact my office to learn more about this nuanced area of IP Law.

Protecting copyrights is also important, as it helps to protect the original works of authorship such as literature, music, and art. You can copyright images and videos, too. It's important to note that you own the copyright to anything you create, however, if you want your rights to be enforceable in a court of law, then you need to register your copyright with the USPTO.

Filing for patents is another important step in protecting your intellectual property. A patent can help to protect an invention or a new and useful process, machine, manufacture, or composition of matter, or any new and useful improvement thereof.

Finally, seeking professional advice from a licensed attorney can help you to understand the best ways to protect your intellectual property. For more information and to set up a consultation with a licensed attorney, refer to www.SholdonDaniels.com.

In this chapter, we will cover all these topics and more, providing you with the knowledge and tools you need to protect your intellectual property and secure your business's future.

UNDERSTANDING INTELLECTUAL PROPERTY

As a Black entrepreneur, it is important to understand the different types of intellectual property and how they can protect your business assets. Intellectual property refers to the creations of the mind, such as inventions, literary and artistic works, and symbols, names, images, and designs used in commerce. These creations can be protected by legal means, such as patents, trademarks, and copyrights.

Trademarks are used to protect the name, logo, or slogan of a business. This can prevent others from using a similar trademark and can help to identify and distinguish a business's products or services. For example, a Black entrepreneur who owns a clothing line could file for a trademark on the brand name to prevent other clothing lines from using the same name.

Copyrights are used to protect original works of authorship such as literature, music, and art. This can prevent others from reproducing or distributing a work without permission. For example, a Black entrepreneur who creates a painting could file for a copyright on the artwork to prevent others from reproducing it without permission.

Patents are used to protect an invention or a new and useful process, machine, manufacture, or composition of matter, or any new and useful improvement thereof. This can prevent others from making, using, or selling an invention without permission. For example, a Black entrepreneur who invents a new type of software could file for a patent to prevent others from using or selling the software without permission.

Clearly, understanding the different types of intellectual property and how they can protect your business assets is important for all, but especially for Black entrepreneurs. Black people are constantly creating treands and coming up with new ideas, and those trends and new ideas often times get appropriated by major corporations and exploited for profit. By filing for trademarks, copyrights, and patents, Black creators and entrepreneurs can protect their business assets and prevent others from using them without permission. By understanding the different types of intellectual property, Black entrepreneurs can take steps to secure and protect their intellectual property, and secure their future.

CONDUCTING A TRADEMARK SEARCH

It is important to conduct a trademark search before choosing a business name or logo. This is because trademarks are used to protect the name, logo, or slogan of a business and can prevent others from using a similar trademark. A trademark search can help you to determine if a similar trademark is already in use and can help you to avoid potential legal issues.

To conduct a trademark search, you can use the United States Patent and Trademark Office (USPTO) database. The USPTO database is a searchable database of registered trademarks, and it can be used to search for trademarks that are similar to the name or logo that you are considering for your business. The search can be done by keywords, class of goods and services, or by the specific trademark number.

It is also important to consider searching for trademarks on the state level, as well as at the federal level. Some states also have their own trademark registration system.

Additionally, it is also important to conduct a common law search. You can do this by searching for unregistered trademarks that are being used in commerce. This can be done by searching online, in business directories, or by talking to industry experts.

It is important to note that even if the name or logo you want is not registered, it could be in use by another company, and it could still be an infringement on their rights.

Once you have conducted your trademark search and determined that your business name or logo is available, you can file for a trademark with the USPTO. This will give you legal protection for your business name or logo, and it will prevent others from using a similar trademark. Trademarks can get expensive to obtain, so if you have a limited budget and a lot of intellectual property, I suggest trademarking your brand logo first.

In any event, conducting a trademark search is an important step for Black entrepreneurs. By conducting a trademark search, Black entrepreneurs can ensure that their business name or logo is available and not already in use, and can avoid potential legal issues. By using the USPTO database and conducting a common law search, Black entrepreneurs can take the necessary steps to protect their business assets and secure their future.

FILING FOR TRADEMARKS

Obviously, it is important to file for trademarks in order to protect your business name, logo, and other branding elements. Trademarks are used to protect the name, logo, or slogan of a business, and can prevent others from using a similar trademark. By filing for a trademark, Black entrepreneurs can secure legal protection for their business name, logo, and other branding elements and can prevent others from using them without permission.

To file for a trademark, Black entrepreneurs should start by conducting a trademark search. This will ensure that the business name or logo is available and not already in use. Once the trademark search is complete, Black entrepreneurs can file for a trademark with the United States Patent and Trademark Office (USPTO). The USPTO is the federal agency responsible for registering trademarks and provides an online application process.

When filing for a trademark, Black entrepreneurs should provide the USPTO with the following information:

- A clear and accurate representation of the trademark
- A description of the goods or services that the trademark will be used for
- The class of goods or services that the trademark will be used for
- The name and address of the person or entity that owns the trademark
- A statement of use or a statement that the trademark is intended to be used in commerce.

It is important to note that the process of filing for a trademark can be complex and time-consuming. It is recommendable to seek the help of a licensed attorney to assist in the process.

Once the trademark is filed, the USPTO will review the application and will either approve or reject it. If the application is approved, the trademark will be registered and you will receive a certificate of registration for your mark.

So, filing for trademarks is an important step for Black entrepreneurs. By filing for trademarks, they can protect their business name, logo, and other branding elements, and can prevent others from using them without permission. By filing for a trademark with the USPTO and seeking the help of a licensed attorney, Black bosses can take the necessary steps to ensure the integrity of their brand in the open market.

PROTECTING COPYRIGHTS

Iit is essential to take steps to protect your copyrights. This includes registering your works with the Copyright Office and including copyright notices on your materials.

Registration with the Copyright Office is a legal requirement for enforcing your copyrights in court. By registering your works, you will have a legal record of your ownership, which can be used to prove your rights in a court of law. Additionally, registering your works allows you to seek statutory damages and attorney's fees in the event of copyright infringement.

Including a copyright notice on your materials is another way to protect your copyrights. A copyright notice is a statement that informs others that your work is protected by copyright law and identifies you as the copyright holder. While including a copyright notice is not a legal requirement, it serves as a reminder to others that your work is protected and can serve as evidence of your ownership in the event of infringement.

It's also important to note that if the material is created by an employee during their work hours, and the company owns the copyright, not the employee.

In summary, Black entrepreneurs should take steps to protect their copyrights by registering their works with the Copyright Office and including copyright notices on their materials. This will ensure that you have the legal tools necessary to enforce your rights and protect your valuable intellectual property.

FILING FOR PATENTS

When starting a business, one important step that entrepreneurs should consider is filing for patents to protect their inventions or innovative ideas. This can help prevent others from profiting from their hard work and creativity. As Black entrepreneurs, it is important to understand the value of protecting your ideas and the potential for financial gain through licensing and selling your patented invention.

Here are some notable patents held by Black entrepreneurs:

- George Washington Carver, a prominent agricultural scientist, held several patents related to his work on crop rotation and crop derivatives, such as over 100 products made from peanuts.
- Dr. Mark Dean, an engineer and computer scientist, holds several patents in the field of computer architecture, including the design of the Industry Standard Architecture (ISA) bus, which is used in most computers today.
- Dr. Lonnie G. Johnson, an engineer and inventor, holds over 80 patents, including the invention of the Super Soaker water gun.
- Dr. Patricia Bath, an ophthalmologist, holds several patents related to her invention of the Laserphaco Probe, a device used in cataract surgery.

- Dr. Shirley Jackson, a physicist, holds several patents related to her work in telecommunications, including the invention of the touch-tone telephone.

It is important to note that patents can be expensive to obtain, but there are resources available to help Black entrepreneurs navigate the patent process, such as the National Black Lawyers and the National Association of Black Women Entrepreneurs. Additionally, there are organizations that support black inventors and entrepreneurs, such as the National Inventors Hall of Fame, which inducts inventors of all races, and the National Black Inventors Hall of Fame.

Filing for patents can be an important step for Black entrepreneurs to protect their inventions and innovative ideas. By understanding the value of protecting your ideas, and the potential for financial gain through licensing and selling your patented invention, Black entrepreneurs can increase their chances of success in the business world.

SEEKING PROFESSIONAL ADVICE

As a black entrepreneur, it is important to protect your ideas and inventions by obtaining patents. But again, the process of obtaining a patent can be complex and time-consuming. To ensure that your patent application is handled properly, it may be beneficial to seek the advice of a lawyer or intellectual property expert. My office is available 24/7 to answer your call at 1-844-SHOLDON.

A lawyer can help guide you through the process of filing a patent application and advise you on the best way to protect your invention. They can also help you navigate any legal issues that may arise during the patent application process.

An intellectual property expert can help you conduct a patent search to ensure that your invention is truly unique and does not infringe on existing patents. They can also help you evaluate the potential market for your invention and advise you on the best way to monetize it.

In addition, both a lawyer and an intellectual property expert can also help you with trademark and copyright registration, as well as advise on other legal matters related to your business, such as contracts and negotiations.

Keep in mind that seeking professional advice can be costly, but it is a worthwhile investment to protect your intellectual property and your business.

In conclusion, as a black entrepreneur, seeking professional advice from a lawyer or intellectual property expert can help you obtain your patents properly and provide you with the necessary guidance to protect your ideas and inventions. This will help you to build a successful and sustainable business.

Chapter Twenty-Four:
Expanding Your Business Internationally

"Expanding your business internationally" is a crucial step for any entrepreneur looking to take their business to the next level. This chapter will explore the various aspects of international expansion, including researching international markets, understanding cultural differences, developing a global marketing strategy, establishing a local presence abroad, complying with regulations, and seeking professional advice. Each of these topics is essential to the success of your international expansion and will be discussed in depth to provide you with the knowledge and tools you need to navigate the complexities of doing business on a global scale. Whether you're a seasoned entrepreneur or just starting out, this chapter will provide valuable insights and practical advice to help you succeed in the global marketplace.

RESEARCHING INTERNATIONAL MARKETS

When it comes to expanding your business internationally, one of the most important steps is researching potential markets to determine their viability and potential for success. As a Black entrepreneur, there may be certain markets that are particularly well-suited to your business, such as emerging markets in Africa and Europe. In this section, I will roll out the specific steps you should take when researching these markets, as well as the key factors to consider when assessing their potential.

The first step in researching international markets is to gather information about the market's size, growth potential, and overall economic conditions. This can be done by reviewing government statistics, consulting with industry experts, and conducting market research. For example, you can use online tools like the World Bank's Data Catalog to access data on GDP, population, and other economic indicators for specific countries.

Once you have a general understanding of the market, it's important to research the specific industry or sector in which you plan to operate. This will help you identify potential competitors, as well as areas of opportunity within the market. For example, if you're looking to expand your business into the technology sector in Africa, you might research the latest trends and innovations in the industry, as well as the number of startups and established companies operating in the space.

Another important factor to consider when researching international markets is cultural differences. As a Black entrepreneur, it's important to be aware of the cultural norms and customs in the market you're considering. This can include things like business etiquette, communication styles, and social customs. For example, if you're looking to expand your business into Europe, it's important to be aware of the different ways in which business is conducted in different countries, and to tailor your approach accordingly.

Finally, it's important to consider the regulatory environment in the market you're considering. This can include things like taxes, tariffs, and other trade barriers, as well as regulations related to labor, intellectual property, and other areas. As a Black entrepreneur, it's important to be aware of these regulations and to seek out professional advice if necessary to ensure that you're able to comply with them.

Therefore, researching international markets is an essential step for any Black entrepreneur looking to expand their business internationally. By gathering information about the market's size, growth potential, and overall economic conditions, researching the specific industry or sector, understanding cultural differences and regulatory environment, you can make informed decisions about which markets to enter and how to best position your business for success in those markets.

UNDERSTANDING CULTURAL DIFFERENCES

When expanding a business internationally, it's crucial to understand and appreciate the cultural differences that may impact operations in different countries. As a Black entrepreneur, it's important to be aware of these cultural nuances and to consider how they may affect your business. In this section, we will use cultural differences between Pakistan and India compared to American business culture as examples to illustrate the importance of understanding cultural differences when expanding your business operations internationally.

One of the most significant cultural differences that Black entrepreneurs need to be aware of when expanding their business operations to Pakistan and India is the importance of building relationships. In these countries, building and maintaining personal relationships is considered a critical part of doing business. This means that it's essential to take the time to get to know your business partners and to build trust with them over time. In contrast, American business culture tends to be more transactional, focusing on the bottom line and getting things done quickly.

Another cultural difference that Black entrepreneurs need to be aware of is the concept of hierarchy. In Pakistan and India, there is a strong emphasis on hierarchy and respect for authority. This means that it's important to be aware of who holds the power in a given situation and to address them accordingly. In contrast, American business culture tends to be more egalitarian and less formal, with a greater emphasis on teamwork and collaboration.

Communication styles also vary greatly between American and Pakistan and India culture. In Pakistan and India, indirect communication is more common, and people may avoid saying "no" directly. This means that it's important to pay attention to nonverbal cues and to be aware of the underlying meaning of what's being said. In contrast, American business culture tends to be more direct, with a focus on getting to the point and being clear and concise.

Finally, it's important to be aware of the different attitudes towards time in Pakistan and India compared to American culture. In Pakistan and India, time may be perceived more flexibly, with a greater willingness to make adjustments and changes as needed. In contrast, American culture tends to be more punctual, with a greater emphasis on meeting deadlines and sticking to schedules.

It is important to note that understanding cultural differences is an essential part of expanding your business operations internationally as a Black entrepreneur. By being aware of the cultural nuances in different countries, you can better anticipate and navigate any challenges that may arise. By understanding the importance of building relationships, the concept of hierarchy, communication styles, and attitudes towards time in foreign countries compared to American culture, you can build a strong foundation for your business in these markets and set yourself up for long-term success.

DEVELOPING A GLOBAL MARKETING STRATEGY

When expanding a business internationally, it's crucial to develop a global marketing strategy that takes into account cultural differences and language barriers. It's important to tailor your marketing approach to the unique needs of the market you're entering, while also being mindful of any cultural nuances that may impact your efforts. In this section, we will explore the specific steps you should take when developing a global marketing strategy and why it is important to learn a second language, or hire a translator for this end.

The first step in developing a global marketing strategy is to conduct market research to understand the target audience and their needs. This will help you identify the most effective marketing channels and tactics to use in the market you're entering. For example, if you're expanding your business to a country where social media is popular, it would be wise to invest in a social media marketing campaign.

Once you have a clear understanding of the target audience, you'll need to consider cultural differences that may impact your marketing efforts. This can include things like color symbolism, communication styles, and social customs. For example, in some cultures, certain colors may have positive or negative connotations, so it's important to be mindful of this when designing marketing materials.

Another important factor to consider when developing a global marketing strategy is language barriers. It's important to ensure that your marketing materials are translated correctly and that the language used is appropriate for the target audience. In order to achieve this, it is highly recommended to learn a second language, and to have a team member who is fluent in the target language. This will allow you to communicate more effectively with potential customers and to better understand their needs and preferences.

Finally, it's important to be aware of regulations related to marketing and advertising in the market you're entering. This can include things like labeling requirements, consumer protection laws, and advertising standards. As a Black entrepreneur, it's important to be aware of these regulations and to seek out professional advice if necessary to ensure that you're able to comply with them.

To recap, developing a global marketing strategy that takes into account cultural differences and language barriers is essential for Black entrepreneurs looking to expand their business internationally. By conducting market research, understanding cultural nuances, learning a second language and being aware of the regulations related to marketing and advertising, you can create effective marketing campaigns that resonate with the target audience and set your business up for tremendous success in the global marketplace.

ESTABLISHING A LOCAL PRESENCE ABROAD

When expanding a business internationally, it's important to establish a local presence in the target market in order to build trust and credibility with customers. As a Black entrepreneur, this can be especially challenging, but by considering the unique needs of the market and working with local partners, you can create a strong presence and position your business for success. In this section, we will explore the specific steps you should take when establishing a local presence, including setting up a physical location or hiring local staff, and working with local ambassadors to meet this end.

One of the most important steps in establishing a local presence is to set up a physical location in the target market. This can include opening a retail store or office, or renting a warehouse or manufacturing facility. Having a physical presence in the market will help you establish trust and credibility with customers and suppliers, and will also make it easier for you to conduct business in the country.

Another key step in establishing a local presence is to hire local staff. By having a local team in place, you'll be able to better understand the market and the needs of customers, as well as build relationships with local partners and suppliers. This will also help you to navigate local regulations and laws, and to better understand the cultural norms and customs of the market.

Working with local ambassadors is also an important step in establishing a local presence. These can include local business leaders, government officials, or community leaders who can serve as advocates for your business and help you to connect with potential customers and partners. This can help to build trust and credibility in the market, and can also provide valuable insights into the local business environment and cultural norms.

Finally, it's important to be aware of regulations related to setting up a physical location or hiring local staff in the market you're entering. This can include things like labor laws, immigration laws, and tax regulations. As a Black entrepreneur, it's important to be aware of these regulations and to seek out professional advice if necessary to ensure that you're able to comply with them.

Again, establishing a local presence is an essential step for Black entrepreneurs looking to expand their business internationally. By setting up a physical location, hiring local staff, working with local ambassadors and being aware of the regulations related to setting up a physical location or hiring local staff, you can create a strong presence in the market, build trust and credibility with customers, and position your business to win in the global marketplace.

COMPLYING WITH REGULATIONS

When expanding a business internationally, it's important to comply with all relevant regulations and laws in the target market. This can be a complex and challenging task, but by understanding the legal requirements and working with local attorneys, you can ensure that your business is in compliance and set yourself up for success. In this section, I will explore the specific steps you should take when complying with regulations and laws in your target market and the importance of working with local attorneys.

The first step in complying with regulations and laws in your target market is to understand the specific requirements that pertain to your business. This may include things like taxes, labor laws, environmental regulations, and intellectual property laws. It's important to research and understand the legal requirements in the market you're entering, and to seek out professional advice if necessary.

Another important step in complying with regulations and laws is to work with local attorneys. Local attorneys will be able to advise you on the specific requirements in the market you're entering and can help you navigate the legal system. They can also assist you in drafting contracts, obtaining licenses and permits, and ensuring that your business is in compliance with all relevant regulations and laws.

It's also important to be aware of any cultural or language barriers that may impact your ability to comply with regulations and laws. This can include things like misunderstandings about business practices or customs, or difficulties communicating with local officials. By working with local attorneys, you can overcome these barriers and ensure that your business is in compliance with all relevant regulations and laws.

Finally, it's important to be aware of the regulations and laws that pertain to your business in your home country. This may include things like export regulations and laws related to foreign investments. By understanding the legal requirements in both your home country and the target market, you can ensure that your business is in compliance with all relevant regulations and laws.

So, complying with regulations and laws is an essential step for Black entrepreneurs looking to expand their business internationally. By understanding the specific requirements in the market you're entering, working with local attorneys, being aware of cultural and language barriers, and understanding the regulations and laws that pertain to your business in your home country, you can ensure that your business is in compliance with all relevant regulations and laws and pave a path for dominance in the global marketplace.

SEEKING PROFESSIONAL ADVICE

Expanding a business internationally can be a complex and challenging task, and as a Black entrepreneur, it can be especially difficult to navigate the process without the right support. One effective way to gain the knowledge and support you need is by seeking professional advice from foreign lawyers or business consultants. In this section, I will explore the practical steps Black entrepreneurs can take to seek professional advice and how it can help them succeed in the global marketplace.

The first step in seeking professional advice is to identify the specific areas in which you need support. This may include things like understanding the legal and regulatory environment in the target market, developing a global marketing strategy, or establishing a local presence. By identifying the specific areas in which you need support, you can better target your search for professional advice.

Once you have identified the areas in which you need support, it's important to research and identify potential advisors. This can include foreign lawyers or business consultants who specialize in the specific areas in which you need support. You can research online, ask for recommendations from other entrepreneurs, or even attend international trade shows or networking events to find potential advisors.

It's also important to consider the language skills and cultural background of potential advisors. As a Black entrepreneur, it's important to have an advisor who can understand your perspective and who can communicate effectively in the target market. It's also important to consider if the advisor has experience working with Black entrepreneurs and has a diverse team.

When you have identified a potential advisor, it's important to schedule a consultation to discuss your needs and determine if they are the right fit for your business. During the consultation, you should ask about their qualifications, experience, and approach to working with clients. You should also discuss their fees and how they intend to bill for their services.

Now you should understand a little more about taking your business international, and seeking professional advice is an essential step for entrepreneurs looking to expand their business internationally. I implore you, do not attempt to expand your business into another country without having ever met with an international business lawyer first. By identifying the specific areas in which you need support, researching potential advisors, considering language skills and cultural background, and having a consultation, you can find the right foreign lawyer or business consultant to guide you through the process and ensure your success in the marketplace.

Chapter Twenty-Five:
Building Strong Customer Relationships

"Building Strong Customer Relationships" is a key aspect of any successful business, and this chapter will explore the various strategies and tactics that all Black entrepreneurs can use to create and maintain strong relationships with their customers. From providing excellent customer service to building trust, listening to customer feedback, showing appreciation, and building loyalty, this chapter will provide valuable insights and practical advice to help Black entrepreneurs create a loyal customer base that will drive their business forward. The chapter also covers seeking professional advice for building relationships. Whether you're just starting out or have been in business for years, this chapter will provide the knowledge and tools you need to create and maintain strong, long-lasting relationships with your customers, which is the foundation for any successful business.

PROVIDING EXCELLENT CUSTOMER SERVICE

Providing excellent customer service is an essential part of building strong, long-term relationships with customers, and as a Black entrepreneur, it's important to strive for the highest level of customer service possible. However, Black entrepreneurs may have to overcome prevalent stereotypes and biases that can make it more challenging to create and maintain strong customer relationships. In this part of the book, we will explore the importance of providing excellent customer service and how Black entrepreneurs can take extra care to combat stereotypes and biases in this regard.

One of the most important things to consider when providing excellent customer service is to be responsive and attentive to your customers' needs. This means being available to answer questions, address concerns, and resolve issues as quickly and efficiently as possible. By being responsive and attentive, you can build trust and credibility with your customers, which is essential for creating strong, long-term relationships.

Another key aspect of providing excellent customer service is to be transparent and honest with your customers. This means being upfront about your products or services, and any potential issues that may arise. By being transparent and honest, you can build trust and credibility with your customers, which will help to create strong, long-term relationships.

It's also important to be aware of the stereotypes and biases that Black entrepreneurs may face when providing excellent customer service. Some customers may have unconscious biases and may make assumptions about the quality of service that a Black-owned business can provide. "Aggressive," "combative," "mean," and "angry" are how mainstream media has portrayed the ADOS to the outside world for decades. For example, I once went to a remote portuguese island known as Terciera. It's in the middle of the Atlantic ocean–basically cut off from the world except by way of internet and television media. When I was there, I saw a few American programs being shown. Besides professional athletes and reality TV stars, the locals had never really seen or interacted with any ADOS. The only portrayals of ADOS that they got were athletes playing ball, and so-called "black housewives" slinging mud and fightinf each other in designer clothes. It was embarrassing to say the least. I often had to explain to people that most ADOS are not like that, and that we occupy all walks of life in America right along with other ethnic groups. As a Black entrepreneur, it's important to be aware of these stereotypes and biases and to take extra care to combat them by providing excellent customer service that exceeds expectations.

Finally, it's important to seek professional advice to ensure that your customer service is at the highest level possible. This can include working with a customer service consultant or attending training workshops. With the right knowledge and tools, Black entrepreneurs can provide excellent customer service that builds strong, long-term relationships with customers.

Clearly, providing excellent customer service is an essential part of building strong, long-term relationships with customers as an entrepreneur. But by being responsive, attentive, transparent, honest and aware of stereotypes and biases, and seeking professional advice, Black entrepreneurs can build trust, create a loyal customer base, and set themselves up for long-term success in the marketplace.

BUILDING TRUST

Building trust with customers and clients is essential for creating strong relationships and driving business success. As a Black entrepreneur, it's important to understand the importance of trust and how it can be built through honesty, transparency, and responsiveness. Unfortunately, when one Black entrepreneur provides terrible customer service, it reinforces in the minds of customers the false notion that all Black entrepreneurs provide sub-par customer service. So, take extra care to uphold the dignity and positive perception of Black entrepreneurs in the minds of consumers. In this section, I will explore the importance of building trust, using quotes from prominent figures throughout history to illustrate the importance of this concept.

"Trust is the foundation of leadership." - John C. Maxwell

Trust is the foundation of any strong relationship, and as a Black entrepreneur, it's imperative that you work to build trust with your customers and clients. One of the most effective ways to build trust is by being honest and transparent in all your business dealings. This means being upfront and honest about your products or services, and any potential issues that may arise. By being honest and transparent, you can build credibility and trust with your customers.

"The best way to gain trust is to be trustworthy." - Ralph Waldo Emerson

Another key aspect of building trust is being responsive to your customers' needs. This means being available to answer questions, address concerns, and resolve issues as quickly and efficiently as possible. By being responsive, you can show your customers that you care about their needs and are committed to providing them with the best possible service.

"Responsiveness is the mark of a reliable and trustworthy professional." - Brian Tracy

It's also important to be aware of any stereotypes or biases that may impact the ability to build trust as a Black entrepreneur. This can include things like preconceptions about the level of service that a Black-owned business can provide. By being aware of these stereotypes and biases and working to overcome them through honesty, transparency, and responsiveness, Black entrepreneurs can build trust and credibility with their customers.

"Trust is not something that you can ask for, buy or borrow. Trust is earned." - Unknown

Obviously, building trust is an essential step for Black entrepreneurs looking to create strong relationships with customers and clients. By being honest, transparent, responsive and aware of stereotypes and biases, Black entrepreneurs can earn the trust of their customers and see long-term success in the marketplace.

LISTENING TO CUSTOMER FEEDBACK

As a Black entrepreneur, it's important to understand the importance of listening to customer feedback and taking it into account when making business decisions. Your customers are the lifeblood of your business, and their opinions and needs should be at the forefront of your mind when making decisions about your products or services.

Listening to customer feedback can be done in a variety of ways, such as surveys, focus groups, or one-on-one interviews. These methods allow you to get a sense of what your customers like and dislike about your business, as well as their needs and wants. Additionally, you can also use social media and online reviews as a way to gather customer feedback. This will help you to understand the customer's point of view and improve your product and services.

Once you've gathered feedback from your customers, it's important to take the time to analyze it and determine what changes need to be made. This may mean making changes to your products or services, adjusting your pricing, or revising your marketing strategy. Whatever changes you make, it's important to communicate them to your customers, so they know that you value their feedback and are taking it into account.

It's also important to keep in mind that customer feedback is not always positive. It may be difficult to hear criticism of your business, but it's important to remember that it's an opportunity to improve and grow. Take the time to consider the feedback, even if it's negative, and determine if there are any valid points that can be used to improve your business.

Remember, listening to customer feedback is an important aspect of being a successful Black entrepreneur. By actively seeking out and considering feedback from your customers, you'll be able to make informed decisions that will help your business thrive.

SHOWING APPRECIATION

As a Black entrepreneur, it is essential to show appreciation to your customers and clients through various gestures such as thank-you notes, special offers, and exclusive events. This not only helps to build and maintain positive relationships with your customers, but it also sets your business apart in a competitive market.

Thank-you notes, for example, can be a simple and effective way to show appreciation for your customers' business. A handwritten note can be a personal touch that goes a long way in making a customer feel valued and appreciated. This can also serve as a reminder to the customer that your business cares about their satisfaction and encourages repeat business.

Special offers and exclusive events are also great ways to show appreciation to your customers. Exclusive events, such as VIP shopping nights or customer appreciation days, can provide customers with a unique and memorable experience that sets your business apart from the competition. Special offers, such as discounts or freebies, can also be a way to thank customers for their loyalty and encourage repeat business.

I host an annual holiday party where I invite my friends, colleagues, clients, and community partners to come celebrate the accomplishments and lessons learned during the year. This gives me an opportunity to rekindle old connections and to show love to the ones that helped make my law firm a successful business. Showing appreciation is always a good strategy.

In addition to showing appreciation to your customers, it is also important to show appreciation to your employees. A positive work environment and a culture of appreciation can lead to a more motivated and productive workforce.

So, showing appreciation to your customers and clients through gestures such as thank-you notes, special offers, and exclusive events is an important aspect of building and maintaining positive relationships in Black entrepreneurship. It sets your business apart and helps to create a loyal customer base that will support your business for years to come.

BUILDING LOYALTY

"The only way to do great work is to love what you do." -Steve Jobs

As a Black entrepreneur, building loyalty with your customers and clients is essential to the success of your business. Consistently delivering high-quality products or services is one of the most effective ways to achieve this.

One key aspect of delivering high-quality products or services is to have a deep understanding and passion for your industry. As Steve Jobs stated, "*The only way to do great work is to love what you do.*" By having a genuine passion for your business, you will be more motivated to go the extra mile to ensure that your customers are satisfied.

In addition to having a passion for your industry, it is also important to be attentive to your customers' needs and concerns. As Oprah Winfrey said, "*The greatest thing you'll ever learn is just to love and be loved in return.*" By listening to your customers and addressing their needs, you are showing them that you care about their satisfaction, which will ultimately lead to increased loyalty.

Another way to build loyalty with your customers is to provide excellent customer service. As Maya Angelou said, "*I've learned that people will forget what you said, people will forget what you did, but people will never forget how you made them feel.*" By providing excellent customer service, you are making your customers feel valued and appreciated, which will lead to increased loyalty.

So, building loyalty with your customers and clients is essential for Black entrepreneurs. By consistently delivering high-quality products or services, having a deep understanding and passion for your industry, being attentive to your customers' needs, and providing excellent customer service, you can create a loyal customer base that will support your business for years to come.

SEEKING PROFESSIONAL ADVICE

"The customer's perception is your reality." - Kate Zabriskie

As a Black entrepreneur, building strong relationships with your customers and clients is crucial to the success of your business. One way to achieve this is by seeking the advice of a customer service expert or consultant. These professionals can provide valuable insights and strategies for improving your customer service and building loyalty with your customers.

One well-known customer service consultant who offers expertise in this area is Kate Zabriskie. Kate is the founder of Business Training Works, a company that specializes in customer service training and consulting. She is known for her ability to help organizations improve their customer service and build stronger relationships with their customers. Kate's famous quote, "*The customer's perception is your reality*" highlights the importance of understanding the customer's perspective and building strong relationships with them.

Kate's approach is to give your employees the right attitude, skills, and tools to handle difficult customers and situations. She helps your employees to understand the customer's needs, wants, and expectations and also how to create a positive experience for them.

Kate's training and consulting services can be helpful for Black entrepreneurs looking to improve their customer service and build stronger relationships with their customers. She can provide valuable insights and strategies for addressing common customer service challenges and implementing best practices in the industry.

Again, seeking the advice of a customer service expert or consultant can be a valuable strategy for Black entrepreneurs looking to build strong relationships with their customers and clients. By working with a professional like Kate Zabriskie, you can gain valuable insights and strategies for improving your customer service and building loyalty with your customers.

Chapter Twenty-Six:

Leveraging Partnerships And Collaborations

"In unity there is strength." - Aesop

As a Black entrepreneur, leveraging partnerships and collaborations is essential to the success of your business. Whether it's working with other businesses, organizations, or individuals, partnerships and collaborations can help you to achieve your goals more efficiently and effectively, and can also open new opportunities for growth and expansion. However, forming and maintaining successful partnerships and collaborations can be challenging, and requires careful planning, clear communication, and a strong working relationship.

In this chapter, I will explore the importance of leveraging partnerships and collaborations as it pertains to Black entrepreneurship. I will cover the following topics: identifying potential partners, negotiating partnerships, building strong working relationships, communicating clearly, enlisting the pros, and expanding your reach. Through these topics, you will learn how to identify the right partners, create mutually beneficial agreements, and develop the communication and teamwork skills necessary to achieve success. By the end of this chapter, you will have a greater understanding of how to leverage partnerships and collaborations to achieve success in your business.

IDENTIFYING POTENTIAL PARTNERS

"Collaboration allows us to go further together than we ever could alone." - Dr. Maya Angelou

As a Black entrepreneur, identifying potential partners or collaborators who share your values, principles, and mission, and those that can bring complementary skills and resources to the table, is essential to the success of your business. Collaborating with other entrepreneurs and organizations can help you to achieve your goals more efficiently and effectively, and can also open new opportunities for growth and expansion. As they say, "your network is your net worth."

One useful online resource for identifying potential partners is LinkedIn. LinkedIn is a professional networking platform that allows you to connect with other entrepreneurs, business leaders, and organizations in your industry. You can use the platform to search for potential partners based on their skills, experience, and values. You can also read their profile and see their past work experience, which can help you identify those who would be a good fit for your business.

You can also use LinkedIn to join industry groups, which can be a great way to connect with other entrepreneurs and organizations in your field. These groups can be a valuable source of information and resources, and can also provide opportunities for networking and collaboration.

In addition to LinkedIn, you can also use Meetup, Eventbrite, and other online platforms to find local events, networking opportunities and meet other entrepreneurs in your area. These events can be a great way to connect with other entrepreneurs and organizations and explore potential partnerships.

You could also look up event venues known for hosting big business events and conferences in your area. In Dallas, we have the Dallas Convention Center. I know that I can visit their website and look at all the upcoming conventions. Oftentimes, I learn about new organizations and potential partners just from the list of sponsors at many of the major conventions. My law practice is my main business, but I own a handful of other companies. I don't spend as much time on my other ventures as I do my law firm, so I have to make even better use of the time that I do dedicate to my auxiliary ventures. A few minutes searching for local conventions online can reap tremendous rewards in the form of networking leads and educational opportunities for me as a Black entrepreneur.

Also, researching conventions in Las Vegas can be a great way to network and gain valuable knowledge and resources for your business because Las Vegas is one of the most popular host cities in America for convention organizers. One convention to consider is the National Black Business Trade Show and Conference, which takes place annually and features keynote speakers, workshops, and exhibitors specifically catering to the needs of Black entrepreneurs. Another option is the National Urban League Conference, which also takes place in Las Vegas and focuses on issues facing urban communities, including entrepreneurship and small business development. Both of these conventions provide opportunities to connect with other business owners, learn from industry experts, and gain access to resources and funding opportunities. Other Cities with major convention centers are Chicago, Orlando, San Diego, Atlanta, Denver, New Orleans, and Washington D.C.

Remember, identifying potential partners or collaborators who share your values and mission, and who can bring complementary skills and resources to the table, is essential for Black entrepreneurs. Platforms like LinkedIn, Meetup and Eventbrite can be useful resources for connecting with other entrepreneurs and organizations, and exploring potential partnerships. As Dr. Maya Angelou said, "*Collaboration allows us to go further together than we ever could alone.*" By working with the right partners, you can achieve more success for your business and for your community.

NEGOTIATING PARTNERSHIPS

"The art of negotiation is not about winning, it's about creating value." - Mark Goulston

One of the most important things to consider when negotiating partnerships is to have a clear understanding of your goals and objectives. This means identifying what you hope to achieve through the partnership, and what you are willing to compromise on. It's also important to have a clear understanding of the other party's goals and objectives, and to work to find common ground between you. Closing deals is probably my strongest skill as an attorney. I'm a dealmaker through and through. This is because I can put myself in the other parties shoes and figure out what it is that they truly want. I can see straight through to the other party's goals and objectives, which help to inform me when I set goals and define objectives for myself.

Once you have a clear understanding of your goals and objectives, it's important to prepare for negotiations by researching the other party and identifying any potential issues or areas of concern. This may include researching their business or organization, their financial situation, and any legal or regulatory considerations.

During negotiations, it's also important to communicate clearly and effectively. This means listening to the other party, expressing your own needs and concerns, and finding ways to create value for both parties. *The art of negotiation is not about winning, it's about creating value.*

If necessary, seek the advice of a lawyer or business consultant. I know I have harped on this concept heavily throughout this book, but that should only illustrate my perceived importance of the act of seeking counsel. Lawyers can provide valuable advice and guidance on legal and regulatory considerations, and can also help you to identify potential issues and areas of concern. They can also assist you in drafting a partnership agreement that is legally binding and protects the interest of both parties.

A business consultant can provide value to a black-owned business in the process of negotiating partnerships through their expertise in strategic analysis and negotiations. The consultant can assist in identifying potential partners that align with the business's goals and objectives. They can also assist in conducting a SWOT analysis to determine the strengths, weaknesses, opportunities, and threats of the potential partnership.

On the other hand, a business consultant can also provide expertise in the negotiation process, helping to establish mutually beneficial terms and conditions for the partnership. They can also assist your attorney in the drafting and review of legal agreements, ensuring that your business and it's interests are protected.

Furthermore, a business consultant can assist in the post-negotiation integration process, helping to ensure a smooth transition and successful execution of the partnership. Frankly, a business consultant can provide extremely valuable expertise and support in the process of negotiating partnerships for a black-owned business.

To recount, it is essential to be prepared, to have a clear understanding of your goals and objectives, to prepare for negotiations by researching the other party, to communicate clearly and effectively, and to seek the advice of a lawyer or business consultant if necessary. By following these guidelines, you will be better equipped to negotiate successful partnerships that create value for everyone involved.

BUILDING STRONG WORKING RELATIONSHIPS

As a successful Black entrepreneur, building strong, mutually beneficial working relationships with your partners and collaborators will be essential to your business. These relationships require trust, mutual respect, and a shared commitment to achieving common goals. One example of a leader who exemplified these qualities is someone you may have heard of–Jesus Christ.

Jesus taught the importance of love, mutual respect, and trust in building strong relationships. His message of "*Love one another as I have loved you*" is a powerful reminder of the importance of treating others with kindness and understanding. By treating your partners and collaborators with love and respect, you can build trust and establish a foundation of mutual benefit.

In addition to treating others with love and respect, it's also important to have open and honest communication. Jesus taught the importance of being transparent and truthful, and the same applies in building strong working relationships. By openly communicating your needs and concerns, and by actively listening to the perspectives of your partners and collaborators, you can build trust and understanding, and work together to find mutually beneficial solutions.

Another key aspect of building strong working relationships is to have a shared vision and a common goal. Jesus taught the importance of working together to achieve a greater good. By aligning your goals with those of your partners and collaborators, you can create a shared vision for success and work together to achieve it.

Building strong, mutually beneficial working relationships with your partners and collaborators is an integral part of the grind for Black entrepreneurs. By treating others with love and respect, having open and honest communication, and having a shared vision and common goal, you can build trust and establish a foundation of mutual benefit. Following the example of Jesus, who taught the importance of love, mutual respect, and trust, can be a powerful guide in building strong working relationships.

COMMUNICATING CLEARLY

"The best way to not feel hopeless is to get up and do something. Don't wait for good things to happen to you. If you go out and make some good things happen, you will fill the world with hope, you will fill yourself with hope." - Barack Obama

"Change will not come if we wait for some other person or some other time. We are the ones we've been waiting for. We are the change that we seek." - Barack Obama

He gets two quotes. Yes. Because communicating clearly and regularly with your partners and collaborators is essential to the success of your business. Effective communication ensures that everyone is on the same page, and that any issues or concerns can be addressed in a timely manner. One elite example of a leader who exemplified effective communication is Barack Obama.

Barack Obama was known for his clear and direct communication style. He was able to convey complex ideas in a simple, relatable way, and he was able to connect with a wide range of audiences. He also used storytelling to convey his message and inspire others.

As a Black entrepreneur, you can take inspiration from Obama's communication style by being clear and direct when communicating important information and using storytelling to connect with your audience. Additionally, it's important to communicate regularly with your partners and collaborators, this can be done through regular check-ins, meetings, or by using various forms of communication, such as email, phone, or video conferencing. Also, shoot them a text every now and again just to make sure they're in good health and spirits personally.

Regular communication is crucial to ensure that everyone is on the same page and that any issues or concerns can be addressed in a timely manner. Furthermore, it allows for better collaboration and helps to build trust and understanding between partners.

So remember, clear and regular communication is a major key for Black entrepreneurship. By following the example of Barack Obama, who was known for his clear and direct communication style, Black entrepreneurs can ensure that they effectively communicate with their partners and collaborators and that everyone is on the same page. Additionally, regular communication and storytelling can be powerful tools to convey your message and connect with your audience. As Obama said "*We are the change that we seek*" by taking the initiative to communicate clearly and regularly, Black entrepreneurs can be the change and the growth they want to see in their business.

ENLISTING THE PROS

"I'm not just an athlete, I'm a businessman and a brand." - Lebron James

As a Black entrepreneur, it can be beneficial to seek the advice of a business coach or consultant to help navigate partnerships and collaborations. One example of a successful entrepreneur who has enlisted the help of professionals is Lebron James, who enlisted his friend, Rich Paul, to serve as his business manager.

Lebron James is not only a successful athlete, but he is also a savvy businessman. He has built a brand that extends beyond basketball and has leveraged strategic partnerships and collaborations to expand his reach and access new opportunities. For example, he has partnered with brands like Coca-Cola, McDonald's, and Nike to expand his reach in the business world. He also has a partnership with the media company SpringHill Entertainment to create content for television, film, and digital media. Throughout this journey, Lebron had the support and guidance of his friend and business manager Rich Paul.

Rich Paul has been instrumental in helping Lebron navigate the business world and make strategic decisions. He played a crucial role in negotiating Lebron's first lifetime endorsement deal with Nike and helped him secure a partnership with the streaming service, WarnerMedia. He also helped Lebron in the development of his production company, SpringHill Entertainment, which has produced several successful shows and films.

In addition to his business acumen, Rich Paul is also known for his ability to identify opportunities and make smart business moves. He's been credited as the one who helped Lebron to become a successful entrepreneur, and his guidance has been key in the development of Lebron's business empire. This is so special because usually, when an ADOS is blessed with the kind of success that Lebron has achieved, they don't hire from within the black community. The fact is, they by-and-large choose to do business with white agents, white business managers, and white attorneys. Partly due to the limited options, but mostly due to the internalized racism[17] that affects many ADOS throughout the U.S.

Now, you may be wondering, "what does he mean by "internalized racism?" The concept of internalized racism, which refers to the way that people who are part of a marginalized group may actually internalize heavily propagated negative beliefs and attitudes about themselves and their group. This can be a significant factor in understanding the experiences of Black entrepreneurs, and that it may play a role in creating barriers and

---

[17] Speight, Suzette L. "Internalized racism: One more piece of the puzzle." The Counseling Psychologist 35, no. 1 (2007): 126-134.

obstacles that they face in their professional lives. The author suggests that it's important to take internalized racism into account when working with Black entrepreneurs, and that addressing it can help to create more equitable and successful outcomes. Remember, love one another.

The sheer act of hiring Rich Paul–his friend and a Black man–was an act of achievement and progress in the eyes of myself and many other black folks witnessing Lebron's career. We only hope to see more successful ADOS following that example.

Therefore, you can take inspiration from Lebron James and Rich Paul by seeking out the advice of a business coach or consultant to help navigate partnerships and collaborations. They can provide valuable guidance on identifying potential partners, creating mutually beneficial agreements, and developing the communication and teamwork skills necessary to achieve success. A business coach or consultant can also help you to identify potential issues and areas of concern, and to develop strategies to address them.

Again, enlisting the help of professionals such as business coaches or consultants can be beneficial for Black entrepreneurs looking to navigate partnerships and collaborations. By following the example of Lebron James and Rich Paul, Black entrepreneurs can seek out the guidance of a trusted advisor to help them make strategic business decisions, negotiate deals and navigate the business world-and they don't always need to look very far.

EXPANDING YOUR REACH

"I'm not a businessman, I'm a business, man." - Jay-Z

Leveraging partnerships and collaborations can be a powerful way to expand your reach and access new customers or opportunities. One great example of a successful entrepreneur who leveraged partnerships to expand his reach–and the reach of hip hop itself– is Jay-Z.

Jay-Z has been successful in many areas of business, from music, to clothing lines, beverage and hospitality, to sports teams. He has been able to leverage strategic partnerships to expand his reach and access new opportunities. For example, he has partnered with fashion brands such as Rocawear and Puma, and with entertainment companies like Live Nation to expand his reach in the music industry. He also has a partnership with the National Basketball Association (NBA) to represent the league as an ambassador.

As a Black entrepreneur, you can take inspiration from Jay-Z by seeking out strategic partnerships that can help you to expand your reach and access new customers or opportunities. This may include partnering with other businesses or organizations in your industry, or with companies that offer complementary products or services.

It's also important to have a clear understanding of the goals and objectives of the partnership, and to make sure that they align with your own goals. By working together to achieve a shared vision, you can create a mutually beneficial partnership that helps to expand your reach and access new opportunities.

Again, leveraging partnerships and collaborations is an important strategy for Black entrepreneurs looking to expand their reach and access new customers or opportunities. By following the examples of Jay-Z and Lebron James, who have been successful in leveraging strategic partnerships to expand their reach, Black entrepreneurs can seek out partnerships that align with their goals and can help them to access new opportunities and grow their business.

It's important to be clear on the goals and objectives of the partnership and to make sure they align with your own goals. Additionally, effective communication and building trust with your partners will help to establish a strong foundation for the partnership to succeed and expand your reach. By leveraging partnerships and collaborations, Black entrepreneurs can increase their impact and achieve greater success in their business endeavors.

Chapter Twenty-Seven:

Developing A Growth Mindset

As Black entrepreneurs, it is essential that we maintain a growth mindset in order to overcome obstacles and achieve success. A growth mindset is the belief that abilities can be developed through hard work and dedication. A belief that no matter what the obstacle is–it can be overcome. This chapter will delve into how understanding and embracing the concept of a growth mindset can lead to making decisions that prioritize growth. I will cover topics such as embracing challenges, seeking feedback, focusing on process rather than outcome, seeking professional development opportunities, and surrounding yourself with like-minded individuals.

By embracing challenges, seeking feedback, and focusing on the process rather than just the outcome, Black entrepreneurs can make decisions that are geared towards growth. Additionally, seeking professional development opportunities and surrounding oneself with like-minded individuals can also help to foster a growth mindset. These strategies will be explored in depth in this chapter, providing practical advice and examples to assist Black entrepreneurs in developing a growth mindset.

In short, this chapter is designed to provide Black entrepreneurs with the tools and strategies they need to develop a growth mindset, which will in turn lead to making decisions that prioritize growth. By understanding and applying these principles, Black entrepreneurs can develop the mindset necessary to achieve success in the face of obstacles and adversity.

UNDERSTANDING THE CONCEPT OF A GROWTH MINDSET

A growth mindset is the belief that abilities can be developed through hard work and dedication. A growth mindset requires that the person believes that their mind can be likened to a muscle–one that needs to be exercised and trained in order to grow stronger. This concept has been extensively studied in the field of psychology, and has been found to have a significant impact on personal and professional development. In the context of Black entrepreneurship, understanding and embracing a growth mindset can be especially important for overcoming obstacles and achieving success.

There are many theories that have been developed to explain the concept of a growth mindset and how it can be applied to entrepreneurship. Some advanced theories include Carol Dweck's theory of fixed and growth mindsets, Angela Duckworth's theory of grit, and Carol S. Dweck and Lisa S. Blackwell's theory of incremental views of intelligence.

Carol Dweck's theory of fixed and growth mindsets explains that individuals with a growth mindset believe that their abilities can be developed and improved, while those with a fixed mindset believe that their abilities are predetermined and cannot be changed. In the context of Black entrepreneurship, understanding and embracing a growth mindset can be especially important for overcoming obstacles and achieving success.

Angela Duckworth's theory of grit explains that individuals who are able to persevere in the face of adversity are more likely to achieve success. This theory is particularly relevant for

Black entrepreneurs who may face additional challenges and barriers in their business endeavors. Making it out of the ghetto and becoming successful as an Black entrepreneur is an amazing feat that most people never achieve.

Finally, Carol S. Dweck and Lisa S. Blackwell's theory of incremental views of intelligence explains that individuals who believe that intelligence can be developed are more likely to achieve success than those who believe that intelligence is fixed.

I am familiar with the work of Dweck, Blackwell, and Duckworth, and according to them, a Black entrepreneur can develop a growth mindset by focusing on the following strategies:

1. **Embrace challenges**: Dweck's research shows that individuals with a growth mindset view challenges as opportunities for growth and learning, rather than as threats. A black entrepreneur can develop this mindset by actively seeking out challenging projects and situations and approaching them with a willingness to learn.
2. **Learn from failure**: Blackwell's research suggests that individuals with a growth mindset see failure as a learning opportunity, rather than as a reflection of their abilities. A black entrepreneur can develop this mindset by reframing failures as opportunities to learn and grow, and by viewing mistakes as stepping stones to success.
3. **Cultivate grit**: Duckworth's research shows that grit, or the ability to persevere in the face of adversity, is a key trait of individuals with a growth mindset. A black entrepreneur can develop grit by setting long-term goals, developing a sense of purpose, and working hard to achieve them, even in the face of setbacks.
4. **Embrace feedback**: A growth mindset means being open to feedback, it allows the entrepreneur to learn from others, and to see how their actions are perceived by others. A black entrepreneur can develop this mindset by actively seeking feedback from others and using it to improve their business and themselves.
5. **Surround yourself with role models**: Seeing others who have been successful in similar circumstances, can help to inspire and motivate the black entrepreneur to adopt a growth mindset.

By embracing these strategies, you can develop a growth mindset that will help you to overcome obstacles and achieve success in your business ventures.

Hence, understanding the concept of a growth mindset and how it can impact Black entrepreneurship is crucial. By studying these advanced theories, Black entrepreneurs can develop the mindset necessary to overcome obstacles and achieve success. Additionally, by embracing a growth mindset, Black entrepreneurs can make decisions that prioritize growth and lead to business success.

EMBRACING CHALLENGES

As a Black entrepreneur, it is important to embrace challenges and see them as opportunities for growth, rather than setbacks. This mindset can be crucial for overcoming obstacles and achieving success. High-level advice from preeminent business coaches can be especially helpful in this regard.

One of the most well-known business coaches, Tony Robbins, teaches that challenges are opportunities for personal growth. He encourages entrepreneurs to embrace challenges and view them as opportunities to learn, grow, and become stronger. He suggests that instead of focusing on the problem, entrepreneurs should focus on the solution and take action to overcome the challenge.

Another preeminent business coach, Jack Canfield, teaches that challenges are a natural part of the entrepreneurial journey and that they should be seen as opportunities for growth and learning. He encourages entrepreneurs to take a positive attitude towards challenges and to view them as opportunities to learn and grow.

In addition, business coach and author, Michael Hyatt, teaches that challenges are opportunities to stretch and grow. He encourages entrepreneurs to embrace challenges and to see them as opportunities to learn new skills, develop new strengths, and build their resilience.

I could tell you of my own personal accounts where I had to overcome adversity to get to where I am today, but I'll save those tales for another book. We all have ourselves as an example of resilience in our own lives, and we should rely on that example to lead us into the light of success in times of darkness. You are everything. You already have within you seeds of achievement and seeds of success, otherwise, you wouldn't be reading this book. You already know that there will be challenges and obstacles lying directly in the path ahead of you, but you are already equipped with the armor of Blackness. You are already fit to take on the challenge of becoming the Boss entrepreneur you are truly meant to be. You only need to tap into yourself to discover a well of inspiration and determination.

SEEKING FEEDBACK

As a black entrepreneur, it is essential to seek feedback from customers, peers, and mentors in order to continuously improve and grow your business. Being open to learning from your mistakes is key to success in any industry.

One way to seek feedback is by conducting surveys or interviews with customers to gather their thoughts on your products or services. This can provide valuable insights into areas where your business can improve, as well as areas where you are excelling. Additionally, reaching out to peers and mentors in your industry can provide valuable advice and perspective on your business.

It is also important to have a growth mindset and be open to learning from your mistakes. Instead of seeing mistakes as failures, view them as opportunities for growth and learning. This mindset will not only help you improve your business, but it will also help you become a more resilient entrepreneur.

In addition to seeking feedback and being open to learning from mistakes, it's also important to diversify your network. Often, the networks of Black entrepreneurs tend to be primarily composed of people who look like them. This is not to say that these networks are not valuable, but it's important to also make connections with people from different backgrounds who can bring different perspectives and fresh ideas to your business.

Don't confuse my passion for uplifting ADOS unapologetically for being racist, bigoted, anti-white or anything of the sort. I believe it to be absolutely crucial for ADOS to avoid harboring hatred for white people in general, as it can greatly impede their success as entrepreneurs.

Holding onto resentment and anger towards a whole group of people can lead to missed opportunities for building connections and diversifying one's network of advisors. In the world of entrepreneurship, having a diverse network of advisors can provide valuable perspective, resources, and connections that can help to overcome barriers and pave the way for success. It is important to approach networking with an open mind and to actively seek out advisors from a variety of backgrounds, including those who may not look or think like you. Doing so can help to foster a more inclusive and equitable business environment, and ultimately lead to greater success for you as a Black entrepreneur.

So, remember that seeking feedback and being open to learning from your mistakes is crucial for Black entrepreneurs. And that by gathering insights from customers, peers, and mentors, and having a growth mindset, they can continuously improve and grow their businesses.

FOCUSING ON PROCESS RATHER THAN OUTCOME

As a black entrepreneur, it is important to focus on the process of growing your business, rather than just the outcome. This approach can help you develop a growth mindset, which is crucial for success in any industry.

A growth mindset is the belief that you can improve and grow through effort and learning. It is the opposite of a fixed mindset, which is the belief that your abilities and characteristics are set in stone. By focusing on the process of building your business, rather than just the outcome, you can develop a growth mindset and become more resilient in the face of setbacks and challenges. It helps you to be more energetically consistent and flexible in your capacity to endure.

One way to focus on the process is by setting specific and measurable goals for your business. This can include goals for revenue, customer acquisition, or product development. By breaking down your overall business goals into smaller, more manageable goals, you can focus on the steps you need to take to achieve them. This approach can also help you stay motivated and focused on the progress you are making, rather than becoming discouraged by setbacks.

Another way to focus on the process is by learning from failure. Failure is inevitable in any business, but it can be a valuable learning opportunity. By analyzing what went wrong and identifying areas for improvement, you can use failure as a stepping stone to success.

Remember, it is important to focus on the process of growing your business, rather than just the outcome. By developing a growth mindset, setting specific and measurable goals, and learning from failure, you can achieve long-term success in your entrepreneurial journey.

SEEKING PROFESSIONAL DEVELOPMENT OPPORTUNITIES

It is also important to seek out professional development opportunities to enhance your skills and knowledge. This can include things like training, workshops, coaching, and mentorship programs. By investing in your own personal and professional growth, you can position yourself for success in the competitive business world.

One way to seek out professional development opportunities is by something I already mentioned–attending conferences and networking events. These events provide an opportunity to learn from industry experts, connect with other entrepreneurs and professionals, and gain valuable insights into the latest trends and best practices. Additionally, many events offer workshops and training sessions that can be tailored to your specific needs.

Another way to invest in your professional development is by seeking out mentorship programs. Having a mentor can provide valuable guidance and support as you navigate the challenges of starting and growing a business. A mentor can help you identify your strengths and weaknesses and provide advice on how to overcome obstacles.

Online courses, webinars and tutorials are also a great way to access a wealth of knowledge and resources. This is a great way to learn from the comfort of your own home, or office and also at your own pace.

It's also important to recognize that professional development is an ongoing process. As your business grows and evolves, so should your skills and knowledge. Continuously seeking out new opportunities for learning and growth will help you stay ahead of the curve and remain competitive in your industry.

SURROUNDING YOURSELF WITH LIKEMINDED PEOPLE

As a black entrepreneur, it is important to surround yourself with individuals who have a growth mindset and can support and encourage your growth. As the old saying goes, "iron sharpens iron."

Having a support system of people with a growth mindset can help to foster a positive and productive environment for your business. These individuals can provide valuable feedback, offer constructive criticism, and serve as mentors and role models. They can also help to hold you accountable for your goals and push you to reach your full potential.

It is also important to surround yourself with people who understand the unique challenges that Black entrepreneurs may face and can offer support and guidance. This can include connecting with other Black entrepreneurs, joining a business organization or networking group specifically for Black entrepreneurs, or seeking out a mentor who is a black entrepreneur themselves.

In addition to surrounding yourself with people who have a growth mindset, it is also important to cultivate this mindset within yourself. This can include setting challenging goals, seeking out opportunities for learning and development, and being open to feedback and constructive criticism.

By surrounding yourself with a growth mindset and actively cultivating this mindset within yourself, you can create a strong support system that will help to drive your success as a black entrepreneur.

Remember, as a black entrepreneur, you are not alone in your journey, and there are people out there who are willing to help and support you along the way. It's important to seek out and build a community of like-minded individuals who share your vision and passion for growth and success. You are not in this by yourself.

Chapter Twenty-Eight:

Giving Back To Your Community

As Black entrepreneurs, we have the challenge and the opportunity to not only build successful businesses, but also to make a lasting impact in our communities. This chapter will explore various ways we can give back, from identifying causes that align with our values to forming our own charity. I will also discuss the importance of supporting black causes and the value of incorporating social responsibility into our business models. Additionally, I will explore the unique challenges faced by rural black communities and the potential of scholarships and grants to empower the next generation of black leaders.

This chapter is important to me because it highlights the importance of using our entrepreneurial success to positively impact the communities around us. Entrepreneurship is not just about making money, it's also about creating a positive change and fulfilling a sense of purpose. This chapter provides readers with practical ways to give back, whether it be supporting causes that align with their values, creating scholarships, or forming their own charity.

By highlighting the unique challenges faced by rural black communities and the importance of supporting black causes, this chapter encourages readers to think about how they can use their resources and platform to make a difference in the lives of marginalized communities that often get left out of the conversation in terms of black progress.

Plus, the chapter provides an opportunity for readers to reflect on their own responsibility to make an impact and the importance of social responsibility in today's business environment. Business, to me, is not just about making a profit, but also making a positive impact in the world.

Finally, it is an opportunity for readers to learn from the experiences of other successful Black entrepreneurs and understand how they have used their success to give back. It also gives you some inspiration on how you can do the same in your own businesses.

IDENTIFYING WAYS TO GIVE BACK

As Black entrepreneurs, it is important to identify ways in which we can give back to our communities. This can take many forms, such as through charitable donations, volunteering, or mentorship. By identifying the causes and organizations that align with our values, we can make a meaningful impact in the lives of those around us.

One example of a successful black entrepreneur who has made giving back a priority is Robert Smith. Robert Smith is the founder of Vista Equity Partners, a private equity firm that focuses on investing in software companies. He is also known for his philanthropy and giving back to the black community[18]. He has donated millions of dollars to support Historically Black

---

[18] "Social Engagement – Vista Equity Partners." n.d. Vista Equity Partners. Accessed January 21, 2023. https://www.vistaequitypartners.com/esg/social-engagement/.

Colleges and Universities (HBCUs) and also established the Fund II Foundation[19], which focuses on supporting black communities and organizations.

In addition to charitable donations, volunteering and mentorship are also powerful ways to give back to the black community. Black entrepreneurs can volunteer their time and skills to support local organizations and causes, such as mentoring black youth in underprivileged communities, supporting local schools and libraries, and participating in community events. Mentoring black youth is also a powerful way of giving back, by sharing knowledge, experience, and guidance with the next generation of black leaders.

By following the example of Robert Smith, Black entrepreneurs can make a meaningful impact in the lives of those around them, while also setting an example for future generations.

SUPPORTING BLACK CAUSES IS IMPORTANT

"In order to change the world, you have to get in it" - Ella Baker

As Black entrepreneurs, it is important to prioritize pro-black causes and support charitable organizations that align with those values and mission. It is foolish not to do so. The Asian-american community does it, and so does the Latin-American community, and they thrive for it. We are gaslighted by the American government and media institutions into believing that if we–as ADOS people–unite for the purpose of uplifting our own black community, independent of any influence from other ethnic groups, that we are somehow a threat. But by supporting these causes, we can make a meaningful impact in our African diaspora and work towards creating a more equitable society for Black people worldwide.

In "*Black Power: The Politics of Liberation in America*", authors Stokely Carmichael, Kwame Ture, and Charles V. Hamilton argue that the fight for civil rights is not just about individual entrepreneurial success, but also about the collective empowerment of the Black community. They stress the importance of building economic, political, and cultural power for the Black community in order to achieve true equality. This message is particularly relevant for Black entrepreneurs, who often face unique challenges and barriers in building their businesses.

By supporting and investing in Black causes, Black entrepreneurs can not only help to level the playing field for themselves, but also pave the way for future generations of Black business owners. By supporting Black-owned businesses, institutions, and organizations, Black entrepreneurs can help to build a more equitable and sustainable ecosystem for Black entrepreneurship. This is not just an act of charity, but an investment in the future success of the Black community. The only people that would discourage this way of thinking are those that would wish to see the ADOS community as a whole remain in a state of arrested development.

INCORPORATING SOCIAL RESPONSIBILITY

"You're either alive and proud or you're dead, and when you're dead, you don't even know you're dead. It's much better to fight for something while alive." - Huey P. Newton

---

[19] n.d. Fund II Foundation – Advancing Social Change. Accessed January 21, 2023. https://www.fund2foundation.org/.

As Black entrepreneurs, it is important to consider incorporating social responsibility into our business model. This can include contracting with black vendors, sourcing products from black producers and distributors, and implementing policies that promote equality and inclusivity within the workplace. By doing so, we can use our businesses as a tool for positive change and make a meaningful impact in the lives of our community.

To truly uplift our community as Black entrepreneurs, we need to build strong black family units and use estate planning laws and other methods to create generational Black wealth. We need to pool our wealth to form our own political party in the United states and end the exploitation of the Black community by the democratic party. We need to elect our own politicians the same way the trans community is working to do. We need to form our own major corporations to provide media, household goods, home entertainment, vehicles, travel carriers, and more. We need to support our HBCU's by getting involved, donating, and sending our best and brightest athletes and students to attend these schools.

One example of a Black entrepreneur who incorporates social responsibility into their business model is Jessica O. Matthews. She is the founder and CEO of Uncharted Power, a clean energy company that designs and installs sustainable energy systems for communities without access to reliable electricity. She realized that the lack of access to electricity in many communities was a hindrance to their development, and decided to use her entrepreneurial skills to tackle this issue. Her company not only provides clean energy solutions, but also creates jobs and improves the quality of life for the communities they serve. By incorporating social responsibility into her business model, Jessica is not only running a successful business but also making a positive impact on the communities she serves, which aligns with the idea of using entrepreneurship as a tool for obtaining equality for Black people.

Another example of a Black entrepreneur who effectively incorporates social responsibility into their business model is Angela Rye. She is the founder and CEO of IMPACT Strategies, a political advocacy firm that works to promote progressive policies and candidates, with a focus on issues that disproportionately affect Black communities. Through IMPACT Strategies, Angela works to increase the representation and influence of Black voices in the political arena. She is also a prominent commentator and media personality that uses her platform to speak out against racism in politics, the media and the society at large. Angela's work aligns with the idea of using entrepreneurship as a tool for obtaining equality for Black people by amplifying Black voices in the political arena and actively fighting against racism in politics, the media and the society.

By following the example of Ayana Parsons, Jessica Matthews, Angela Rye, and other Black entrepreneurs, we can use our businesses as a tool for positive change and make a meaningful impact in the lives of our community. Incorporating social responsibility into our business models is not only ethical but also a way to create a more just and equitable society for black people.

SUPPORTING RURAL BLACK COMMUNITIES

Rural black communities in the United States have long faced a unique set of challenges when it comes to economic development and social mobility. These challenges include limited access to capital, educational opportunities, and healthcare, as well as systemic discrimination and racism. Despite these challenges, rural black communities are rich in culture and history, and have a wealth of untapped potential for economic and social advancement.

One way to support rural black communities is through philanthropy from successful Black entrepreneurs. Black entrepreneurs who have achieved success in business can use their wealth and influence to empower and uplift their communities. This could include investing in local businesses, providing education and training opportunities, and supporting pro-black community-based organizations.

Remember Robert Smith, the CEO of Vista Equity Partners. Smith paid off the student loan debt of Morehouse College's 2019 graduating class, a historically black college. This move greatly impacted the lives of those students and their families, many of whom come from rural black communities. We need more of this from our best and brightest.

Another example is Oprah Winfrey, the media mogul who has invested in various initiatives to empower rural black communities, such as the Oprah Winfrey Leadership Academy for Girls in South Africa and the Oprah Winfrey Scholars Program at Tennessee State University.

In addition to individual acts of philanthropy, Black entrepreneurs can also join or create coalitions of like-minded individuals and organizations to maximize their impact. The National Black Child Development Institute (NBCDI) is a great example of an organization that has been working to empower rural black communities for decades. NBCDI's mission is to improve and protect the lives of black children and their families through advocacy, education, and research.

The NBCDI works towards this goal by providing resources, training and education to parents, caregivers, educators and other professionals who work with Black children. One of their main programs is the "Rural Black Child Development Institute" (RBCDI) which focuses on improving the lives of Black children and families living in rural communities. The program provides training and resources to educators and other professionals working in rural areas, as well as support to parents and caregivers. Through this program, NBCDI aims to improve the educational outcomes and overall well-being of Black children in rural communities by addressing issues such as poverty, lack of access to quality education, and discrimination.

This kind of work can inspire Black entrepreneurs to support rural Black communities by providing resources, training and education, and creating opportunities for them. Entrepreneurs can also support rural Black communities by investing in and creating businesses that provide goods and services that are tailored to meet the specific needs of these communities. They can also actively look for ways to create jobs and opportunities in these communities, as well as support organizations like NBCDI that are working to improve the lives of Black children and families in these areas.

Rural black communities face unique challenges in terms of economic development and social mobility, but these communities also have a wealth of untapped potential. Philanthropy from successful Black entrepreneurs can play a crucial role in empowering and uplifting these communities by investing in local businesses, providing education and training opportunities, and supporting community-based organizations. It is important that both individuals and organizations work together to support rural black communities and to create a more equitable future for all.

SCHOLARSHIPS AND GRANTS

Black students in the United States face unique challenges when it comes to higher education, including limited access to financial resources and systemic discrimination. Despite these challenges, a college degree can be a powerful tool for social and economic mobility for black students.

One way to support black students in their pursuit of higher education is through scholarships and grants. Scholarships and grants can provide financial assistance to help cover the cost of tuition, books, and other expenses associated with attending college.

There are many organizations that provide scholarships and grants specifically for black students, such as the United Negro College Fund (UNCF), the Thurgood Marshall College Fund, and the National Black Nurses Association (NBNA). These organizations provide support to thousands of black students each year and are a valuable resource for those seeking financial assistance for higher education.

In addition to these organizations, many successful Black entrepreneurs have also created scholarships and grants to support the education of black students. For example, Oprah Winfrey, the media mogul, has invested in various initiatives to empower black students, such as the Oprah Winfrey Leadership Academy for Girls in South Africa and the Oprah Winfrey Scholars Program at Tennessee State University.

Black entrepreneurs can also join or create coalitions of like-minded individuals and organizations to maximize their impact. For instance, organizations such as the Black Economic Alliance and the National Black MBA Association offer scholarships, grants, and mentorship programs to support the education of black students and young professionals.

Clearly, black students face unique challenges when it comes to higher education, but scholarships and grants can be a powerful tool for providing financial assistance and empowering them to pursue their educational goals. Concerted philanthropy from successful Black entrepreneurs and organizations can play a crucial role in providing support for black students and helping to create a more equitable future for all.

POLITICAL ACTIVISM PART 1

When many people today think of strong political movements in support of black causes, they most likely think of Black Lives Matter. The Black Lives Matter (BLM) movement has brought attention to the issues of police brutality and racism, and has sparked important conversations and policy changes in the United States. However, the BLM Organization itself has been plagued by scandal and internal conflicts, leading some to question its effectiveness and longevity. I personally do not support the formal BLM organization, but I absolutely believe that black lives do matter. The BLM leaders are decorated veterans in the war on the traditional black family unit, but they don't fight for traditional black families. The number one enemy of the Black Lives Matter movement is the 'living, breathing, free-thinking, heterosexual, black man.' Despite this, the Black Lives Matter 'movement' can be seen as a valuable learning lesson in the potential for organized black action and the importance of accountability and transparency within social justice movements.

One of the key lessons from the Black Lives Matter movement is the need for strong and effective leadership. The movement's decentralized structure, while initially successful in amplifying a wide range of voices, has also led to inconsistencies in messaging and a lack of clear decision-making. This has resulted in internal conflicts and public criticism, which have damaged the movement's credibility and public perception.

Another important lesson is the need for transparency and accountability. The movement's lack of clear financial practices and the accusations of self-dealing by certain leaders have led to distrust and skepticism among supporters. Clear financial practices and transparency can help to build trust and credibility, which are essential for sustained success and impact.

Despite these challenges, the Black Lives Matter movement has also been successful in raising awareness about issues of police brutality and racism, and has led to policy changes and reforms at the local, state, and federal level. It has also inspired similar movements around the world and has brought attention to the importance of intersectionality in social justice movements. Like I said, I don't personally like BLM, but I'm not a hater and I have to give props where they're due.

POLITICAL ACTIVISM PART 2

Political activism is an important aspect of the fight for social and economic equality for Black Americans. Black entrepreneurs, in particular, have the ability to empower the Black community through the creation of new political institutions and a new political party.

Black entrepreneurs working with black political organizers can create new political institutions by founding organizations that work to promote Black political representation and participation unapologetically. These organizations could focus on voter registration and education, voter mobilization, and candidate training and development. They could also work to build a Black political network, connecting Black leaders and activists across the country to share ideas and strategies for political change.

Another way entrepreneurs can empower the Black community is by founding a new political party. This party could focus on the specific needs and concerns of Black Americans and provide a platform for Black candidates to run for office at all levels of government. This party could also work to build a Black voting bloc, which would immediately have significant political power and influence.

Black entrepreneurs can also use their resources and influence to support Black candidates running for office. They can provide financial support, use their networks to raise awareness, and encourage their employees and customers to vote for Black candidates. This is real Black empowerment for equality. Marching, T-shirts, and Protests are cool, but real political action is needed to get the change we deserve as ADOS. The only institution standing vehemently opposed to this idea is the American Democratic Party. This idea and line of thinking is precisely what got civil rights leaders like Medgar Evars, Malcolm X, and Dr. Martin Luther King Jr. killed.

Black entrepreneurs can use their platforms and influence to raise awareness of Black political issues and advocate for policy changes that would benefit the Black community. They can also use their businesses as a tool for social change by implementing policies that promote diversity and inclusion, and by supporting organizations that work to improve the lives of Black Americans.

USING TECHNOLOGY TO SERVE BLACK INTERESTS

A Black-owned social network, backed by powerful Black entrepreneurs, has the potential to make a significant impact on the Black community. Such a network would provide a platform for Black voices to be heard and for Black culture to be celebrated. It would also provide a space for Black people to connect, share information, and organize for political and social change.

By being owned and controlled by Black people, the social network would be able to prioritize the needs and concerns of the Black community in a way that mainstream social networks may not. It would also allow for a more diverse range of perspectives and experiences to be represented, as well as fostering a sense of community and belonging.

With the support of powerful Black entrepreneurs, the social network would have the resources and influence to reach a large audience and make a real impact. Entrepreneurs can use their networks and platforms to promote the social network, and also use the social network as a tool to raise awareness of Black issues and advocate for policy changes that benefit the Black community.

Additionally, the social network could be a powerful tool for Black entrepreneurs and businesses to connect with customers and promote their products and services, which can also have a positive economic impact for the Black community and the global economy at-large.

Overall, a Black-owned social network, backed by powerful Black entrepreneurs, could provide a valuable resource for the Black community and play a vital role in promoting social and economic equality.

In conclusion, Black entrepreneurs have a unique ability to empower the Black community through the creation of new political institutions, a new political party, and the creation of an Afro-centric social networking application. By using their resources and influence to promote Black political representation and participation, Black entrepreneurs can play a vital role in the fight for social and economic equality for all Black people. We truly have the power to reset the world if we only unite behind a common cause that is greater than us all.

Chapter Twenty-Nine:
Mentoring The Next Generation Of Entrepreneurs

As the business landscape continues to evolve, it is crucial that the next generation of entrepreneurs is equipped with the skills and knowledge needed to succeed. Mentoring is an essential tool for helping young entrepreneurs navigate the challenges of starting and growing a business, as well as for passing on valuable lessons and insights.

One of the key lessons that can be passed on to the next generation of entrepreneurs is the importance of soft skills in business. Soft skills refer to the personal attributes, behaviors, and social intelligence that are needed to navigate the complexities of the business world, such as communication, collaboration, and adaptability. These skills are often more important than traditional testing scores and academic qualifications in determining success in business.

As Black entrepreneurs, we have a unique perspective and understanding of the challenges that come with being a minority in the business world. By mentoring the next generation, we can share our experiences and knowledge and help to create a more inclusive and equitable business environment for all. This includes encouraging hiring based on soft skills and not placing so much emphasis on traditional testing scores, as well as promoting diversity, equity and inclusion in the workplace and in the community.

In this chapter, I will explore the various ways in which Black entrepreneurs can mentor the next generation, including through mentorship programs, networking events, and educational initiatives. I will also discuss the benefits of mentoring, both for the mentor and the mentee, and provide practical tips and strategies for effective mentoring. By working together, we can empower the next generation of entrepreneurs to achieve their full potential and create a more prosperous future for all.

IDENTIFYING OPPORTUNITIES TO MENTOR

One of the most important ways Black entrepreneurs can support the next generation is through mentorship. Mentorship can take many forms, from formal mentorship programs to informal relationships. Black entrepreneurs should be proactive in identifying opportunities to mentor the next generation of Black entrepreneurs and to invest their time, resources, and networks.

One way to identify opportunities to mentor is through mentorship programs. Many organizations, such as the National Black MBA Association and the National Association of Black MBAs, offer mentorship programs that connect Black entrepreneurs with students or young professionals. By participating in these programs, Black entrepreneurs can share their experiences and knowledge, and help to guide the next generation on their path to success.

Another way to identify opportunities to mentor is through informal relationships. Black entrepreneurs can also mentor the next generation of Black entrepreneurs through informal relationships, such as through networking events, social media, or even within their own organizations. By building relationships with young entrepreneurs and sharing their experiences, Black entrepreneurs can serve as role models and provide guidance and support.

Furthermore, Black entrepreneurs can also identify opportunities to mentor through volunteering in schools, community centers, and non-profit organizations where they can share their knowledge, experiences and skills to the next generation. They can also create their own mentorship programs within their own companies and organizations, creating a culture of mentorship and development within.

SHARING YOUR KNOWLEDGE AND EXPERIENCE

One of the most important aspects of mentorship is sharing your knowledge and experience with your mentee. As a black entrepreneur, you have unique insights and perspectives on the challenges and opportunities that come with building and growing a business. By sharing your knowledge and experience with your mentee, you can help them to navigate the complexities of the business world and to achieve success.

One way to share your knowledge and experience is by providing guidance on specific business challenges and opportunities. For example, you can provide advice on how to secure funding, how to create a marketing strategy, or how to navigate the legal and regulatory landscape. By sharing your own experiences and providing concrete advice, you can help your mentee to avoid common pitfalls and to capitalize on opportunities.

Another way to share your knowledge and experience is by providing guidance on the soft skills that are essential for success in business. For example, you can provide advice on how to communicate effectively, how to build a strong network, or how to manage stress and maintain a work-life balance. By sharing your own experiences and providing guidance on these important personal attributes, you can help your mentee to become a well-rounded and effective business leader.

Additionally, sharing your network with mentees can also be of great benefit for them. Introducing them to potential investors, partners, or clients can help to open up new opportunities and to give them a foothold in the industry. Furthermore, you can also provide them with resources and information that you have gathered throughout your career and that can be useful for them. By providing guidance on specific business challenges and opportunities, soft skills, and sharing your network, you can help your mentee to navigate the complexities of the business world and to achieve success. Investing in the next generation by sharing your knowledge and experience can help to create a more inclusive and equitable business environment for all.

BEING A SUPPORTIVE AND ENCOURAGING ROLE MODEL

Mentorship is not only about sharing knowledge and experience, but also about being a supportive and encouraging role model for the next generation of Black entrepreneurs. By being a positive and supportive role model, you can help to empower your mentee to believe in themselves and to persevere through the challenges of building a business.

One way to be a supportive and encouraging role model is by offering guidance and advice as needed. This means being available to your mentee when they have questions or need support, and providing honest and constructive feedback. It also means being a sounding board for their ideas and providing guidance on how to move forward.

Another way to be a supportive and encouraging role model is by celebrating their successes and encouraging them to continue to push forward. Celebrating their small wins, offering words of encouragement, and congratulating them on their achievements can help to build their confidence and to keep them motivated. This can help them to overcome the inevitable setbacks and obstacles that they will encounter along the way.

Additionally, Black entrepreneurs should also be role models in terms of resilience, perseverance and determination. Black entrepreneurs have often had to face and overcome many obstacles in their journey, and by sharing these experiences and how they overcame them, they can be a valuable source of inspiration and encouragement for mentees.

The main takeaway here is that Black entrepreneurs should be supportive and encouraging role models for their mentees. By offering guidance and advice as needed, celebrating their successes, and being a source of inspiration and encouragement, Black entrepreneurs can help to empower the next generation of Black entrepreneurs to believe in themselves and to persevere through the challenges of building a business.

SETTING EXPECTATIONS

Mentoring is an essential aspect of entrepreneurship, and it is even more critical for Black entrepreneurs who face unique challenges and barriers in the business world. As a mentee, it is crucial to set expectations for your mentorship relationship and establish clear goals and objectives. This will ensure that you and your mentor are on the same page and that the mentorship is productive and beneficial for both parties.

When setting expectations, it is essential to discuss the following:

1. **Time commitment**: How often will you meet with your mentor, and for how long? It's essential to establish a schedule that works for both of you and to stick to it.
2. **Communication**: How will you communicate with your mentor? Will you meet in person, via phone, or video call? How often will you check-in?
3. **Goals and objectives**: What specific areas do you want to focus on during the mentorship? What are your short-term and long-term goals?
4. **Feedback**: How will you receive and give feedback during the mentorship? It's essential to establish a process for giving and receiving feedback so that you can continue to improve and grow.

By setting clear expectations, you and your mentor can work together to achieve your goals and objectives. It's also important to remember that mentorship is a two-way street, and as a mentee, you have a responsibility to take initiative and actively engage in the mentorship relationship. Also, by setting expectations, establishing clear goals and objectives, and actively engaging in the mentorship relationship, Black entrepreneurs can ensure that the mentorship is productive and beneficial for both parties.

BE GENEROUS BUT DISCERNING

As a Black entrepreneur, it is important to pay it forward and give back to the next generation by mentoring young entrepreneurs. One way to do this is by exhibiting measured generosity towards your mentees. This can include spending money to enrich the mentorship experience, but it's essential to be careful not to make the nature of the relationship one based on financial dependency.

When it comes to spending money on your mentorship relationship, it's essential to be strategic and consider the value it will bring to the relationship. For example, if your mentee is interested in a specific industry, you could invite them to attend a conference or trade show with you. This would give them valuable exposure to the industry and networking opportunities that they might not have otherwise.

It's also important to remember that mentorship is not just about money, but also about sharing your knowledge, experience, and networks. Black entrepreneurs can provide mentees with valuable insights and connections that can help them grow their businesses.

However, it's also important to be mindful of creating a dependency relationship. It's crucial to provide mentees with the tools and resources they need to succeed, but also encourage them to be self-sufficient and take ownership of their own success.

It's essential to pay it forward and give back to the next generation by mentoring young entrepreneurs. While it's important to spend money to enrich the mentorship experience, it's crucial to be strategic and not make the nature of the relationship one based on financial dependency. Black entrepreneurs should focus on sharing their knowledge, experience, and networks to help mentees succeed on their own.

GIVE CREDIT WHERE CREDIT IS DUE

"This Little Light of Mine" is a gospel song that was written by an African American woman named Harry Dixon Loes in the 1920s. The song is based on a Bible verse from Matthew 5:16, where Jesus says, "Let your light shine before others, that they may see your good deeds and glorify your Father in heaven." The song encourages individuals to let their light, or their faith, shine for others to see, and has been a popular gospel song in the black community for many years.

This theme parallels the expectation of a mentor to promote the accomplishments and growth of their mentees to members of their own network. Have faith in your mentees and let that faith shine like a light. Just as the song encourages individuals to let their light shine, a mentor should promote the accomplishments and growth of their mentees in order to help them achieve their goals and reach their full potential. By introducing them to potential clients, investors, or industry contacts, and sharing their successes on social media or in professional circles, a mentor is providing valuable opportunities and exposure that can help mentees take their business to the next level.

Furthermore, the song also encourages individuals to let their light shine without any hidden agenda, in the same way, a mentor should promote their mentee's accomplishments without any personal gain, but rather to give from the heart and help others to succeed.

By opening doors for your mentees and showcasing their potential, you are providing them with valuable opportunities and exposure that can help them take their business to the next level. This act of generosity and support can also serve as a powerful source of motivation and encouragement for your mentees, and help them to believe in themselves and their abilities.

Chapter Thirty:
Celebrating Your Success While Staying Grounded

"I ain't no role model, I ain't trying to be nobody's role model, I do what I do, and people can look at it and do what they want with it." - Mr. T

As Black entrepreneurs, it's essential to celebrate your business success while remaining grounded and humble. This can be a challenging balance to strike, but it's crucial to remember that success is not the only thing that matters. It's important to stay true to yourself, your values, and to remember where you came from.

One example of a successful Black entrepreneur who embodies this balance is Daymond John, the founder of FUBU and famous Shark Tank Investor. Daymond is a self-made millionaire, who despite his success, remains humble, and always stays true to his values and his mission to empower other entrepreneurs. He is a great example of someone who has kept his head in the sky while keeping his feet on the ground.

This chapter will explore the importance of recognizing your accomplishments, sharing your success, staying grounded, recognizing your limitations, seeking feedback and not giving up. It will touch on the following topics:

- **Recognizing Your Accomplishments**: Learn how to acknowledge and celebrate your successes without becoming arrogant or complacent.
- **Sharing Your Success**: Understand the importance of sharing your story and inspiring others.
- **Staying Grounded**: Discover how to stay true to your values and remain humble despite your success.
- **Recognizing Your Limitations**: Learn how to identify and overcome your limitations in order to continue growing and expanding your business.
- **Seeking Feedback**: Understand the importance of seeking feedback and how to use it to improve your business.
- **Don't Give Up**: Learn how to overcome obstacles and stay motivated on your entrepreneurial journey.

By exploring these key topics, this chapter will help you understand how to balance celebrating your business success while remaining grounded and humble.

RECOGNIZING YOUR ACCOMPLISHMENTS

It's essential to recognize and celebrate your accomplishments. Acknowledging your successes is not only important for your own personal growth, but it also serves as a source of inspiration and motivation for others. However, it's crucial to do so without becoming arrogant or complacent.

One way to recognize and celebrate your accomplishments is to keep a record of them. This can include a journal, a file, or even a simple list. By keeping a record of your accomplishments, you can refer back to them when you need motivation or inspiration.

Another way to recognize and celebrate your accomplishments is to share them with others. This could be through social media, a blog, or even in conversations with friends and family. Sharing your accomplishments not only helps you to acknowledge and celebrate them, but it also serves as a source of inspiration for others.

It's also important to remember that success is not the only thing that matters. It's essential to stay grounded and humble, and to remember that success is not the end goal but rather a part of a journey.

Remember, recognizing and celebrating your accomplishments is an essential part of being a Black entrepreneur. By keeping a record of your accomplishments, sharing them with others, and staying grounded and humble, you can acknowledge and celebrate your successes without becoming arrogant or complacent.

SHARING YOUR SUCCESS

It's also essential to share your success story with others. Not only does it help to acknowledge and celebrate your accomplishments, but it also serves as a source of inspiration and motivation for others. The importance of sharing your success story can't be understated, particularly for Black entrepreneurs who often face unique challenges and barriers in the business world.

Sharing your story can take many forms, such as writing a book, speaking at events, or even just sharing your experiences on social media. It's an opportunity to let others know what you've been through, the challenges you've faced and overcome, and the lessons you've learned. It's an opportunity to inspire others to pursue their own entrepreneurial dreams, and to show them that it's possible to succeed despite the odds.

It's also important to remember that sharing your success story is not about boasting or showing off. It's about being transparent, honest, and authentic, and offering valuable insights and advice to others who may be facing similar challenges.

STAYING GROUNDED

A successful Black entrepreneur may lose touch with their community if they become disconnected from the experiences and struggles of everyday Black people. This can happen when an entrepreneur becomes too focused on achieving success and accumulating wealth, and forgets about the issues and challenges faced by the Black community.

Here are a few signs that a Black entrepreneur may have lost touch with their community:

- They are no longer in tune with the needs and concerns of their customers and clients, and their products or services no longer align with the values and priorities of the Black community.
- They are no longer active in the Black community, and do not participate in events, organizations, or initiatives that support the Black community.
- They are no longer involved in advocacy or activism, and do not use their platform, resources, or influence to speak out against racial injustice or support Black causes.
- They are no longer mentoring or investing in Black businesses, and do not use their success to support the next generation of Black entrepreneurs.

It's important to note that it's not uncommon for entrepreneurs to get caught up in the day-to-day work of running a business, and it's not a bad thing to have a focus on business growth. But, it's important for successful Black entrepreneurs to remain connected to the Black community, to remain in tune with their needs and concerns and to continue to support them. This is especially important for Black entrepreneurs, who may have a unique perspective and understanding of the challenges faced by the Black community and can use their platform, resources and influence to make positive change Black people in general.

As a Black entrepreneur, it's essential to stay grounded and humble despite your success. This can be a challenging balance to strike, but it's crucial to remember that success is not the only thing that matters. Staying true to your values and remaining humble can help to keep you grounded and focused on what's truly important.

One way to stay grounded is to remain connected to your community. This could be through volunteer work, mentoring, or even just staying in touch with friends and family. By staying connected to your community, you can remain grounded and focused on the things that matter most.

Another way to stay grounded is to practice mindfulness and self-reflection. This could be through meditation, journaling, or even just taking a few minutes each day to reflect on your values and priorities. By practicing mindfulness and self-reflection, you can stay grounded and focused on what's truly important.

It's also important to remember that success is not the only thing that matters, and that it's essential to stay true to your values and to remember where you came from.

Remember, staying grounded and humble is essential for Black entrepreneurs. It helps to keep you focused on what's truly important, and to stay true to your values and priorities. By remaining connected to your community, practicing mindfulness and self-reflection, and remembering that success is not the only thing that matters, you can stay grounded and focused on what's truly important.

RECOGNIZING YOUR LIMITATIONS

As a Black entrepreneur, it's essential to recognize and acknowledge your limitations. This can be difficult to do, but it's crucial in order to continue growing and expanding your business. Identifying and overcoming your limitations can help you to improve your business and reach your goals.

One way to recognize your limitations is to conduct a self-evaluation. This could be through journaling, setting goals, or even just taking a few minutes each day to reflect on your business and your performance. By conducting a self-evaluation, you can gain a better understanding of your own strengths and weaknesses, and take steps to improve.

Once upon a time, there was a successful black entrepreneur named Helaine. She had built a thriving tech company that had gone public and made her a millionaire many times over. Despite her incredible success, Helaine always remained humble and grounded.

One day, a reporter asked her how she had managed to achieve so much success while remaining so humble. Helaine smiled and replied, "*I always try to stay aware of my own limitations. I know that I am not perfect and that there is always room for growth and improvement. That's why I make a point of seeking out feedback from my employees, customers, and mentors. They help me to see things that I might not be able to see on my own.*"

Helaine also made it a point to surround herself with a diverse group of people, who had different skills and experiences, this helped her to broaden her perspective and identify the areas where she could improve. She also believed in setting realistic goals, and when she achieved them, she celebrated them with her team and family, and shared her success with her community. Helaine's humility and willingness to learn and grow had served her well and helped her to build a successful and sustainable business that was respected in the industry.

SEEKING FEEDBACK

"The biggest room in the world is the room for improvement." - Unknown

As a Black entrepreneur, it's essential to understand the importance of seeking feedback and how to use it to improve your business. Most employees strongly agree that the feedback they receive helps them to do better work. By actively seeking feedback and using it to improve your business, you can increase employee engagement, improve customer satisfaction and ultimately achieve better business results.

One way to seek feedback is to conduct customer surveys. This could be through online surveys, phone interviews, or even just asking customers for their honest opinions during in-person interactions. By conducting customer surveys, you can gain valuable insights into areas where you may be lacking and take steps to improve.

Another way to seek feedback is to solicit feedback from employees. This could be through employee evaluations, team meetings, or even just informal conversations. By soliciting feedback from employees, you can gain a better understanding of their needs and perspectives, and take steps to improve employee engagement and satisfaction.

It's also important to remember that seeking feedback is not a one-time event but rather a continuous process, and it's crucial to continuously seek, evaluate and act upon feedback.

DON'T GIVE UP!

"I can accept failure, everyone fails at something. But I can't accept not trying." - Michael Jordan

As a Black entrepreneur, it's essential to learn how to overcome obstacles and stay motivated on your entrepreneurial journey. Entrepreneurship can be a challenging and unpredictable journey, and obstacles and setbacks are inevitable. However, it's crucial to not give up, to learn from the obstacles and to stay motivated to achieve your goals.

One way to overcome obstacles and stay motivated is to set realistic and achievable goals. By setting goals, you can stay focused on what you want to achieve, and measure your progress. By achieving small goals along the way, you can build momentum and stay motivated to achieve your ultimate goal.

Another way to overcome obstacles and stay motivated is to surround yourself with a support system. This could be through mentorship, networking, or even just having a circle of friends and family who understand and support your entrepreneurial journey. By surrounding yourself with a supportive community, you can stay motivated and inspired, and get the help and support you need when obstacles arise.

It's also important to remember that failure is a natural part of the entrepreneurial journey, and that learning from failure can be an essential part of success.

As we come to the end of our journey exploring the world of Black entrepreneurship, I want to thank you, dear reader, for joining me on this enlightening and empowering journey. I hope that through the stories, insights, and strategies shared in this book, you have been inspired to pursue your own entrepreneurial dreams, and to overcome any limitations you may have encountered along the way.

As a black entrepreneur, you have the power to create wealth, generate jobs, and drive economic growth within your community. And by staying aware of your limitations, and continually striving to improve, you can achieve tremendous success while remaining humble and grounded.

Remember that the road to success is not always easy, but with hard work, perseverance, and a positive attitude, you can overcome any obstacle. I encourage you to stay connected with the black entrepreneurial community, to seek out mentorship, and to continue learning and growing as a business leader.

Once again, thank you for reading this book, and I wish you all the best in your entrepreneurial endeavors.

For comments, questions, and feedback send mail to:

Attorney Sholdon Daniels , Esq
1910 Pacific Avenue
Suite 14225
Dallas, Texas 75201

If you like this book, please follow me on Twitter at @SholdonDaniels, Instagram at @EntertainmentLawya, and visit me at my website at https://www.sholdondaniels.com/.